THINK BIG

Nine Ways to Make Millions from Your Ideas

Don Debelak

Entrepreneur Press

Entrepreneur Press
Irvine, California

Managing Editor: Marla Markman
Cover Design: TLC Graphics
Composition and production: Eliot House Productions

This publication is designed to provide accurate and authorita-
tive information in regard to the subject matter covered. It is
sold with the understanding that the publisher is not engaged in
rendering legal, accounting or other professional services. If
legal advice or other expert assistance is required, the services
of a competent professional person should be sought.

Debelak, Don.
Think Big: Nine ways to make millions from your ideas/Don Debelak.
p. cm.
Includes index.
ISBN 1-891984-22-5
1. New products--Management. 2. New products--Marketing. I. Title.

HF5415.153.D45 2001
658.5'75--dc21

ISBN 1-891984-22-5

Printed in Canada

09 08 07 06 05 04 03 02 01   10 9 8 7 6 5 4 3 2 1

Contents

Preface

$\mathcal{T}$wenty years ago I was hired by a company that was founded by the man who invented the first reclining dental chair. Since then I have worked with three other inventor-oriented companies, and since 1989 I've worked on new products as an independent consultant and as a part-time consultant for the University of St. Thomas Small Business Development Center. During that time I've worked with over 50 new products, about half of which have made it successfully onto the market and that together have sold over $100 million. I also write a monthly column on new products and inventors for both *Entrepreneur Start-Ups* and *Entrepreneur* magazines. While writing those columns, I've talked to over 50 successful inventors. I've also talked to dozens of inventors for my two previous books on new products, *How to Bring a Product to Market for Less than*

$5,000 and *Bringing Your Product to Market* (both by John Wiley and Sons). My experience has given me a unique perspective on just how products are being introduced today and on how introduction strategies have changed rapidly over the last ten years.

The most interesting assignment over the last few years has been my magazine columns. I feature at least one inventor in each column, and this has introduced me to the vast range of strategies inventors are employing to reach the market. The business world is rapidly evolving, and inventors are constantly trying new approaches to keep up. And that's the goal of this book: to show inventors the wide variety of tactics they can use to get their product on the market in today's brave new world. Most successful inventors try at least three or four different introduction methods before they find one that works. Hopefully, this book will make it a little easier for you to choose the best strategy for your product the first time.

Most inventor books typically concentrate on two options: either licensing or starting your own company. These are standard, tried-and-true methods, but they are no longer the only ones, and they are not equally available to every inventor; some inventors don't have the knowledge or money to start their own company nor the clout to negotiate a licensing agreement. What's the inexperienced new product marketer to do? In this book, I will describe the many new ways inventors of all kinds are using to introduce their products, and I will offer strategies to get your creative juices flowing so you can discover your own way to market based on your particular circumstances. I believe everyone has a real chance of success if they are persistent and know all of the options available to them, and I want to encourage you to take your product out on the market. Inventors are supposed to be able to think "outside the box," and successful inventors today are doing so, both by creating new products and by developing new manufacturing and marketing methods to sell them. If your eyes are open and you're willing to roll up your sleeves and work hard, you can discover myriad ways to succeed in today's market.

And it is hard work. This book is not for the inventor looking for someone else to make him or her rich. Many inventors tell me they don't have the time to introduce their idea but that they are instead looking for someone who can market it for them. One line I often hear is: "I am really good at coming up with great new product ideas. But I'm not good at marketing them. All I need to succeed is to find someone to sell my inventions." I tell inventors looking for a "rescue ranger" to forget they ever had the idea in the first place. Getting a product idea is not like winning a lottery; it is the starting point on a rough road to success.

If you want to find the person who will do the best job of marketing and selling your idea, look in the mirror. Taking a product to market is an extremely time-consuming activity, and you will need to work on it at least 10 to 15 hours a week and maybe more. Most inventors must do this for two to five years before the product finally clicks and begins bringing in a decent income. No one is going to do that development work for you and then let you have a major share of the profits. Nor will someone else stay true to your vision of the product. A few inventors might get lucky and have a company license their idea, but most inventors succeed only after plenty of hard work developing and marketing their product themselves.

The need to put in a major effort to sell your idea doesn't mean that you should quit your day job. That can be a disastrous mistake, putting yourself in financial distress at the worst possible moment. Instead, develop and market your product at your own pace, making sure not to make any drastic life changes until your product has proven itself. Take, for instance, the experience of 24-year-old Gary Kellmann of St. Charles, Missouri, who came up with his first commercial idea, the Hair Holder Holder, after watching his girlfriend constantly search her apartment for hair accessories. The product has a large outer loop and a smaller inside loop, both with easy-opening latches, and it holds barrettes, hair clips, and assorted hair accessories. Everybody Kellmann showed the product to liked it, so Kellmann decided to introduce it. Since Kellmann didn't know a thing about introducing a product, he volunteered at the local Small Business Development Center, where he could meet and network with people who knew about product development. He read trade magazines and attended trade shows, and once he was able to line up a marketer, he bought 20,000 units of his product on his credit card and he was off and running.

The marketer was able to get the product into Claire's Boutique, a chain of mall stores geared to teenage girls. But the product didn't sell the way Kellmann hoped, primarily because teenagers don't buy organizing products, their mothers do. So Kellmann revamped his marketing strategy and looked for a partner to market his product to drug and discount stores. He prowled the aisles of local stores looking for the names of any manufacturer that might sell a plastic hair accessory product. He was able to line up a royalty agreement with Fit-All Sportswear of Pilot Mountain, North Carolina.

During this entire time, Kellmann kept his full-time day job, devoting nights and weekends to the Hair Holder Holder, since he didn't have enough income from sales to pay his bills while still funding his invention. In reality, Kellmann worked two full-time jobs for three years. But finally, when Kellmann was 27, his Hair Holder Holder became well-enough established to allow him to quit his day job and devote himself entirely to his new company, Beyond Mars.

As you will see, regular everyday people are becoming successful inventors all the time, and I include many of their stories in this book. If you have a success, drop me a line with your story, and I'll try to include it in a future magazine column or book. Your story might be just the ticket to help others take that first step to try and introduce their product.

Don Debelak
PO Box 120861
New Brighton, MN 55112

Introduction

*B*elieve it or not, there was a time not all that long ago when college graduates wanted nothing more than to get a job with a big corporation and stay there for their entire career. A successful, satisfying life seemed to hinge on that type of cradle-to-grave security. But those times are long gone. Today I talk to inventors and entrepreneurs who knew in their teens that they wanted nothing else but to go into business for themselves. Most of them even started little businesses in high school or college—everything from selling T-shirts to leasing area rugs and refrigerators to new college students. In fact, the 20 year olds of today are going into business on their own at a faster rate than of any past generation.

This has meant sweeping changes for the invention business. In the seventies and eighties, new inventors were, for the most part, already successful businesspeople, and they either introduced products on their own or they licensed them to a big corporation. Tactics were pretty stagnant. But today the range of tactics being employed by inventor/entrepreneurs is staggering. When Kristine Penta of Hillsdale, New Jersey, graduated from college, she wanted to start a cosmetics company for teenage girls, but she didn't have any money. She convinced a cosmetics company to hire her and then to start a new line based on her own designs. Once her line was established, she convinced some investors to buy the line from the company, and she included herself as part of the package sale. In addition, Penta negotiated for herself 20 percent ownership of the new company, Fun Cosmetics, Inc. Some inventors are giving their ideas to companies in return for the right to sell their products for a 10 percent commission. Other inventors have become, in effect, virtual entrepreneurs, arranging for one company to market and distribute the product and then arranging for another company to manufacture the product. This way, the inventor retains control of the product while still pulling in a 10 to 15 percent profit on every sale. Even as I write, I'm sure there are inventors creating new ways for bringing their product to market.

The Nine Tactics

Most inventors only consider two options when they decide to cash in on their idea—either licensing it or starting their own company. Instead, this book covers nine tactics, and they incorporate different strategies than most inventors usually consider. Inventors should put every one of these tactics into their introduction arsenal. That way you can switch tactics if you find your original strategy isn't working. Remember, your goal is to put your product on the market, and it really doesn't matter how you get it there.

Here are the nine tactics:

1. *Fairs, Craft Shows, and Events:* Some of those people you see selling products at home shows and state fairs are bringing in over $25,000 per weekend.

2. *Selling Locally:* Many inventors start selling their products, especially food products, in their own hometown.

3. *Home Shopping—TV and Mail-Order Catalogs:* QVC, the Home Shopping Network, and the hundreds of mail-order catalogs provide a low-risk sales opportunity.

4. *Internet Sales:* All you have to do is put up a Web site and people will come? Not exactly. But you can succeed on the Internet by implementing a simple strategy.

5. *Selling on Commission:* You can get a manufacturer to pick up all the costs of producing and marketing a product as long as you agree to sell the product on a commission basis.

6. *Joint Ventures:* Inventors can introduce complex and expensive products if they team up with a manufacturer or marketer, or both.

7. *Private Label Marketing:* Some companies don't want to buy from small one-line inventors. But inventors can still get their products on the shelves with a private label agreement, where another company sells the product under its own name.

8. *Licensing:* You come up with a marketable idea and another company makes and sells the product, paying you a royalty, or a fixed percentage on every sales dollar.

9. *Your Own Company:* Most inventors dream of being the president and CEO of their own growing company that produces and markets their own inventions.

The Book's Format

Each of the nine tactics is explained over the course of
two chapters: the first covers the "inside scoop," and the
second explains how to "make it happen." I give you
everything you need to know for each tactic, from what
products work best with it and how much money you
need to start to what concrete steps you need to follow
to be successful. Each chapter contains the following
sections.

The Inside Scoop

▶ *The Basics:* a brief description of the tactic, how it is
   used, and its major benefits

▶ *Perfect Products:* types of products that work well
   with this tactic

▶ *Your Goals:* typical goals for this tactic

▶ *Other Choices:* other tactics you can use to meet the
   same goals

▶ *Money Matters:* how much money inventors need for
   the tactic and how it can best be raised

▶ *Protection:* what patent strategies are best

▶ *Prototypes:* whether or not a prototype is needed,
   and if so, what type to get and how to get it paid for

▶ *Research:* what research you should conduct before
   spending any money

▶ *Manufacturing:* strategies for getting your product
   made with or without your money

▶ *Key Contacts:* the people inventors really need to
   know to succeed

▶ *Pros and Cons:* good and bad points about the tactic

▶ *Up, Up, and Away:* how the tactic can be used as a
   starting point for a successful business

▶ *Key Resources:* places, publications, people, or organizations that the inventor can contact for useful information or important help with the tactic

▶ *What to Expect:* problems and opportunities the inventor will encounter using the tactic

Making It Happen

▶ *Keys to Success:* the three or four factors that will determine if you will succeed or fail

▶ *Momentum Makers:* tactics that will give a product a quick start in the marketplace

▶ *Before You Start:* steps you should take before you actually start your product introduction

▶ *First Steps:* the first few activities inventors should implement for the tactic

▶ *Off and Running:* activities and programs inventors should use to build a customer base

▶ *Building a Business:* the necessary steps for an ongoing successful business

▶ *Are You Making Money?:* how to determine quickly whether or not your product is making money and what corrective actions to take if it's not

The Appendices

There are certain basic tasks that every inventor must tackle no matter what their invention—that is, applying for patents, building prototypes, and raising money—and I have created a separate appendix devoted to each subject. The appendices cover how to proceed with little or no money if needed, and they cover a range of ways you can get the results you desire. There is no single strategy that is always right. Inventors have different products, different amounts of cash, and they are comfortable with different amounts of risk. In each appendix, I list the pros and cons of each strategy so you can choose the one you feel most comfortable with. In the main book chapters, I include brief discussions of patents, prototypes, and raising money as they pertain to each of the nine tactics, but for more thorough descriptions, turn to the appropriate appendix.

Two experts in their fields helped me here, ensuring that I have the most accurate information. Al Davis, a retired patent agent who spent part of his career at the U.S. Patent Office, helped me with the patent appendix, and Jack Lander, a leading expert on low-cost prototypes, helped me write the prototype appendix.

Tips and Inventor's Stories

Throughout the book, you'll find five boxes, each offering different types of information:

▶ *Buzzwords:* These offer definitions of words that are commonly used with new products but that are not always well known by new inventors.

▶ *Success Tips:* These are tactics to improve your chances of success.

▶ *Market Reality:* Here I give information about both positive and negative factors in the market that will influence an inventor's product introduction strategy.

▶ *Inventor's Story:* Each chapter includes a story about an inventor who implemented the highlighted tactic. These stories should help give you a better understanding of how inventors use their creativity and implement a wide variety of strategies to introduce their products.

▶ *Insight:* Here you'll find answers to questions I'm commonly asked by inventors, such as, "How do I set my price?" and, "How much money will I need to introduce a product?"

Teaming Up for Success

I've worked with inventors for over 20 years, and most of the successful ones have created and developed their product on their own and love being independent. "Being my own boss" is the answer I usually get when I ask them what they like best about being an inventor. Indeed, the independent "eccentric" inventor—embodied by everyone from Thomas Edison to Doc Brown in the *Back to the Future* movies—has been lionized in American culture, and it's an image that has strong attraction today for most inventors. But in fact, successful inventors are not Lone Rangers—which, for inexperienced inventors, should be regarded as a good thing. I've talk to over a hundred successful inventors over the last five years, and they frequently don't have a lot of business management experience, don't have any more money than the average person, and

> ▶ **BUZZ** WORD
>
> *Standard dating*, which indicates when payment is due, is 30 days. *Extended dating* or *extended terms* indicates that you don't have to pay for 60, 90, or 120 days. Extended dating is a tremendous benefit for underfinanced inventors. It allows them to wait to pay a contract manufacturer until after their customers pay them.

typically have never tried to introduce a product before. The key moment in their invention process has been when they recognized their shortcomings and sought help from other people. That help is exactly what they need to succeed, and it can come in hundreds of forms, such as these:

1. A manufacturer willing to extend dating on orders.
2. An independent sales agent or industry insider who offers tips on getting a product out into the market.
3. A retailer who heavily promotes your product at its expense.
4. A manufacturer who funds your research and development for the option on a private label contract.
5. A marketer who shares a booth with you at a major convention, or provides an introduction to key industry buyers.
6. An industry connection who helps you fund your initial production run.
7. Another inventor who tells you the best fairs and events to attend, and helps you price your product.
8. A manufacturer who lets you use his or her model shop to produce your products in return for help filling back orders on Saturday.
9. An industry insider who first invests in your company and then comes to work with you to make the product a success.
10. A retailer who gives you a provisional order (they'll buy when and if you can deliver) so you can get a manufacturer to fund an initial production run.

INVENTOR'S STORY

It Takes a Village to Sell a Product

Fatima Sokera was a 23-year-old working her way through college at a beauty salon in Atlanta, Georgia. At the salon, she became frustrated with the job of removing artificial braids and hair extensions—it was always messy and inevitably damaged the customer's hair. The problem was the glue used to hold the extensions in place, and Sokera went to work on creating a product that would dissolve the glue. Once she'd done that, she called her product Hair Down and was ready to go to market. There was just one small problem. Sokera didn't know how to get there. She had several salons try out her product, and some of them started to buy from her, but she wasn't getting her product into stores or to distributors.

So Sokera got creative and did a college research project on the beauty products distribution network. Her field research included an interview with Roscoe Thomas, the vice president of purchasing for Jinny Corp., a Georgia-based distributor of beauty products. Thomas gave her the ins and outs of how to get a product to the market. He also suggested that a new entrepreneur should enlist the aid of a successful independent sales agent, and he suggested that Sokera contact Chester Cavil of Target Marketing Group.

Cavil was a little wary at first, but he took Sokera's product to ten major salons to see if they felt it would work. The salons endorsed it enthusiastically, and Cavil went to work with Sokera to create packaging, pricing, and both salon and store displays. With those in place, Cavil and Sokera were able to line up beauty supply store distributors and major consumer stores to carry the product. In just one year, Sokera's company, Beautiful Braids, Inc., had sales that jumped from $15,000 to $150,000, and Sokera was on her way with more than just a little help from her friends.

You should think about the kind of help you will need right at the start, before you even begin to introduce a product to market. If you can prototype and make your product at home, you can probably survive on your own until you're ready to sell. But most inventors have products that require a little more investment up front, and they could go broke if they wait too long to get experienced advice. Not only that, but getting help early will prevent a lot of mistakes in creating your product, and this will help you save money for the crucial tasks that lie ahead.

The Lone Ranger Is Dead

The product life cycle today is short, very short. Products can come and go in just two to three years, and this dramatic change presents both problems and opportunities for inventors. On the one hand, inventors can't afford to work alone and follow the normal, slow two- to five-year process to get their product to market—since in that time the market may pass them by. This means inventors can't be independent, can't control everything that happens with their product, and may have just a few short years of successful selling. The good news is that established marketers and manufacturers have an even harder time getting to market quickly, so nimble inventors can beat them to the punch. The big manufacturers are responding to this challenge by working with an increasing number of outside companies, including inventors, to keep on the leading edge of their markets. This also means that manufacturers, marketers, distributors, and retailers are generally willing to help inventors. All you have to do is ask.

The simple fact is that teamwork equals success. In today's crowded market, individual inventors have a hard time standing out and getting noticed. To build up the necessary size and momentum, you need resources, and if you don't have them, you must team up with someone who does—someone who has the money, the manufacturing prowess, or the distribution reach required to turn a new product into a success. Every month I hear of at least one new story of an inventor forming alliances to succeed. Below are examples of three inventors who've done this, and they are just the tip of the iceberg. If you keep alert, you'll read about other examples in your local newspapers and business magazines. Might that other person's experience work for you? Remember to always be on the lookout for opportunities to make alliances.

1. Karen Alverez of Dublin, California, invented the Baby Comfort Strap, a product that keeps children safely strapped into shopping carts. When she first started her company, the Baby Comfort Company, LLC, she sought advice from Sharon Trupiano, owner of Kazoo's Consignment Shop for Kids, which sells a fair amount of new children's accessories. Among other things, Trupiano suggested that Alverez also contact the Safe Strap Company, a manufacturer that

 INSIGHT

The Bottom Line

An inventor of a plastic product typically needs a partner because a product that expects to sell $1 million per year (producing an average income of $50,000) will have the following estimated expenses.

Patents	$5,000 to $7,000
Prototypes/Models	$2,000 to $4,000
Tooling	$12,000 to $25,000
Manufacturing Fixtures	$5,000 to $10,000
Up-front packing costs	$3,000 to $7,000
Marketing materials	$5,000 to $10,000
Trade shows	$5,000 to $15,000
Working capital (including inventory)	$150,000 to $250,000
Total	**$187,000 to $328,000**

sells straps to supermarkets for their carts. Alverez asked Safe Strap for help, and the company president, Paul Giampvolo, agreed to make low quantities of Alverez's product at a quantity price as well as agreeing to 90-day payment terms to help launch the product.

2. Nathaniel Weiss's company, G-Vox, based in Philadelphia, Pennsylvania, hit $5 million in sales in 1999. He got his start with a hardware/software product package that automatically transcribes notes played on a guitar into sheet music. His product allows guitarists to work on a new song without having to stop constantly to write down each note. Weiss has had a board of advisors from the beginning. His big break came when he formed an alliance with Fender Guitar Company. Fender agreed to sell his product to guitar stores, both as an accessory and as an option on Fender guitars. Once his company generated some initial sales success, Weiss went out and found several marketing people with extensive experience selling to retail music stores to push his product into the market.

> ▶ **SUCCESS** TIP
>
> Nathaniel Weiss had on his initial advisory board David Horowitz, a former MTV president. Horowitz knew one of Weiss's relatives and was willing to help out when asked. I've found this to be true for myself as well: Many of my friends and relatives have an astounding number of interesting contacts. Ask your family and friends if they know anyone who might be able to help you. Make a list of those contacts and call them when you need them.

3. Vic Pella of Studio City, California, created several new products to cash in on the year 2000, including a baseball hat with an LCD display on the front that says "Happy 2000," a teddy bear that shouts "Happy Millennium" when squeezed, and the

Countdown Candle, which burns down in seven days. Pella didn't have the funding to finance the large volume he needed for his products to cash in on this one-time event. So he struck a deal with a Hong Kong manufacturer who gave extended terms in return for the manufacturing and distribution rights to his products in the Far East. The deal was win-win for both parties. Pella's company, Idea Express, Inc., received products it couldn't afford to pay for in advance, and the Hong Kong manufacturer had its own products to sell in its primary markets.

INVENTOR'S STORY

Virtual Entrepreneur

Vijay Malik loves coming up with product ideas. To date he has come up with seven, primarily storage products for shoes, CDs, and videos. (You can see Malik's products at his Max Space Web site: www.maxspace.com.) Malik, who lives in Kansas City, Missouri, uses a partnership approach every time, which lets him invent products without worrying about manufacturing or marketing each one. One of his successes is the Hang 10, a modular storage strip that holds CDs, DVDs, and computer Zip drives. Malik used his standard tactics to introduce the Hang 10. When Malik felt he had created the right product, he went to the 1997 Housewares Show in Chicago looking for a marketing partner. He found Maverick Ventures, which sells plastic impulse items that are similar in price to the Hang 10. After signing an agreement with Maverick Ventures for them to market and distribute his product, Malik found a contract manufacturer that was willing to make the product, and he was ready to go. The contract manufacturer makes the product, Maverick Ventures sells the product, and Malik's profit is the difference between what he charges Maverick Ventures and what he pays the contract manufacturer. Everyone makes a profit, and Malik is happy, as the arrangement allows him to move on to developing his next idea.

The Invention Factory

There are three tasks involved in launching a successful product.

1. Finding an opportunity in the marketplace, and then creating a product to meet that opportunity. The well-conceived product meets a consumer desire or need and can be produced at a price that provides buyers with value. This is normally an inventor's strength.

2. Manufacturing the product. Tooling, manufacturing fixtures, working capital, quality control, value engineering, product liability insurance, regulatory approvals, and a host of other complicated concerns are the realm of the manufacturer.

3. Marketing the product. Pricing, packaging, promotional allowances, and connecting with major buyers are some of the simpler tasks of marketing. Understanding customer needs, positioning the product so it will sell, creating a memorable brand and product image, and finding customer hot buttons are some of the tactics marketers use to successfully introduce a product.

As you look at these three tasks, ask yourself: Does it make sense for inventors to try and do everything involved in bringing a product to market? I don't think so. Each of the jobs of inventing, marketing, and manufacturing requires in-depth expertise. Your goal as an inventor is to learn to utilize other people so that both you and they make money. Once you do that, you'll be able to devote your time to being creative and inventing new products. Unfortunately, there is no single way to find partners. Each market and each product are different and require a particular approach; for

▶ MARKET **REALITY**

Before you decide exactly what course to take, I recommend you talk to at least one inventor who has succeeded and get his or her insights. You should be able to find at least two or three inventors in your area. Visit the local paper and ask to look through its electronic archives for stories on entrepreneurs. Most successful inventors are happy to talk to new inventors.

each new endeavor, you'll need to go to shows, make industry contacts, and find just the right marketing and manufacturing partners. But once you become skilled at finding partners, you'll only be limited by your creativity and your ability to come up with new ideas that the market wants.

Team Player Advantages

Creative deals are being struck by inventors every day to help launch their products. Teaming with other people improves your market intelligence, gives you access to key market contacts, helps guide you to the best products, and gives you the funding you need to make an impact in the market. Teaming up also offers one more incredible benefit to inventors. It dramatically cuts the financial risk of taking a new product to market. I have heard hundreds of stories of inventors who have spent as much as $30,000—and sometimes much more—on a new product that failed. Countless inventors have put themselves in financial peril by trying single-handedly to put a product on the market. New product introductions are an inherently risky business. Inventors are much better off spreading the risks and taking advantage of other people's expertise.

The advantages of being a team player are overwhelming. This is just a short list of the most important ones.

1. By teaming with marketing organizations, inventors gain the resources and contacts needed to push their product into the market with momentum.

2. Inventors lower their investment and risk. Lowering risk gives inventors the opportunity to start over again if their products should fail.

3. Concentrating on inventing allows inventors to introduce several new products each year.

4. Teaming up may cost the inventor profits on each unit sold, but the inventor typically makes more money because the volume of sales will be much higher.

5. Inventors minimize the number of costly marketing and manufacturing mistakes by teaming up with experts in these fields for each type of product.

The Best of Times

I believe new and underfinanced inventors have never been in a more favorable position. The reason for this is that companies simply cannot keep up with the pace of new products on their own. They are forced to work jointly with other companies. Small to midsize companies are also unable to fund research and development, manufacturing, and marketing of new products. Companies are specializing more and more into one of these three areas, so that it is rare to find a company that isn't selling at least one product developed by someone else. Marketers and manufacturers no longer believe they can develop all the products they need, nor do they believe they can keep up with all the changes in the market. As a result, marketers and R&D engineers have become much more receptive to inventors, and inventors can typically find at least one company to consider a worthwhile proposal.

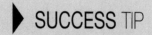

▶ SUCCESS TIP

The costs of taking a product into the market have risen so fast that companies no longer expect inventors to finance too much of a product's development. They are aware that they'll have to pick up most of the product's cost if they want to take advantage of an inventor's ability to spot opportunities and create customer-driven products. Don't try to hide the fact that you are low on cash.

Of the nine tactics in this book, some are brand new, such as setting up an agreement to market your invention on a commission basis or becoming a virtual entrepreneur. Others are more traditional, such as licensing an idea, setting up a private label agreement, or selling at fairs and trade shows. But what inventors should like best is that they can now, more easily than ever before, find partners willing to take over the jobs of manufacturing and marketing—partners with experience, expertise, and resources. And because of this, the types of arrangements are growing and changing every day. By seeking out the best arrangement for each product, you leave yourself free to invent, which is exactly what you want to do, how you will make the most money, and how you can get the most products to market.

2

Fairs, Craft Shows, and Events–
The Inside Scoop

The Basics

County fairs, state fairs, renaissance fairs, craft shows, home shows, home and garden shows, sports shows, and auto shows are just a few of the events inventors can attend to sell their products. And don't think these things are small potatoes. Many experienced showgoers consider $5,000 a bad weekend. I would say most inventors wouldn't think it was a bad weekend at all, since they could slug it out for months trying to sell $5,000 worth of products to stores. This tactic requires only that the inventor pack up the van, drive to the show, set up a booth, and start selling. You control everything, and substantial sales success can point the way to a big future market.

Perfect Products

Products should fill a real need most people who attend the show have, they must be amenable to a demonstration, and they must have a simple, direct message. Fairs are the perfect starting points for products with broad appeal that would ideally be sold in supermarkets, department stores, and mass merchandisers. Normally, those markets are difficult to penetrate for a small inventor. But inventors can build up sales at fairs, selling sometimes as much as $60,000 to $70,000 over a weekend, which can give them the success they need to crack the big retailers.

▶ MARKET **REALITY**

Yes, you can make $70,000 at a weekend fair. People do. But you don't get to this level by just laying your product on a card table. You must develop an entertaining booth that attracts people. The key is to have a little show business flair. Attend several events and note the type of showmanship that brings the people in. Then develop your own style, but don't go to the show until you've polished your act.

Other perfect products are those that lend themselves well to demonstrations. A real-life demonstration is best, but pictures, videos, slides, or posters can also work. Your product or demonstration should have some sizzle and catch people's eye. Being able to show a before-and-after result simply and quickly is a good way to convince people to buy in the atmosphere of a fair. Other types of products that can do well are ones that people can play with or try out, such as toys, musical instruments, or sporting goods. Finally, food products and family recipes can do especially well. People can taste a sample, and if they like it, buy it.

Your Goals

Shows are traditionally regarded as the outlet for a part-time inventor/entrepreneur who only wants to make a

INVENTOR'S STORY

Make It Shine till It Glows

Max Appel got his start about 14 years ago at his local Denver Home Show selling the Hokey Carpet Sweeper. It didn't take Appel long to realize the potential of small shows; some of his fellow retailers were taking home about $20,000 per weekend. He then started to look into products of his own and created Brewax, a finish based on beeswax that turned a dull piece of furniture into a highly polished masterpiece right before your eyes. One of the advantages of Brewax was its convenience, as it dried quickly into a beautiful finish. Appel sold Brewax at fairs and home shows throughout the country until he became aware that some of the chemicals in the formula were considered unsafe.

So Appel started working on a new formula. He was convinced that cleaning products were the best ones for his marketing and demonstration techniques. Finally, he created his current product line, Orange Glo, which includes OxiClean, Orange Clean, New Life for Wood, and Orange Eliminator. This product demonstrates well at fairs, and Appel was able to pick up at the same point where he left off with Brewax. But then something strange began to happen—people started to call for reorders, repeatedly. Instead of a one-time sale, Appel was flooded with reorders, which is when he decided it was time to pursue other avenues: infomercials, Sams Clubs, the Home Shopping Network, QVC, Wal-Mart, and other mass merchandisers.

Appel concentrated on adding business through traditional retailers, home shopping networks, and catalogs. He took on 15 distributors, who were really salespeople with geographic rights to certain home shows, state and county fairs, and other sales outlets. Today, the bulk of his sales occurs through regular sales channels, and Orange Glo's top-selling location is at supermarkets, which account for 30 percent of all sales. From his beginnings at state fairs and home shows, Appel has turned his Orange Glo product line into a $100-million business, Orange Glo International.

little extra money. These inventors don't want to invest much money and are happy making $15,000 to $35,000 extra per year. But shows and fairs can help you meet many other goals, such as:

▶ *Immediate cash flow*: You get the money immediately when you are at a show, money that can help you expand into other markets in the future.

▶ *Test market period*: If you are getting manufacturing support from a company (see appendix C), you may need a test period to entice the manufacturer into paying for permanent tooling or for investing in the operating capital for your product.

▶ *Securing investors*: Sales success at a show helps convince potential investors that your product has a chance for success. Shows work even better for attracting potential investors if you invite them to the show to see firsthand how consumers react to your product.

▶ *Setting up a distribution network*: If you are going to a show, contact potential retailers in the show's town. Let them know you will have a booth and that you will be passing out a flyer saying where the product is available in the area. Many retailers will give you a stocking order in return for being listed on a show flyer.

Other Choices

If your goal is generating part-time income, or you need some initial sales success either to help get funds from an investor or to build up cash flow, other options are selling locally (see chapters 4 and 5) or selling through catalogs or home shopping networks (see chapters 6 and 7).

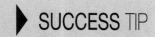

▶ SUCCESS TIP

Shows can be an effective tactic to encourage retailers to stock your product. If that is your goal, keep accurate records of the sales at each show. Take pictures both of your booth and of people watching your demonstration and buying your product. Use these pictures when talking to retailers. They demonstrate that consumers respond positively to your product.

Money Matters

Attending shows is one of the least expensive methods of introducing a product. You simply need to build enough inventory for the first show, and then use the proceeds from that show to build inventory for the second show. For some products, such as cleaning, food, and craft products, inventors can make the product in their garage and take it to the show themselves. Your other costs are booth space and travel expenses. Start out with local shows in your hometown first to keep those expenses low.

Protection

The level of protection you want depends on your long-term goals. Many people will sell at shows initially with just a design patent pending. You can apply for a design patent for under $100, and that allows you to post patent pending on your product. Once you start to sell your product, you have one year to apply for a utility patent.

▶ BUZZ WORD

Patent pending status is a tactic often used to delay competition. Patents that are pending have been filed with the patent office but not yet awarded. They are not on public record, so competitors don't know how to design a product that won't infringe on your patent. You can file for your own patent and post patent pending on your products without ever intending to finish the patent process.

Inventors can apply for a utility patent on their own as the one-year "on sale" time-limit approaches, and this way you can retain your patent pending status for a total of two to three years. That period gives you time to establish your product in the market. You might want to consider using a patent attorney and obtaining a utility patent if your plan is eventually to take your product into the general market.

Trademarks are even more important for show products than for most other products, since you want a name that people will remember—and one they can't turn around and use on their own products at a neighboring booth. (See appendix A for more details on trademarks.) One common tactic to make your product memorable is to use your own name. Don Debelak's Super Lure gives people an extra point to help remember the product.

Prototypes

Most inventors who use shows make their own prototypes or models to get people to evaluate the idea. You can also work a deal with a manufacturer to make your prototype at a reduced price if you promise to use the manufacturer for future production.

Research

Shows are a form of research in themselves. Typically, people start selling at a show in their hometown, where costs will be lower, before committing to a more aggressive show schedule. One disadvantage of a show is that you'll talk to many people who maybe aren't ideal target customers. Since what you really want to know at a show is how well your product sells to your target customers, make sure you have a clear profile of exactly who that is before you go. Then develop one to three questions you can ask people to determine if they fit your ideal profile. For example, Max Appel's target customers for his Orange Glo furniture polish are people who use furniture polish at least once a month. Appel can ask people what type of furniture polish they use now and how often they buy it to determine if they are in the target customer group.

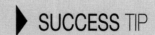 ▶ SUCCESS TIP

Are you having trouble getting investors to give you the money you need? One tactic inventors use, even when they don't have enough inventory for wide sales, is to ask investors to come and spend time in a booth at a show. Investors are typically impressed if you get a strong consumer reaction, and they will be more likely to get behind your product.

If you talk to a target customer and he or she doesn't buy, ask why. Before asking, explain that you have the booth at the fair as a research tool. Then say it would help you decide if you should invest in the product if the person could explain why he or she decided not to buy. I've found that most people will give you an answer immediately if you ask without using any additional sales pressure to convince them to buy the product.

Manufacturing

You should be able to make the product yourself, or the up-front manufacturing costs charged by a contract manufacturer should be minimal. If your product isn't cheap to make, shows don't provide a good long-term strategy, since either your product will be too expensive or you won't be able to sell enough to cover your up-front costs.

 INSIGHT

When You Need a Little Help to Get By

Many inventors wonder, How can I get a contract manufacturer to help me fund my new product's introduction? In fact, successful attendance at shows can be a critical tool for this. Two of an inventor's biggest expenses are operating capital and tooling, which is a broad category that covers the making of molds, dies, fixtures, and any other accessory specifically needed for the manufacturing of a part. If a manufacturer believes an inventor has a winning product, it will often offer extended terms, which reduces the inventor's need for operating capital. Manufacturers may also offer to amortize tooling costs to reduce an inventor's up-front expense. Amortized tooling is the practice of paying for tooling on a per unit basis rather than paying for the tooling all at once when the manufacturer purchases or makes it. For example, if your product requires $15,000 for new tooling, you could pay that cost up front, or you could agree to pay an extra five cents per part to cover the tooling cost, which means that you only have to pay for the tooling as you actually sell products.

Manufacturers are usually reluctant to offer favorable terms to an inventor unless they know the product will sell. If a manufacturer is unwilling to commit a major expense, try asking for a small run of the product to sell at a show. The manufacturer may agree to produce a small run made without new tooling, as the financial risk will be low. While this means your costs per unit will be high—since the manufacturer will have to machine the parts, make them with temporary or prototype tooling, glue them together, or use another labor-intensive manufacturing method—and you may not be able to make any money at the show, the effort can still be worthwhile. Once you've proven your product will sell, it may convince the manufacturer to extend you the terms you need to do a full manufacturing run.

Key Contacts

Show promoters are essential for placing your booth where you will have the best chance of success. They also can help you find other shows where your product will sell. Show promoters are the people who put on the shows, assign the booths, attract visitors, and determine booth regulations. Max Appel recommends that you always visit the show promoter before signing up for a booth. He or she can help you find a booth location where you won't be fighting another busy booth, plus the promoter can tell you what types of booth displays have worked well in the past and what types of demonstrations do best at that particular show.

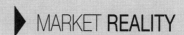

▶ MARKET **REALITY**

Don't tell the promoter that you are attending the show just for market research. That will convince the promoter that you are only going to attend one show, and he or she will probably put you in a poor booth location. However, do tell show promoters that you are attending your first show. They will typically bend over backward to help you succeed.

Pros and Cons

Pros

▶ Low-cost method of introducing a product.

▶ Creates very fast cash flow.

▶ Establishes that a product will sell.

▶ Helps set up an initial distribution network.

Cons

▶ Only products with broad market demand and a $10 to $30 price point will sell well at fairs.

▶ Can't get preorders to help fund production. When using other strategies, marketers can often get a provisional order, which is an order from a distributor, retailer, or other company that they will buy your product if you can produce it as specified. These orders will encourage investors and contract manufacturers to invest a significant sum in your product.

▶ Limits sales to $200,000 to $400,000 in the first year.

Up, Up, and Away

Max Appel started selling Orange Glo at fairs and shows, and the product now sells over $100 million per year. Sales at shows and fairs can easily turn into a profitable company with wide distribution throughout the nation. The reason they are effective is that they establish that consumers want your product. They can also build brand recognition, especially in a small geographic market, and your success here can help you get investors, line up a manufacturer offering extended terms, and even sign up distributors, manufacturers' sales agents, and other distribution outlets. Fairs and shows are an excellent starting point for many inventors, and they are not used nearly as often as they should be.

 SUCCESS TIP

Achieving success through direct-response TV advertising, both through infomercials and one-minute or two-minute spots, has become increasingly difficult over the last two years for inventors with show products because advertising rates have risen steeply. If you want to know more about direct-response TV, subscribe to the industry's leading magazine, *Response*. It's published by Advanstar Communications, Inc., 201 Sandpointe Avenue, Suite 600, Santa Ana, CA 92707-5761; or call 714-513-8482.

However, products that rely heavily on a demonstration to be successful often don't make the transition easily from shows to retail sales. Unusual musical instruments sell well at renaissance fairs but usually don't sell well in stores. People just won't buy an instrument that they haven't heard. Toys and other fun items also frequently fail to make the transition because the product's appeal isn't apparent when the product is in a package. If you have this problem, you can move beyond the show circuit by targeting TV shopping networks or by attracting enough funding to run an infomercial or direct-response TV campaign.

Key Resources

Your city or state visitors and convention organization will have a complete listing of all the shows in your area. You can find the closest group to you by calling the local chamber of commerce. Several Web sites that give show listings that might apply to your product are:

www.tsnn.com
www.scheduleearth.com
www.expoguide.com
www.tradegroup.com
www.renaissancefaire.com
www.fairsnet.org

Frequently, local inventor groups have a booth at state fairs that several inventors share. You can find most local inventor groups through the United Inventor's Association of the USA, PO Box 23447, Rochester, NY 14692; 716-359-9310; www.uiausa.com.

The best listing for craft shows is available from Sunshine Artists, 2600 Temple Drive, Winter Park, FL 32789; 407-539-1399 or 800-597-2573.

MARKET **REALITY**

I've found that one of the biggest reasons inventors give up on shows is that they get discouraged when some people don't like their product. Remember, you will be a runaway success if just 10 percent of the people who stop by your booth like and buy your product. That leaves 90 percent who won't buy. Don't set your expectations too high when you go to the first show. If you convince 10 out of 100 people to become customers, you've had a great sales performance.

If you plan to do a lot of selling at fairs and shows, you'll need an organized accounting and show-scheduling system. A good book that covers this topic is *The Craft Business Answer Book & Resource Guide: Answers to Hundreds of Troublesome Questions About Starting, Marketing & Managing a Homebased Business Efficiently, Legally and Profitably* by Barbara Brabee (M. Evans & Co).

What to Expect

▶ Your product and booth demonstration are all important. You won't sell any products if you expect people to buy just because you show up.

▶ Only 15 to 20 percent of the people who talk to an inventor will buy even a great product. You should feel happy if 10 percent of the people you talk to buy.

▶ You will need to attend 25 to 30 big shows a year to make a profit of $50,000 to $75,000 per year.

▶ A successful booth needs a staff of three to four people for a busy show.

▶ Unless you are using fair or show sales as a test, you probably will need to pay for most of the manufacturing costs yourself.

▶ Successful fair products are frequently knocked off by other fair sellers, typically because the products are relatively easy to make. You need to consider patent protection as soon as you're confident the product will sell. Your other choice is to accept a two-year to three-year life cycle for your product.

▶ Show sales can be a major accounting nightmare at tax time if you don't set up a simple accounting system before you begin.

3

Fairs, Craft Shows, and Events—
Making It Happen

Keys to Success

▶ *Demonstration:* Your best selling tool is a dramatic before-and-after demonstration. Lea Cavender turns a ribbon into a beautiful bow (see "Make It, Take It," page 28). Max Appel's Orange Glo products turn a dull tabletop into a shiny, highly polished, beautiful piece of furniture. Greg Bamaneck—a.k.a., Dr. Juice—sells a product you rub on your hands before handling fishing lures and bait. Dr. Juice claims that people's hands have an odor that repels fish, and his product removes it. Dr. Juice demonstrates his product at shows with a tank full of fish. When people first put their hands in the water, the fish move away. But the fish don't seemed to mind a person's hand at all once he or she has on "the miracle juice."

Another type of demonstration that sells involves people having fun. Rosemary and Omar Barreto sell their own four-legged marionette puppets at renaissance fairs. They set up their booth with stands of the four-legged, easy-to-use puppets; demonstrate the puppets so kids can see them; and then let kids play with them. The kids get into it, attracting more children and parents, and the new "puppeteers" frequently buy puppets.

INVENTOR'S STORY

Make It, Take It

One thing that Lea Cavender learned while working in a ribbon outlet near her hometown of Sevierville, Tennessee, was that people don't know how to make bows. With some help from her father, she created a wooden bow maker that anyone could use, and she started selling it at her ribbon outlet. However, Cavender soon discovered that people only bought the item when it was demonstrated. Otherwise, customers didn't see how easy it was to use or how great the bows turned out. Cavender introduced her EZ Bow Maker at the Hobby Industry Association Craft Show in Las Vegas. Since the product was unique but a little hard to understand in a package, Cavender set up a table in front of her booth with eight stations where people could make a bow and then take it with them. She says, "There was a line at our booth for the entire show. There would be people with one of our bows everywhere you looked, and everyone wanted to take home a bow." Many people also took home an EZ Bow Maker. The EZ Bow Maker is a great demonstration item that was also picked up by the Home Shopping Network, where demonstrations helped Cavender's company, EZ Bows, LLC, sell $1.5 million of product in its first year.

➤ *Single Focus:* Concentrate on just one simple-to-understand benefit when selling at a show. People are not going to take five or ten minutes to understand all the great things about your product, and your sales will go down with every extra benefit you try to sell. Max Appel sells the benefit of a quick beautiful polish. Lea Cavender sells the benefit of a beautiful bow. Dr. Juice sells the benefit of catching more fish.

 MARKET **REALITY**

You won't sell anything if people don't notice you. Dr. Juice claims he created his formulas while visiting medicine men in Africa, and he wears an African safari outfit that people can't miss. You can make your booth stand out by having a big graphic or a wild-and-woolly product display, or you yourself can stand out the way Lea Cavender does, by being the bubbliest person around.

➤ *The Right Shows:* Max Appel sold his Orange Glo primarily at home shows. Appel feels that at least 50 percent of the people attending a show need to be potential customers in order for the show to produce profits. At state or county fairs, be sure you're located in an area, such as a home and garden pavilion, where the most likely prospects will come.

➤ *The Right Locations:* Appel offers these do's and don'ts:

1. Don't be right in front where all the traffic has to pass by. People won't want to create a major traffic jam into the show.
2. Do be in an area where there is enough aisle space for 10 to 20 people to watch you demonstrate a product.
3. Don't be next to a busy booth where people will be attracting a large number of visitors or giving their own demonstrations.

4. Don't be next to a booth with large products or graphics that will cut down on your visibility to potential customers.

5. Do be in the middle of the show where people are likely to walk by.

▸ *The Right Price:* Appel feels products that sell best are priced from $10 though $30. Appel also recommends that you price your product at five to six times what it costs to manufacture. Your goal, after all, is to make money, and you need to clear $4,000 to $10,000 a weekend to make a show worthwhile. Lea Cavender's bow maker is $12.95, and Dr. Juice's products generally sell for under $15, both in the target price range. You'll have trouble generating enough revenue if you sell a product too much below $10.

Momentum Makers

▸ *Unique products:* People won't purchase a product if it is readily available in other locations. Make sure your product stands out as a one-of-a-kind item at the shows.

▸ *Customer involvement:* If possible, have people participate in a demonstration or interact with you doing your presentation. That involvement will dramatically increase sales.

▸ *Carry-around items:* One of the reasons that people kept lining up at Lea Cavender's booth

▸ **SUCCESS** TIP

Enthusiasm is infectious—everybody is attracted to an upbeat, outgoing person. But even if you're not comfortable entertaining crowds and strangers, you can dress in a noticeable way or have some gimmick that will start a conversation. For example, you might have a small model to demonstrate, a squeaky toy to catch people's attention, something good to eat, a great video, or even music in your booth.

was because they had seen hundreds of other people walking around carrying a pretty bow made on her bow maker.

▶ *A busy booth:* Have your booth look active at all times, and then be sure people don't pass by your booth because no one is available to talk to them.

Before You Start

▶ *Locate potential shows:* You want shows that appeal to your target customer, have plenty of visitors, and allow you to sell products. Start first with local shows. Your expenses will be much less, and you will be able to work more closely with the show promoter. Follow these steps to find the best shows.

1. Contact your local chamber of commerce or convention center to get a list of upcoming shows. You can also check out the Web sites mentioned under "Key Resources" in chapter two (see page 23).
2. Get the name of the show promoter—that is, the person who rents the space from the convention center manager and then sells space to exhibitors.
3. Call the show promoter and ask for a copy of last year's convention guide.
4. Call at least three or four past exhibitors. Ask them how many years they have exhibited, and how the show does for them. Exhibitors will keep going back to good shows, so be sure that at least half the people have exhibited at the show for two or more years. Also ask the exhibitors what types of products sell best at the show, and what prices do best.

▶ *Investigate all leads:* When you talk to other exhibitors, be sure to ask them where else they exhibit. Frequently, your city or town will host smaller shows that aren't listed in convention guidebooks, such as a festival in the park, other community celebrations, or even a small miniconvention at a local community center. These can still be good shows to start selling your product.

Community newspaper event calendars are potential sources of smaller, profitable local shows that cater to your target customer group. These could include garden shows, bridal fairs, hobby club events, or fishing demonstrations. Your library may carry three to six months of back issues of the local paper. Call up past event sponsors to find out what events are coming up. Associations can be another source of small shows. In Minnesota, the Hockey Coaches' Association has meetings and conferences periodically throughout the year. Each meeting has tables with exhibitors trying to sell products. I've also seen similar exhibits at the local meetings of the Christian Day Care Centers Association. You can find a list of associations in *Gale's Encyclopedia of Associations,* which is available at most larger libraries.

▶ *Inventory needs:* You only need enough inventory for the next show, and that's all most show exhibitors keep on hand. The ideal situation is to run out of product just as the show closes. Predict how much you might sell at the show based on your discussions with past exhibitors, then take 20 to 30 percent more inventory than you think you will sell. If by chance you sell out, you will still have had a successful show.

▶ *Pricing:* As I mentioned earlier, products priced in the $10 to $30 range sell best. Your best show strategy is to create impulse sales based on a demonstration or a person trying out a product. Though some inventors who sell higher priced products feel they can get leads at a show and sell prospects later on, I find that this is a mistake. The urge to buy drops dramatically once people leave a show, and so these are not sales you can count on.

First Steps

▶ *Visit other shows:* Before exhibiting at your first show for a promoter, try to visit one of the promoters other shows, as most promoters do similar shows in a variety of cities. You want to see what other booths are like so you can design yours to stand out. This is also another great way to talk to exhibitors and get more information about how the show works, about how much merchandise you can expect to sell, and what steps you can take to maximize sales.

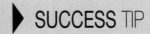

▶ **SUCCESS** TIP

Booth promotions can double or triple your sales—so use them. Free giveaways, two-for-one specials, combination packages of products, buy-two-get-one-free: Try a variety of promotions at different shows to get figure out what works best for your product. And don't forget to check the types of promotions other people are offering.

▶ *Start at a low-cost show:* Start at a small show with a low-cost booth where past exhibitors have had success. Pitching a product and closing a sale is more difficult than you might first expect, and it pays to practice at a lower volume show. A small show will give you a better idea of what sales levels you can expect in the future.

▶ *One show at a time:* When you're just starting out, make sure your first show is successful before committing to a heavy show schedule. If it isn't successful, figure out what went wrong, make adjustments, and then sign up for only one more show to be sure your changes are effective. You can't get refunds on booth rental fees, so don't make extended commitments until you know you will make money.

Off and Running

▶ *Sign up:* Once you've proven you can be successful, set up a show schedule for the next six months. Call the shows you plan on attending and see what booth location you can obtain. If you can't get a good location, select another show. A good location will do two to three times the dollar sales of a bad one, and it's better not to attend a show than to go to one and suffer bad sales because your booth is far from the action.

▶ *Sell, sell, sell:* Products, no matter how great they are, don't sell themselves. *You* are the one who generates excitement and gets people to buy. Before you exhibit, be sure to attend at least two or three shows to observe the various styles and tactics people use to attract and interest a crowd. Find a tactic that fits your personality and that you feel comfortable with. Don't go to a show till you've decided just how you will grind, flash, and tip, or you'll find sales will be very disappointing.

▶ **BUZZ** WORDS

Here are three terms you'll hear experienced show sellers use:

Grind: When few people are at the show and sellers need to call every person over to their booth to pitch their product.

Tip: Getting the first person to come over to the booth and start listening to a pitch or observing a demonstration.

Flash: Moving around in and outside the booth to attract people.

Building a Business

▶ *Set a show schedule:* You have several considerations when setting your show schedule.

> ▶ MARKET **REALITY**
>
> I recommend you only attend one show per month for the first six months. Shows are a lot of work: You must prepare your product, set up the booth, run the show, and then tear it down, package everything up, and prepare for the next show. You can't anticipate all the problems you'll encounter, such as how long it takes to get a booth from one location to the next, until you've done several shows.

1. How many shows are available at which you can make money? Sell-ers of musical instruments or outdoor toys might do well at renaissance fairs but do poorly at indoor shows. Since there are only so many renaissance fairs, you'll need to try other outdoor venues, such as other types of fairs, art festivals, outdoor concerts, and summer festivals to find other shows that will work.

2. What is your desired income? If you net $5,000 from a show after expenses, and desire an income of $60,000, you'll need to attend 12 shows.

3. When are the shows? Many times, there are similar shows running in different parts of the country at the same time or very close together. Give yourself adequate time to recover from one show before scheduling the next.

4. What booth location can you get? Most shows give this year's exhibitors the option of keeping the same booth space for the next year. As a result, you might not be able to get a good booth location for a particular show, and you might not even be able to get a booth at all. If this is the case, call vendors who've attended the show (you can get their names from past show directories) and ask

what other shows they have attended with good results.

▶ *Hire helpers:* Shows entail quite a few expenses, including booth rental, literature, handouts, travel expenses, and the cost of the booth itself. Realistically, one person usually can't sell enough products to cover all those expenses and make a healthy profit. You need two or three people in the booth selling at the same time, or else too many prospects will walk by without talking to you. It is expensive to travel with your own salespeople, so most people recruit help in the city where the show is. You can find salespeople through the convention center, through a temporary agency, or through an ad in a local paper.

▶ *Expand your network:* Once you've become an adept show seller, you'll discover there are two limits to what you can accomplish: time and energy. Working a show is exhausting, especially if you have two or three in a row; and you can only get to so many in a year. One way to get around this is to set up franchisees or sales agents with specific territories. For example, you might give a person in Milwaukee the rights to all the shows in Wisconsin. As the inventor or product owner, you would typically agree to sell the product to the franchisee for a specific price (typically about 40 to 50 percent of the consumer

---

▶ **SUCCESS** TIP

A great salesperson can sell 20 times the amount of a poor salesperson. To get great people, offer a 20 percent commission. That way your workers can make a bundle on each show, which is fine with you because the more the salesperson makes, the more you make. And if you're offering a good commission, those same excellent salespeople will be more willing to travel with you to distant shows.

price), and the franchisee would agree to purchase a certain amount of product every year, attend the shows, and pay all show expenses. Typically, the inventor doesn't charge the franchisee an up-front fee but settles for selling products to the franchisee or sales agent. There are quite a few people who enjoy working fanatically for 10 weeks in order to have the rest of the year off. How do you find them? At shows, of course. Attend shows in the area where you would like an agent or franchisee, then talk to the other exhibitors and find out if they are the owner of the product, an agent franchisee, or an employee. If they are either of the latter, ask them if they know other people who might be interested in being your agent.

Are You Making Money?

▶ *Profit check:* For each show, keep a detailed record of these expenses:

1. Booth rental
2. Travel, food, and lodging, including the cost of shipping the booth and products to a show
3. Literature. Put a value on each piece of literature by adding up the creative and printing costs and dividing that total by the number of brochures printed. A typical flyer or brochure should cost between 50 cents and a dollar each.
4. Money paid to all employees or helpers, including sales commissions—along with any other expenses, such as booth set up, related to the show.
5. The manufacturing cost of any items you've sold. For example, if your product costs $1 to make,

and you sell 2,500 during the show, your manufacturing cost will be $2,500.

6. The costs of giveaways and other promotional items.

You need to make about $3,000 to $5,000 per show over and above these expenses, and of that, $1,000 to $2,000 needs to be applied against your one-time start-up expenses, such as tooling, booth design and purchase, legal fees and so on. The rest can be considered profit. If you are not clearing this amount, you'll find you just won't make money in the long run.

> ▶ **BUZZ** WORD
>
> *Creative expenses* refers to artwork, design, photography, writing, and any other work that prepares a product for production or printing. In many cases, creative charges can exceed the actual cost of printing a brochure or preparing a package.

▶ *Corrective measures:* The most common problem at shows is that you are not selling enough. People often claim that the problem is not enough traffic, but I've found it's usually that the inventor hasn't put the work into creating an effective display, demonstration, or sales presentation. At each show, determine how much you've sold versus what other booths are selling. Traffic is not the problem unless nobody is being successful. Analyze what is working at other booths, and then adjust your presentation for the next show.

▶ *Cutting costs:* All the expenses of a show are pretty well set except for travel and shipping expenses. Many show sellers hold down both those expenses by traveling to shows in travel homes and carrying all their inventory and booth materials with them. If you ship your booth and inventory to a site prior to a

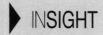

Testing for Sticker Shock

Another common problem is that inventors set their price too low. You simply can't succeed unless you mark your product up at least four times your manufacturing cost. Don't be afraid to experiment with various prices on different days of your first shows. Remember, people are making impulse purchases, and they don't expect show sellers to have Wal-Mart pricing. Rarely will sales be impacted by a $2 to $3 price differential, and raising your prices even that much can dramatically increase your profits. In general, as you gradually raise your price, sales won't change much until you reach the point where people feel the price is too high—at which point sales will plummet. A typical price sales chart for a single day might look like this:

Price	Units Sold	Unit Profit	Total Profit
$12.95	300	$8	$2,400
$14.95	280	$10	$2,800
$15.95	270	$11	$2,970
$19.95	240	$14	$3,360
$24.95	100	$19	$1,900

You get the most income if you keep raising your price until sales fall off dramatically.

show, the convention's freight and drayage charges can often be 50 to 100 percent of the actual booth expense, so eliminating those costs can save you a significant amount of money.

4

Selling Locally–
The Inside Scoop

The Basics

Inventors face many obstacles when they start to sell. They have no sales history, retailers and distributors worry about getting paid, and everyone wonders how the inventor will create demand for an unknown product. The one place where you have the best chance of breaking through these restrictions is in your home market. Every community is interested in seeing its own people succeed. When you begin by selling locally, you can personally support your product, it's easier to get press coverage, and you can have friends buy your product and create a "word of mouth" advertising program in the neighborhood. Inventors of food products almost always use this tactic, as it gives them the opportunity to pass out samples and do virtually everything a large manufacturer can do locally except advertise. People with fishing products can do demonstrations at local stores and have a booth at local fishing stores. Some inventors use selling locally as a stepping stone to build initial sales and market momentum, while other inventors—primarily those who make their product at home—may be completely satisfied with the level of sales the local market can produce.

Perfect Products

▶ *Products that generate press coverage:* Publicity will get retailers to try out a product, but to get press coverage, you need an interesting personal story or an interesting product that appeals to a large number of people. Candace Vanice, the woman who invented a fat-free french fry (see "Fifteen Minutes of Fame," page 43), had a lot of angles to her story. The more angles a story has, the more press coverage the product is likely to get. Products that appeal to a broad range of people, such as food, will also generate more coverage than products that appeal to a small group of people, such as a new air filter for clean rooms.

> ▶ **BUZZ** WORD
>
> In journalism, an angle refers to the focus of a story. Candace Vanice had several angles to her french fry story: One was her age, since she was just 28 when she started; another was the fact that the fries are fat free, since they offer a big health advantage for a favorite American food; and a third angle was taste. People will want to know: How do these "healthy" fries stack up against the regular "bad" ones?

▶ *Products frequently used by consumers:* People pay more attention to products they use frequently, and they are more likely to buy these sorts of items on impulse. In addition, publicity is usually a one-shot deal. If consumers purchase the item only occasionally, they are unlikely to remember a six-month-old news story when it comes time to buy.

▶ *Products that work well in demonstrations:* Many local stores will allow you to put on a demonstration on a weekend. This could be a product demonstration or just a food sample giveaway. Toy inventions also do well in demonstrations, as do products with a specialized use, such as wallpaper tools, paint applicators, or easy weeding tools.

INVENTOR'S STORY

Fifteen Minutes of Fame

Candace Vanice loved french fries, but she didn't love what they did to her figure. Remembering how her mother used an egg coating to make bread crispy, Vanice conducted a series of culinary experiments to do the same with fries. Once she had a winning formula, she got a patent and was ready to go. Unfortunately, supermarkets are a very tough sell for inventors. One problem is that sales usually go through wholesalers, who don't like small one-product companies. Another is that supermarkets expect a big marketing and advertising program to create demand for a new product. Vanice couldn't deliver a big advertising program. But she could kick up a big publicity and demonstration program in her hometown of Kansas City, Missouri.

Vanice started by convincing a small local grocery store to carry her product, promising them that she would be in the stores on Fridays and Saturdays handing out samples to consumers. Once Vanice had her product established in the one small chain, she hit the publicity circuit of local papers, radio stations, and TV shows. She was able to get coverage in every media, and she even started hosting special taste events at the supermarkets. The blitz of publicity brought most Kansas City supermarkets on line, and her product started to sell throughout the metropolitan area. Vanice kept the publicity and sampling blitz operating for six months till she had a secure customer base who liked her product, Eighth Wonder Fat Free Fries. Then Vanice used the same strategy to build success in regional supermarkets like HiVee, Kroeger, and Albertson's. That success has allowed her company, Marvel, LLC, to branch out into markets throughout the Midwest, though she is careful to launch a publicity blitz in every new market.

Your Goals

Inventors typically sell locally for four reasons:

1. The product is specialized for the local market. Stores in Minnesota carry specialized Norwegian foods that probably won't sell well in many other places. Other inventors sell products associated with a particular state, and still others sell products based on local situations, like an infestation of fire ants or an overabundance of rabbits. Other people will sell a product based on a particular state or regional activity, such as black powder hunting, which is a type of hunting with a rifle that's very popular in Pennsylvania and Michigan.

2. An inventor wants to build momentum for an eventual regional or national product launch. You are much better off concentrating your initial efforts on a single, smaller market, where success will be easier, than spreading your efforts among three or four markets. Once you've built sales success in a small market, you'll develop a steady cash flow, you may be able to obtain additional financing, and you'll have market momentum for further growth.

3. An inventor is happy with the level of sales one market can produce. If you make your product in your basement, or at a small manufacturing facility, you can run literally most of the business operations

for a small market yourself. Expanding nationwide calls for a whole new outlook, hiring lots of employees, and raising a substantial amount of money. Some inventors are happier keeping things low key and making enough money to give themselves a decent salary.

4. The product requires a high level of sales support. One inventor I worked with had a product he sold to apartment owners. The product required an extensive sales process, installation, and ongoing monitoring. The inventor had to do all the work himself, and he didn't feel he could expand until he could train additional salespeople or licensees.

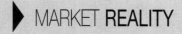 ▶ MARKET **REALITY**

Many inventors start out excited about selling their product, and then after a year or two get discouraged if they don't land a major sale. One reason for their lack of success is that they spread their efforts out with a national sales campaign, rather than focusing on a small market. However, once you have proven your product will sell locally, you usually can find someone to buy your product or company—either another entrepreneur looking to own a company in your area, or a bigger company that wants to take advantage of your local distribution network.

Other Choices

Inventors sell locally because they want to build market momentum or because they want to keep their business from growing too large. While selling locally is the best tactic for building market momentum, inventors could also strike an exclusive deal with one retailer or distributor, or they could restrict themselves to a certain store category, such as selling a cosmetic only through skin salons. The only other choice is to gear up a full nationwide promotional campaign and sell nationally.

▶ BUZZ WORD

If you haven't already, you're bound to hear *market niche* a lot as you run your business. It refers to a smaller, clearly defined market of end users or applications within a larger, general market. For example, a company might sell door hardware, the general market. One market niche would be owners of Victorian homes, who would want Victorian door hardware. An application niche would be day cares and preschools, since they might want hardware that would prevent children from accidentally locking themselves in a room.

Inventors who are trying to keep their business small and still profitable can also do that by selling through catalogs and home shopping networks, through direct mail and Internet sales, through a private label contract, or through an alliance with a distribution group. Catalogs, direct mail, and Internet sales all work well with products targeted at a market niche. For example, if you sell products to firefighters, you can sell through special catalogs or form an alliance with another company targeting the same market.

Money Matters

If you plan to sell locally, you'll want to keep your expenses low. Selling locally is best for inventors who make their product themselves or can have it made without purchasing expensive tooling. This is one reason food products work so well in a local market, since inventors don't need to spend much start-up money. You can get a local food manufacturer to make the product for you, and the local food manufacturer usually has the equipment for smaller production runs and packaging, so you don't need to make an up-front investment. Selling locally in a limited market isn't advised for products that have huge up-front costs because you might not be able to recoup your investment.

Inventors who sell locally often finance their efforts with credit cards, personal savings, or investments from family or friends. Another common tactic is to ask stores for a down payment with orders to help get the product made. Indeed, this tactic only works in local markets, or if you offer an exclusive sales agreement, where the retailer is anxious to help you.

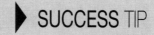

SUCCESS TIP

Inventors often strike exclusive sales agreements with companies in order to entice them into buying. An exclusive agreement just means you won't sell to anyone else for a certain period of time. If you are having trouble landing that first customer, promise a short-term exclusive agreement to coincide with a publicity program and a weekend sampling program.

Protection

One of the risks of selling locally is that people might notice your success in one market and try to duplicate it in another. This is a big risk if you are selling locally to build market momentum in order to develop nationwide sales. If you plan to have broader sales eventually, you should pursue the best patent protection you can obtain. If you only plan to sell locally, full patent protection may not be needed or worth the expense, and instead you might either pursue a patent pending strategy or apply on your own for a design patent, both of which will discourage competitors until you become established.

Prototypes

Most inventors who sell locally typically don't start production until they actually have orders, as this cuts down on the inventor's financial risk. Typically, you get orders by having a convincing prototype. Inventors often make the prototype themselves, as in the case of food, in which they prepare the initial samples and use those to get orders. It's important to have a prototype that is exactly like or very similar to the product you will deliver. If required, use

MARKET **REALITY**

Inventors of simple products can frequently buy the equipment needed to make the product for the same cost or less of having a prototype built. If that's the case, you should buy the equipment. You can then make two or three prototypes to be sure the product is right for your market. Your local inventor club can help you find the new or used equipment you need.

a prototype service or a manufacturer to make the prototype.

Research

The absolute best market research anyone can do is to try and sell a product, so selling locally in itself is research. If people buy your product, they clearly like it and you have it in the right place. If they don't buy, you can begin to determine why: perhaps people aren't in a buying mode, they are buying a competing product, they don't like some aspect of your product, or they aren't finding your product (and you need a different store or more publicity). The one big mistake inventors make is they set their expectations too high. You should be happy if 10 percent of the retailers you call on actually buy. You should also plan on calling on every contact at least four or five times. Many buyers and retailers want to be sure you have staying power before they buy, so you have to make repeated calls. It is common for buyers to wait four or five times before they will buy from a first-time inventor.

Manufacturing

Selling locally is a low-volume option. You want to avoid spending too much money on fixed equipment during this phase. Unless you can make the product at home, in a garage, or in a small building, you should work with a small to midsize local manufacturer. The per unit costs may be higher at first, but your initial goal is to find out if

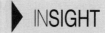

Orders Without Products

It's a classic Catch-22: You need money to make your product, and yet you can't get money or orders until you have the product in hand. Actually, what you need is a prototype. If you're looking for funding, a good prototype is a great way to convince either an outside investor or a contract manufacturer to help you. Getting orders with a prototype can be trickier. Since you might not be able to deliver for several months, some buyers may be reluctant to place an order on a far future delivery, and other buyers may be reluctant to order without seeing the actual final product. One way around this is to ask for a provisional order. This is just like a regular purchase order, but it has two escape clauses for the buyer. The first is the buyer can cancel the order if the final product doesn't meet his or her expectations, and the second is that the buyer has seven days to cancel the order once he or she is notified of a delivery date. Another advantage of asking for a provisional order is that it helps you determine whether a buyer is just brushing you off (and really isn't interested in buying) or if he or she is genuinely concerned about your ability to produce a future shipment.

Another strategy is to get an order from a retailer for a future delivery date, or to get a supporting letter from the retailer or distributor that they like your product concept and that they will strongly consider buying your product once it's available. I've found people relatively willing to give an inventor a supporting letter if the inventor explains that he or she needs it for a potential investor.

the product will sell and for how much. Once you know that, you can decide how you want to have the product made. For example, Candace Vanice had a small food manufacturer make her fat-free french fries for over a year. She paid extra for that, but it kept her expenses low until she was ready to reevaluate how she would make the product on her own.

Key Contacts

▶ *Chambers of commerce*: Members of the local chamber of commerce are interested in promoting local businesses. The chamber will give you the names of local members, and they may also have meetings you can attend to network with potential customers.

▶ *Small Business Development Centers (SBDCs)*: These government-sponsored centers often have information about manufacturers, sales organizations, and sales agents in your city or area that might be able to help you. They also offer classes in business organization. Contact the Small Business Administration office in your state to find the phone number of the SBDC closest to you.

▶ *Local equipment dealers*: The best manufacturers to work with are small to midsize companies that are looking for production. You could look for a long time before you find the right manufacturer on your own. A better approach is to call up the distributors that sell the equipment in that industry. For example, Vanice could have called distributors of food manufacturing equipment and asked them which manufactures were likely candidates to produce her product.

▶ *Local sellers*: People who sell your type of product are good contacts. Start subscribing to trade magazines, and send away for new products. New products usually arrive with descriptive literature that includes the name of a salesperson or the manufacturers' sales agent. Contact that individual, explain that you are an inventor with a new product, and meet the person for lunch. Usually local salespeople will offer you a considerable amount of helpful advice.

Pros and Cons

Pros

▶ Low-cost method of selling a product.

▶ Most effective way to generate market momentum.

▶ Provides inventors with extensive market feedback before they invest in a national campaign.

▶ Ideal for inventors who just want to run a small business on their own.

▶ Success during this phase will encourage investment from outside sources.

> ▶ **SUCCESS** TIP
>
> You should always subscribe to every trade magazine that applies to your industry. Trade magazines are directed usually at all the people in an industry, including retailers, distributors, and manufacturers. You can locate trade magazine publishers in either the *Standard Periodical Directory* or *Gale's Encyclopedia of Publications and Broadcast Media*, which are available in libraries. Trade magazines help you keep informed about competitive new products and industry events.

Cons

▶ Inventor's success may encourage competitors to go after other markets with a similar product.

▶ Local manufacturers will be less interested in offering favorable terms for products only sold locally.

▶ Income potential is limited.

▶ Difficult to implement the lowest-cost manufacturing options, as the lower volume may not justify expensive tooling.

Up, Up, and Away

Your success selling locally is often driven by the publicity you generate and on-site demonstrations. You won't have

MARKET **REALITY**

Many inventors I've talked to feel that the second market they sell to will be much easier than the first. But actually the opposite is true. In their first market, inventors typically have many network contacts that help them get their product into the market. Those contacts provide introductions and help the inventor get sales. In the second market, inventors don't have that network help, and they can often flounder.

these advantages when going to other markets, where you may have trouble repeating your success. To overcome this, make sure you set up some local stores where you don't provide extensive sales support. At these stores, create displays and use other strategies to produce an impact on consumers as they walk by. Once you've proven that your product will sell without a demonstration, you should be able to succeed at other locations. Then, when you launch at each new city, do a publicity and promotion campaign. Your second city, one where you are not considered a local person, is probably your most important market. You won't be able to get as much favorable press coverage, and you won't be able to spend as much time in that city promoting your product. Spend at least four to five months concentrating only on your second target market to be sure you can still sell in markets where you aren't the "local hero." If you succeed in the second city, you should be able to succeed on a nationwide basis.

Key Resources

By far, your key resource is your card file—that is, all the individuals you know and the contacts you've made. You probably know dozens of helpful contacts in your community, even though you may not realize it. Our church did a survey of its members once when it was searching for volunteers. That list included a purchasing manager at

J.C. Penney, three manufacturing representatives, retail store owners, vice presidents of manufacturing companies, and dozens of other people in potentially helpful positions. One person was a salesperson at the Schwinn Bicycle Company, and on one project, he presented and recommended my product to the president of his division. I knew all of these people at our church, I just didn't know what they did. The same is true for parents of kids on my son's baseball team, and it's true of individuals I meet all the time in the community. You have to make a point of asking people what they do for a living, and then keep a file on all your contacts. You can also attend network meetings in your community. Take classes at local colleges for small business owners, and become active in local business associations. Then, once you have the file, don't be afraid to use it. Call those contacts when you need help. They will prove indispensable with any number of aspects of your product introduction.

What to Expect

▶ You'll do almost everything yourself to keep your expenses low.

▶ Most evenings, you'll be preparing invoices, packaging product, or even making product well into the night.

▶ You'll spend the day demonstrating and selling your product.

▶ You should be able to get into a minimum of 10 percent of the local distribution outlets with an aggressive promotion program.

▶ After six months, about 25 percent of the distribution outlets will come on board if your product is successful.

▶ You'll find it is very tough to get into over 25 percent of the distribution outlets without a major
advertising program unless you have a runaway
product winner.

Selling Locally—
Making It Happen

Keys to Success

▶ *Get into as many stores as possible:* To do this, you need a two-pronged approach—enticing stores and enticing customers. Some stores will probably only take products on a consignment or guaranteed sales basis. They may also want a commitment from you that you will be working

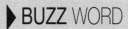

▶ BUZZ WORD

Consignment sales means that a store agrees to carry your product, but the store only pays for the items that are sold. *Guaranteed sales* is a payment clause that many retailers insist on even from successful companies. It means that the seller guarantees to take back any unsold products and to issue a refund to the retailer for any returns.

independently to create demand for the product. Since you should be doing this anyway, your answer will always be yes, and indeed, a strong demand-generating program greatly increases your chances of landing retailers.

▶ *Create buyer demand:* Publicity is one method to generate demand. Other tactics include hosting events, giving prizes away at events, running classes for or giving demonstrations to targeted local groups, having booths at major fairs or conventions, getting endorsements from local celebrities, and offering to participate in a co-op advertising program. Brad Young invented HeadBanz, a headband that contains headphones. Since his primary market is skiers, he built demand by having ski race sponsors run a give-away contest during the events. Whenever there was a delay in the race, the announcer would play a radio song. The first person who could name the artist would receive a free HeadBanz. One mother invented a bumper guard for baby walkers, and she passed out coupons to day care centers and preschools to build demand. An inventor of a flashlight holder paid a hardware store $150 to have his product included in a sales flier the store was sending out.

> ▶ **BUZZ** WORD
>
> When a sales flier from a store comes to your house, the advertisement is probably not paid for completely by the retailer. The retailer also gets money from manufacturers, which is called *co-op advertising.* This refers to the practice of manufacturers paying part of the cost of a retailer's ad or flyer when it features the manufacturer's products.

▶ *Build rapid momentum:* You need to convince buyers, especially buyers in the distribution channel, that you are going to be a major force in the market. You can't convince people you are a winner if you add two to three stores per month. Ideally, you should aim for 10 to 15 stores a month. Even when you sell locally, be sure to carefully plan out your introduction so your idea looks like a "hot" product.

INVENTOR'S STORY

The Secret Ingredient: Persistence

Daniel Cugino's family has a 150-year-old recipe for an Italian dressing that Cugino felt was far better than anything else on the market. He christened his product the Absolutely Delicious Authentic Italian Dressing and Marinade, and he started selling in his local market— Chicago. Cugino encountered heavy sales resistance at first because he couldn't cash in on many of the benefits of selling locally. It is difficult to generate publicity in a big city because there is so much local news and so many local companies are vying for press coverage. By simply going out and hustling sales, however, Cugino overcame this initial cool response and eventually built the customer list for his company, Cugino Gourmet Foods, to over 500 stores.

To start, Cugino offered sales incentives to prospective stores. Cugino offered to do demonstrations and sell the product himself, while the store only paid for products Cugino sold. The store could decide to order after seeing the results of the demonstration. This technique built a small customer base for Cugino in finer food stores, but this tactic wasn't working fast enough to build market momentum. Cugino started asking stores he sold to for the names of the independent sales representatives who sold other products to them. He contacted those representatives and asked them to carry his product. When Cugino promised to pay for demonstrators at new stores, representatives started signing on and promoting the product.

Cugino then took an extra step that probably clinched his success. He attended every craft fair he could in the Chicago area. At each show, he gave away samples, sold products, and, most importantly, passed out fliers that listed every store that carried his line. Cugino knew he had to create demand for the product or it would just sit on the store shelves. Getting on store shelves was the first step, but sales depended on his convincing Chicagoans to find those stores and buy.

Momentum Makers

▸ *Create a memorable name:* Publicity is great, but your success depends on people remembering your product name when they are ready to buy. If people read a story about your company, hear about your great product from a friend, or see you at a local community event, you want them to recall your product's distinctive name as they browse the aisle of the supermarket or hardware store. Cugino's product starts with the phrase "Absolutely Delicious," which sets it apart from other names in the market.

▸ *Know the distribution network:* You want to get into as many stores as quickly as you can, building market interest and making your product easy to buy. To do this, you need to understand all the different ways your target stores buy products. Do they buy exclusively through distributors? Do they buy from representatives, or do they buy direct from the company? You will expand the fastest if you tap into the distribution network that the stores normally use. Know who the contacts are and how to approach them before you start selling.

▸ *Make the right contacts:* The secret to a fast-track introduction is to have a core of stores presold, those that take your product immediately, and then to use those sales to line up other customers. You need two contacts to start. First, you need store owners or other customers who will bring the product into their stores and help you promote it. Next, you need to identify one person or company, and preferably more, who can take the initial success at those first stores and sell additional customers. Usually that person is a manufactures' representative or a sales manager of a distributor.

Before You Start

▶ *The right plan:* Nothing succeeds like success. That statement is never truer than with new product introductions. The most successful introductions are well-coordinated one-month blitzes. Start by having inventory on the shelves of a group of retailers on a date when your demand-generating activities—events, contests, newspaper stories—start impacting customers. Use the success at those stores in that initial week to ten days to land other retailers, and then in week three, make sure to have additional demand-creating activities. Your goal is to make a product look like a runaway winner, something retailers want to have on their shelves. You want momentum to sweep the market, which will in turn generate additional publicity for you.

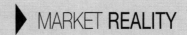
▶ MARKET REALITY

Too many inventors place their product in a couple of stores and then wait to see what happens. Then they are surprised when the product doesn't sell. I'm not surprised. After all, why should anyone else think an introduction is a big deal when the inventor doesn't treat it that way? If you stage the introduction with a marketing blitz, people will notice, and you just might enjoy the sight of everyone jumping onboard your bandwagon.

▶ *Packaging:* If you are selling a retail product, packaging is critical. Talk to your retail contacts and get their approval of your packaging design before you set a launch date. Retailers usually won't buy a product that isn't packaged to meet their needs, which include eye-catching graphics, size, how it is displayed, and UPC code requirements. To obtain a UPC code for both your company and your product, contact the Uniform Code Council for an informational pamphlet; write to them at 8163 Old Yankee Road, Suite J, Dayton, OH 45458.

▶ *Incentives:* Your first introduction is not the time to worry about how much money you'll make; it is a time to worry about getting into stores. So use as many incentives as you can think of to get that first order. You can offer discounts for all orders received for the first month. For retailers, you can promise demonstrations at each store, co-op advertising programs, and free tickets to events related to your product; you can offer to pass out fliers that include the store name at events or locations where your target customer visits. For people in the distribution channel, you can offer bonuses for those who sell a certain number of customers in the first month. You can also offer extra commissions, training aids, or a night on the town to encourage salespeople to sell more products.

▶ *Inventory needs:* If you did your homework with key contacts, you should have a reasonable idea of how many products a store might sell each month. Multiply that number times about 20 percent of the stores in the local market, and go with that number. You run a risk of running out of inventory, but that will only reinforce that your product is a "hot" seller. Don't overinvest in inventory in case you need to make product adjustments.

▶ *Pricing:* You have a big introduction for a red-hot, innovative product, so don't lowball the price or you'll detract from that image. You don't want to be priced higher than everyone else, but do set your price between the upper half and the upper three-fourths of products on the market. That pricing reinforces the message that you have a quality product. If you don't feel your product can justify that price, ask yourself why you are introducing it. The strategy of pricing a product low to increase volume is a myth unless you have a generic me-too product, which is rarely the case in a small market.

First Steps

▶ *Target lists:* First, list all of the retailers or business customers that could purchase from you. Then list each contact you have and which places they could help you get sales. You should also have a list of distribution companies (for when you expand distribution) along with the contacts who can help you sell to those companies.

▶ *Launch date:* You need to set a launch date for your introduction. This forces you to determine who your first retailers will be, what distributors you'll use, and what type of demand-generating activities you'll plan.

▶ *Presells:* You want to start building momentum by preselling retailers, the distribution channel, and consumers. You presell retailers and distributors by getting orders to coincide with your launch date.

INSIGHT

Timetable for Success

Once you select a launch date, work backward to set up a timetable for your product launch. For example, an inventor of a new shock absorber for mountain bikes might set this schedule.

December 1, 2001	Identify a retailer and a distribution-channel member who will be advisors on the introduction.
January 15, 2002	Secure commitment from the promoter of the Summer Mountain Trail Rally on July 10 for sponsorship of the drink station at the three-quarter point of the race.
March 1, 2002	Set schedule for attendance at spring bike shows in the area.
March 15, 2002	Obtain commitments from a minimum of six area stores to stock product on introduction July 1, 2002. In return, they will be listed on the show flyer as future retail locations.
May 1, 2002	Prepare publicity plan and story. Include in releases photos of people looking at the product during spring shows.
May 1, 2002	Prepare a flyer on the co-op advertising plan and other retailer incentives for final sales push.
June 1, 2002	Obtain orders from local stores.
June 15, 2002	Contact manufacturers' sales agents and distributors about product plans to get them lined up for follow-up sales right after introduction.
July 1, 2002	Product launch.

You'll need to have a presentation on your demand-generating plan to get the orders, and you'll need to explain your incentives. It also pays to presell consumers. Attend trade shows and other area events where you show, demonstrate, and sell your product. On everything you offer to consumers, state when the product will be available and what stores will carry the product.

▶ *Events:* Your first key goal when introducing a product is to get noticed by end users, retailers, and distributors. The most cost-effective way to get noticed is to be involved in an event. Brad Young, the inventor of the HeadBanz, got involved in an event by having his product given away as a prize. Ronald Demon invented a new running shoe, the Raven, and he planned his introduction to coincide with the Boston Marathon, where several leading runners used Demon's new shoe. You can sponsor an event, run an event that other companies help sponsor—such as a garden show in a local community center—or you can be a part of a significant race, for example by hosting a drink station at a big bike road rally.

▶ *Restocking plan:* Retailers are not always attentive when it comes to restocking their inventory of a new product. Sometimes retailer's computer software will show they have a few products left on the shelves when in fact they don't. After a few weeks, the retailer believes the product isn't selling, when in fact the store doesn't have any product to sell. You need to plan on checking on the inventory of your first stores at least once a week. Tell the buyer when he or she needs to reorder, and ask for a better store location for your product if it isn't selling as well as you expected.

Off and Running

▶ *Wrap up customers:* Getting a store or customer to order the first time is just a foot in the door. You need to make that store successful. Talk to the store and see what you can do to help. Demonstrations in the parking lot, sales incentives for buyers, contests, and other promotions can all be utilized to prove to the store that your product is a winner.

➤ *Build a story:* Compare these two versions of the same story by the inventor of a microwaveable dinner tray for leftovers. Story one: "I invented the product because my sons are often late for dinner, and they thought it was too much work to reassemble the dinner." Story two: "My two sons are constantly on the go, and they just miss dinner. They always seem to be working, playing sports, or working on a school project. They were both thin and were starting to lose energy. It finally hit me one night when they came home late and were demolishing a bag of cheese nachos—they had stopped eating dinner and were simply getting most of their "nutrition" from junk food. I had to find a better way to feed them." A good story speaks to the experience of your target customers and brings to life the predicament that led you to invent your product in the first place.

➤ *Milk publicity:* Most newspaper reporters are concerned about their next story, or maybe their next few stories. If you send out a publicity release and the paper doesn't pick it up, that doesn't mean the writer didn't like the story. It just might mean that the paper didn't have room to run a story based on your publicity. So keep sending out new releases with new information, and you'll eventually get one or more articles published. Also be sure to contact the producers of talk radio shows in town. Radio shows will often have you on as a guest, and that publicity can be just as valuable as a written article.

The radio shows and their formats are listed in *Gale's Source of Publications and Broadcast Media,* which is available at many local libraries.

BUZZ WORD

A *press release* is what you send to writers or producers to catch their interest with newsworthy information they might turn into a news story. Include a picture of yourself holding or using the product, information about the product—including how it works and its benefits—and a story about what inspired you to create the invention. You'll find writers and talk show hosts are more interested in you, as the inventor, than they are in the product.

▶ *Expand distribution:* You want to get distributors or sales agents involved with your product for two reasons. The first is that you are only capable of doing so much. Your product's sales will go up as you get more people involved in selling your product. The second reason is that when you expand outside your local markets, you will need outside distribution. You will have an easier time getting additional distribution in new markets if you have established it in your local area.

Building a Business

▶ *Hire helpers:* The first employees inventors hire are usually assigned to do the office work, to package and ship the product, or to help with in-store demonstrations. Actually, the best person to hire is a salesperson experienced in the industry. You can get established in a local market with help from your contacts and people's desire to help a local start-up business. But as you go out into new markets, you won't have the contacts or the local edge. A knowledgeable person in the industry will know how to secure business in different markets, which is the most effective way to accelerate your company's sales.

▶ *Secure key supporters:* I recommend that all inventors, no matter how they are taking their product to market, have an advisory board of industry professionals. You can meet with the advisors once or twice per year and compensate them with either stock options or a small payment. An advisory council can help you grow your business, prevent you from making costly mistakes, and give you introductions to important new customers. But most important, it helps you get those key supporters firmly on your team, where they will continue to support your products.

> ▶ **SUCCESS** TIP
>
> Industry professionals can often be attracted to a start-up if they have a chance to own a significant part of the company, or if they can make significant commissions. Don't be cheap when hiring an outside person. It pays to hire the best even if you need to offer that person a big stock and commission plan. Top professionals will help your company grow.

▶ *Write a marketing plan:* The three key words in marketing a new product are *momentum, momentum, momentum.* You can't generate continued momentum for your product without a well-thought-out plan. Without one, it is too easy to let several months go by without significant marketing activity. Most libraries have several good books on writing a marketing plan that can guide you through the process.

▶ *Support the product:* You can't rest on your laurels. You need to have a plan for improving your product, adding new products to the line, and continually creating innovations that the market will notice. Daniel Cugino, who sold his family's marinade recipe, eventually introduced nine products within the first few years of his business. The new products kept interest high in his product line, allowed his products to occupy more shelf space, and provided an excuse for new sampling programs in stores. To stay on top in the market, you need to rejuvenate your product at least once every two years.

Are You Making Money?

▶ *Profit check:* When you first introduce a product, you will be losing money hand over fist because you need to promote the product until it is successful. Of course, sooner or later you want to make money, and as you do, you need to know if you are operating at or above the standard industry ratios for your business. For example, plastic manufacturers with sales under $1 million will have a standard average ratio for costs of goods sold, which includes manufacturing costs, marketing expenses, sales expenses, administrative expenses, and so on. They will also

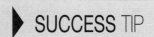

▶ SUCCESS TIP

As a general guideline, if you make your product yourself, you need to be able to sell it for four to five times your manufacturing cost in order to make money. If you buy the product from a contract manufacturer, your end-user price needs to be two and a half to three times the cost of the product.

have ratios for sales per employee and return on investment. You can find those ratios in the *Prentice Hall Book of Ratios,* a reference book that's in many large libraries. You won't be successful long term if your ratios aren't in line with, or better than, the industry standards.

▶ *Corrective measures:* If you can't turn an adequate profit, the three most common problems are that your manufacturing costs are too high, your sales price is too low, or you are giving away too many discounts. If your costs are too high, start by leveling with all your suppliers. Tell them that your costs are X percent higher than they should be, and that you won't be able to continue selling the product unless you can get the costs down. The suppliers will almost always have some suggestions on how you can cut your costs. If that doesn't slow your costs enough, try contacting your local university (one that has a course in manufacturing) to see if they have a program to help outside companies. A third choice is to look for new vendors.

If your price is set too low, this is a hard problem to correct unless you add new features to the product, since the distribution channel and end users resist price increases. One way to give yourself flexibility is to have a sticker on your product stating it has special introductory pricing. That way you can raise the price if needed. Otherwise, to raise the price you need to add features and say the product is new and improved, or you could put the product in a more upscale package. One last tactic is to include value-added features. Cugino, for example, could include small recipe cards with his Italian marinade that explain different ways of preparing meat.

Finally, inventors frequently need to offer extra discounts at first to get

---

▶ **BUZZ** WORD

Value-added is an adjective frequently used in marketing for all types of products. It means including features or auxiliary products that help customers meet their objectives. In the case of Cugino and his dressing, his customers want to prepare tasty meals. Offering his customers recipe cards can help them with that goal and would be considered a value-added feature.

retailers or distributors to carry their products, but they can't maintain these discounts indefinitely and stay profitable. You need to be careful to put a time limit on those extra incentives, typically 90 to 180 days, so that you can bring your discounts back to the industry norm.

▶ *Cutting costs:* Your first goal is to generate significant sales so that your manufacturing and marketing costs will be in line with your sales level. Once you have achieved 10 to 15 percent market penetration, you want to be sure your spending levels match your sales level. Sales and marketing costs should be no more than 20 to 25 percent of your sales, and your total manufacturing costs should be no more than 30 percent of your sales price if you sell direct, and no more than 60 percent of your sales if you sell through distribution.

If your costs are high, evaluate all the items you spend money on and prioritize them by their sales/cost ratio. For example, if a show produces $10,000 in sales, but costs $5,000 to attend, its sales/cost ratio is $10,000/$5,000, or 2. Ideally, your marketing programs should have a 10-to-1 cost ratio, which means a marketing program should produce $10 of sales for every $1 of expense. Drop expenses where the sales/cost ratio is below 5. Also, don't run programs where you can't measure the sales the program produces. Always use coupons, bounce-back cards, or sales order forms to gauge a program's impact. For example, if you run an ad, don't tell people they can get $10 off at a retail location. Have a coupon the customer has to cut out and turn in to the store to get the discount. That way you can measure the ad's effectiveness.

Home Shopping: TV and Mail-Order Catalogs–

The Inside Scoop

The Basics

TV shopping networks like QVC and the Home Shopping Network along with mail-order catalogs have proven for years to be two of the top ways for inventors to sell their products. These sales channels can be used to accomplish a wide variety of goals.

▶ You can sell effectively to a small market that can't be reached in any other way. Steve Niewulis of Fort Lauderdale, Florida, created the Just Tap It rosin wristband, which baseball players can use to stop their hands from getting sweaty. His company, Tap It!, Inc., sells the vast majority of his wristbands through the Baseball Express catalog, which is mailed to high school and youth baseball coaches. This market is difficult to reach through any other distribution network.

▶ You can create initial sales momentum. Often retailers are reluctant to handle a product until it has some degree of sales success. Jack

Panzarella of Wayne, New Jersey, created neon lights that go around an auto's license plate, in the glove box, and even under the car body to highlight a car's "hot" look. Retailers at first were reluctant to carry the product. But the product was picked up by two catalogs, J.C. Whitney, an auto-parts catalog, and Crutchfield, an auto-parts stereo catalog. Primarily using catalogs, Panzarella was able to build Street Glow's distribution network of retailers and raise sales to $16 million.

➤ They can be a primary sales channel. Tim Wilson's first product was the Drain Blaster (see "TV Blast Off," page 85), which uses a high-speed rotating nozzle to pressurize tap water into a high-velocity stream—a perfect solution for a clogged drain. Wilson sold the product exclusively through QVC, and he has continued to sell his follow-up products through TV shopping networks. While Wilson has added some retail outlets, the driving force behind his $4.5-million company, Jet Blast, Inc., continues to be TV sales.

➤ MARKET **REALITY**

Are you looking for fast results? Catalogs decide on what to buy six months before they need delivery and eight months before you'll receive payment. TV shopping networks put items on TV one to three months after they are submitted, and you'll receive payment 45 days after you ship. TV networks can't be beat when it comes to quick sales.

Perfect Products

Virtually any type of product can be sold through catalogs. All you need to do is find the catalogs that appeal to your target markets, since most catalogs are aimed at specific niches. (See "Key Resources" page 80 for help finding the best catalogs.) As such, catalogs work best for inventors with specialty products, while TV shopping networks are better for products with a very wide appeal, as the shows aim at a broad target audience. Both catalogs and TV shopping networks prefer products that appeal to almost all of their readers or viewers. Most perfect products have these four characteristics:

▶ They match a need buyers already know they have. People usually skim catalogs, and they are often doing something else while watching TV shopping shows. They notice products that catch their interest, which happens when the product meets a specific, known customer need.

▶ They have a new or unique positioning statement. Most people think of products in categories. A consumer might see a new sleeping pillow and think it is just like the neck-bracing pillows sold in the past. Products have to stand out in the market, and it's the inventor's job to make that happen.

> ▶ **BUZZ** WORD
>
> *Positioning strategy* refers to how marketers want end users to remember their product. Consider the Ironing Board Caddy, a U-shaped rod that attaches to an ironing board and allows people to hang clothes on the rod while ironing. The positioning strategy could be any one of the following: It allows people to iron while watching TV; it keeps clothes wrinkle-free after ironing; it allows ironing in any room in the house; or it holds 15 pounds of clothes.

▶ They must be easily understood. Inventors are lucky if people give their products even a glance. You need your invention to be understood in one to two seconds or the prospect will move on to the next item.

▶ They should be priced in the $10 to $50 range. Catalogs and TV shows both look at how many dollars a product generates relative to the space it takes, which in the case of a catalog is the page space it occupies, and for TV shopping networks is the air-time during which the product is sold.

Your Goals

Neither catalog nor TV sales require an extensive distribution network, and both can be executed by a very small company with a minimal investment. That allows inventors to start out small, build up substantial sales levels of up to about $5 million, and generate a nice income. Some inventors will stay at this level of sales, while others will use TV or catalog sales to establish their product and company and then launch a national retail sales effort.

INVENTOR'S STORY

Catalogs: Reading the Fine Print

Chris McKay is the coinventor of the hit toy Doodle Top, which is a spinning top with a marker pen that draws spirals while it spins. Based in Carmel, California, McKay sold the product in toy stores across the country. But he switched to catalog sales with his second product, the Magnawatch, which is a watch that has an extra lens that pops up for reading maps and other small print. McKay had several marketing challenges with the Magnawatch. One was that the product was aimed at a narrow market of travelers and was therefore not a product that most people would buy. A second challenge was that the product couldn't be understood without it being seen in use.

While these challenges were daunting in the retail market, McKay was able to recover in the catalog market. His company, Direct Hit Products, sold through catalogs like *National Geographic*, *Signal*, and *Norm Thompson*, all of which sell items for upscale travelers.

In the process of selling to catalogs, McKay learned about a few additional benefits they provide inventors. One is that he doesn't have to actually produce the product before obtaining an order. He shows catalog buyers two or three options for his products, and then he produces the version the catalog buyer selects. A second benefit McKay discovered is that catalogs want products that aren't generally available. At the retail level, McKay couldn't compete with giants like Casio. In catalogs, those buyers avoided manufacturers that sold through wide distribution.

Other Choices

For inventors who want to make only enough income to live on, catalogs serve the same purpose as selling in a small local market. Inventors looking to establish a sales base can also sell through a private label (chapters 14 and 15), sell by commission (chapters 10 and 11), or sell through a joint venture (chapters 12 and 13).

Money Matters

Catalogs and TV sales are both low-cost ways of getting started because you can wait until you have an order to start producing product. Once you have orders, you can always get financing from a contract manufacturer or even possibly a bank to get the product made (see appendix C for more on financing). Your actual costs to obtain an order are just the expenses of building a prototype or model, of a sales flyer, and of contacting the catalog or TV program. For inventors, selling to catalogs is probably the most common initial sales strategy because of its low cost.

Protection

The drawback to catalog sales is that your product is exposed to a wide variety of people. Potential competitors know that inventors with limited funding often sell through catalogs. They can see your product, realize it has at least some potential (or it wouldn't be in the catalog), and can decide to compete with you. You should at least be in patent pending status if you can afford it. Otherwise, you take the risk of someone with more money taking your idea and running with it.

Prototypes

Sometimes inventors will send sales literature and a price sheet to catalogs to see if they will buy. If they like the product, catalogs will respond by asking for a sample. Catalog buyers rarely ask for a sample unless they have a strong interest in the product. In fact, catalog buyers and TV shopping networks won't buy a product unless the inventor presents at least a prototype and sometimes a production model.

 SUCCESS TIP

Catalog buyers probably see more products in a given market than anyone else. An effective research tool is to send sales flyers and price sheets to buyers. The catalog buyer will be able to tell you if someone else has tried to introduce a product like yours before, how well products like yours have sold before, and if your pricing is too high or too low.

Market Research

Get a copy of each catalog before mailing to its buyer. Look at the different products and find where yours would fit in. When you mail to the catalog company, it helps to include a mock-up of a typical page from the catalog that includes your product alongside other complementary products already in the catalog. This helps the catalog buyer know what volume to expect from your product, and it also helps you show the catalog buyer how your pricing and product features are a perfect fit. Do the same with the TV shopping networks. Watch the networks and find products that appeal to the same target audience as yours. For example, if you are selling an organizing product, refer to other organizing products that the TV network sells. The TV networks don't require you to show more than one product in your submission package, but you'll find it does help your chances when you can make a convincing case of why your product should sell better than the one the TV channel is already selling.

Manufacturing

As noted above, one of the nice features of selling to catalogs or TV shopping networks is that you receive the order before you have to produce your product. If you've found a manufacturer to make the product, you can produce only the necessary amount of inventory. Frequently, contract manufacturers will allow you to pay them once you get paid. This allows inventors to start producing products with very little operating capital. You can also produce the product yourself, in which case you will have to fund inventory, equipment, tooling, and accounts receivables.

> ▶ **BUZZ** WORD
>
> A *contract manufacturer* is any manufacturer that makes a product that someone else markets and sells. The product is owned by the selling party, who agrees to pay a fixed (or contracted) price to the manufacturer for each product. The difference between a contract manufacturer and a *private label manufacturer* is in the ownership of the product. A private label manufacturer owns the product and arranges for another company to sell the product under the selling company's name.

Key Contacts

The buyers at catalogs and at the TV shopping networks are the key contacts. There are some agents who can help you sell to catalogs and TV networks, but I've found that most inventors are able to present their ideas to catalog buyers and TV shopping networks on their own. After sending out a mailing, be sure to make follow-up calls to see if buyers have any questions.

PROS AND CONS

Pros

▶ Low-cost method for starting sales, as contract manufacturers will often offer extended terms if they know inventors have a purchase order from a substantial buyer.

▶ Can produce sufficient sales to support a business.

▶ Requires very few people to run the company. In many cases, inventors can get by with just one or two employees.

▶ Success in catalogs can help an inventor establish a nationwide distribution network.

Cons

▶ Competitors that copy the product can establish a retail network before the inventor does.

▶ Successful sales through catalogs and TV shopping networks doesn't necessarily mean the product will sell through retail.

▶ Sales can be erratic, since catalogs will switch products so the catalog always has new merchandise.

 INSIGHT

One Product—Two Names

Catalogs and TV shopping networks like to carry exclusive merchandise that isn't commonly available. Inventors who want to sell to broader markets without compromising their catalog sales will either sell a variation of the product to catalogs or even sell their product under a different company and brand name. Inventors might also add features for the catalog market, make catalog products out of better materials, or customize products for various applications to sell to specific catalogs.

The strategy of offering two products offers two big benefits for inventors. The first is that the inventor can gear his or her products for the right price range. Many catalogs carry higher priced items, and a two-product strategy allows inventors to configure their products to meet the right price range for both retailers and catalogs. Inventors are also able to maximize their profits by offering different products to catalogs. Frequently, a catalog will target a certain type of customer who may prize certain features that aren't desired by most buyers. Inventors can receive a premium for those features in a catalog without having to offer them to retailers, where the features wouldn't increase the product's perceived value.

Up, Up, and Away

Catalog and TV shopping network sales build up a history of success with a new product that is attractive to most retailers. Catalog and TV shopping network sales also build up cash flow for the inventor and establish a base of business. This cash flow helps inventors generate the momentum they need to establish a nationwide network. But the most important task catalogs can perform is to secure favorable terms from a contract manufacturer. Inventors are left with a familiar chicken-and-egg problem. Contract manufacturers are willing to put

> ## SUCCESS TIP
>
> A contract manufacturer will offer favorable terms when an inventor's product adds 10 to 20 percent more volume to the manufacturer's existing production. If your product can sell $1 to $2 million, you want to approach manufacturers that currently produce $5 to $10 million worth of products. That increase will add substantially to the manufacturer's profits.

financial support behind a winning product, but inventors often don't have the resources to make their product into a winner without a manufacturer's financial help. Catalogs and TV shopping networks overcome this problem because they will give an order before you are in actual production.

Key Resources

▶ *The Catalog of Catalogs VI: The Complete Mail Order Directory* by Edward Palder (Woodbine Publishing, $25.95). Lists more than 15,000 catalogs in 920 different categories. Available in many libraries. To order, write 6510 Bells Mill Road, Bethesda, MD 20817, or call 800-843-7323.

▶ *The Directory of Mail Order Catalogs* by Richard Gottleib (Grey House Publishing, $275). Available at libraries, or by calling 800-562-2139.

▶ *The Directory of Overseas Catalogs* by Leslie MacKenzie and Amy Lignor (Grey House Publishing, $190). Call 800-562-2139 to order.

▶ National Mail Order Association (NMOA), 2807 Polk Street NE, Minneapolis, MN 55418-2954; 612-788-4193. NMOA occasionally features new products in its *Mail Order Digest,* which is sent to mail-order catalogs.

▶ Home Shopping Network, New Business Development, 1 HSN Drive, St. Petersburg, FL 33729. You can get a complete information package for submitting a product at www.hsn.com.

▶ QVC Studio Park, Vendor Relations, Mail Stop #128, West Chester, PA 19380-4262; www.vendor.studiopark.com.

▶ *Response* magazine, Advantsar Publications, 201 Sandpointe Avenue, Suite 600, Santa Ana, CA 92707; 714-513-8400; www.responsemag.com. This magazine covers infomercials, direct-response short form ads, mail-order catalogs, and TV shopping networks. The magazine also sponsors a yearly trade show where inventors can meet with direct-response marketers who license inventors' products.

What to Expect

▶ Catalog and TV buyers are easily turned off by a non-professional approach. They count on their vendors delivering quality products on time, and they won't count on you if your initial presentation is slipshod.

▶ Buyers won't respond unless they are in the process of deciding what products will go into the next catalog. Call a catalog first to find out when its product selection dates are, and then send your materials only when the catalog is actually deciding to buy products.

▶ TV shopping networks look for products that can be effectively demonstrated. Include pictures of demonstrations at fairs or trade shows to show how people are interested in the product.

▶ Orders typically have a two- to four-month lead time.

▶ Catalogs and TV networks both worry a lot about an inventor's ability to deliver unless you are either an established manufacturer or are using an established manufacturer as your production arm.

▶ Catalogs and TV shopping networks usually pay within 45 days. They typically pay much more promptly than retailers.

▶ Catalogs expect a discount of 50 percent off the suggested retail price when they purchase the product from you.

▶ Catalogs frequently ask for a payment from a company to help pay catalog printing costs. They will often accept this payment in additional product supplied at no charge.

▶ TV shopping networks often will suggest product changes, and they expect inventors to make those changes. My experience is that changes are suggested about 20 to 25 percent of the time.

▶ QVC will air products every 40 days and expects a minimum of $2,500 in sales per minute. They require a discount of 45 to 55 percent off the suggested retail price for every order. About 10 to 15 percent of inventors' products on both QVC and the Home Shopping Network are presented on the air more than a few times.

▶ The Home Shopping Network expects discounts of 45 to 60 percent off the suggested retail price and will air a product once a week for as long as it keeps selling.

▶ MARKET REALITY

Many catalogs have gone out of business over the last few years, and many more are operating on a shoestring. Ask for credit references from a catalog. Don't pay any money for printing costs before the catalog is printed. Pay only in free goods or in discounts off your invoice. A drawback to catalog sales is that one order could bankrupt you if you don't get paid.

Home Shopping: TV and Mail-Order Catalogs—

7

Making It Happen

Keys to Success

▶ *The right catalogs:* General-purpose catalogs like J.C. Penney or Wards have either lost influence or gone out of business. Catalogs today cater to specific audiences with a narrow product line. Levenger's, for example, is a catalog of upscale products for serious readers. You need to concentrate on finding catalogs that sell to your target audience, sell products that are priced similarly to yours (that is, have economy, midrange, or premium pricing), and sell products that are complementary to, but not the same as, yours.

▶ *Visual image:* You need to create a clear visual that lets people immediately connect to your product. This image can be of the product itself, or it can be of the situation the product solves. People easily understand from a product picture the easy dispensing racks that hold multiple drink cans in the refrigerator. But they may need a visual of a dandelion-removing tool in action to quickly understand how it works.

▶ *Immediate customer response:* Customers have to decide to buy a product quickly if it is going to succeed in catalogs and TV. Products need to satisfy a need or desire that is important to the customer to generate an impulse order. If people have trouble with gophers in their yard, they will buy a product that promises to solve that problem quickly. You can also get an immediate response if you tie your product to a customer's self image. People who want to appear successful at the office will not hesitate to buy a product that clearly helps them project that successful image.

> ▶ **BUZZ** WORD
>
> Catalogs and TV buyers like to group complementary products, which are products that target the same end goal for customers but that are not the same. Wallpaper, wallpaper paste removers, wallpaper pasting trays, devices for keeping wallpaper straight, and wallpaper smoothing tools are complementary products. You have the best chance of selling to a catalog or TV shopping network if they already sell products complementary to yours.

▶ *Promotional programs:* Immediate buyer response is increased on TV sales when a sales offer includes extra components, a free add-on product, or some other promotion, such as buy-two-get-one-free.

Momentum Makers

▶ *Unique products:* Catalogs do not want to carry products that everyone else has. Inventors can often get a foothold in the market if they tell buyers they will only be in one or two catalogs the following year. This tactic only works if your product is considerably different than other products on the market. Promising an exclusive sales option is also helpful to inventors because it encourages an earlier commitment from the catalog.

▶ *Strong customer desire:* Products that either meet a huge user need or connect with a big consumer desire sell best in catalogs because readers only see a product for an instant. A product that holds several extra towels in small bathrooms will do well in a catalog because people with small bathrooms recognize the problem. A temperature gauge for baby's bath water will sell in a catalog for expectant mothers. A new style of upscale but casual business shirt will sell to businesspeople who still want to look sharp in today's more casual business world. The same holds true for TV shopping networks, where strong-selling products include fitness and beauty aids—two categories that meet well-known consumer desires.

▶ *Product needed by many people:* TV shopping networks sell to a much broader spectrum of people than catalogs, and they look for products that appeal to a broad spectrum of their target customer group—which primarily consists of women who spend time caring for their homes. Cleaning products, jewelry, cooking products, home decorating projects, craft kits, and yard products all appeal to a wide range of TV network target customers and will generally sell well.

INVENTOR'S STORY

TV Blast Off

Tim Wilson and his company Jet Blast, Inc., based in Baltimore, Maryland, have introduced several inventions through TV shopping networks. They include the Drain Blaster, a high-speed rotating nozzle that turns tap water into a drain-clearing high-velocity stream; the Pro-Jet 2000, which converts ordinary water pressure from a garden hose into a high-pressure stream; and the Aqua Helix Shower Nozzle, which accelerates water flow from a shower head.

When Wilson started out, retailers wouldn't handle his product; in general, retailers feel it is too expensive to carry a product from a one-line company. Unique products from small companies, on the other hand, are just what catalogs and TV shopping networks are looking for, and by using the TV networks, Wilson has built his company's sales to over $4 million. One secret Wilson learned early on was the importance of demonstrations. Even if he has only a prototype when presenting a new product, he takes the time to create a video, sometimes spending as much as $5,000 to show how well the product will demonstrate on TV. Wilson feels that without a video buyers won't understand a product's appeal.

Wilson has also tried to sell his products on his own through direct-response ads. But he has learned that TV networks have two huge advantages. One is that they have a proven sales process. They know what types of products will sell and what types of demonstrations produce the best results. The second advantage is that they have a huge built-in audience that likes to buy from the TV shopping network. Those advantages overcome the 50 to 60 percent discounts off suggested retail that the networks ask for.

Before You Start

▶ *Identify the target:* Catalogs and TV shopping networks all do a careful job identifying their target customer. Then they look for products that also target those customers. Inventors need to understand who the target customer is for each catalog or TV network they approach, and then they need to demonstrate why the product is perfect for those customers.

▶ *The right copy:* You want to match the style of copy on your sales materials to the style of each catalog. Many marketers who sell to various catalogs custom-write the materials each time. Having the right style helps convince the buyer that your product is perfect for the catalog.

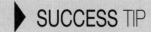

▶ SUCCESS TIP

Copy—the words on a brochure or ad—can vary in style. Some catalogs use image-enhancing copy: "the perfect suit for the woman executive." Others use a practical style: "Two tops and two bottoms offer four different outfits." Copy may be personalized, frequently using the pronoun you, or it may be more impersonal, using third-person descriptions like executives, young women, or teenage girls.

▶ *Exclusivity:* The Home Shopping Network and QVC do not like to carry the same products, and many catalogs also prefer a more exclusive line of merchandise. A good strategy when starting out is to tell mail-order catalogs that you will only have the product in two catalogs in the first year. This gives them a little more incentive to buy, and it allows you to ask the buyer for a response by a certain date, so that you can contact other buyers if the first catalog doesn't want the product. You should only approach one TV shopping network at a time, and you should make it clear to them that you are only approaching one network to start.

▶ *Publicity:* If you have any past publicity, include it in your presentation to show buyers the potential of your product. If don't have any, manufacture some. Host an event—it doesn't have to be big—that allows people to use your product, and then ask them to offer testimonials. For example, you could organize a five-kilometer bike ride for 10 people to showcase a new, more comfortable seat. Or you could offer a cooking demonstration at your local church. What's important is that you bring people together to try your product, take pictures, and write a story that could be used for publication by your local media.

▶ *Inventory needs:* You don't need to produce any product until you have an actual order. All you need is a few prototypes or units to offer as samples if they are requested.

▶ *Pricing:* Products from $12.95 to $29.95 seem to do best in general-merchandise catalogs and the shopping networks. Specialty and premium catalogs prefer products that are priced anywhere from $40 to $500. If prices are too low, you need to sell too many units before the catalogs or shopping networks make money. If your prices are too high, the products move out of the impulse category and become a more difficult sale. Check your pricing against other comparable products in the catalog or on the shopping network to be sure it is similar. For example, electrical devices for the kitchen might sell for $29.95 to $49.95. Make sure your three-in-one can opener falls in that same range and maintains the same price/value relationship.

▶ **SUCCESS** TIP

Lillian Vernon has had a successful catalog since she started out at the age of 21. Currently, her catalog sales exceed $200 million per year. Lillian Vernon still selects many of the products for the catalog herself. What are Vernon's criteria for including products? They must be distinctive, not generally available anywhere else, and aimed at her target audience—women looking to add style to their lives.

First Steps

▶ *Target lists:* See Chapter 6, page 80–81, for a list of several directories of catalogs. Find catalogs that look appropriate, and call the company to request one. Double-check that each catalog's target market and pricing fits your product, then make a list of the top ten catalogs to which you will send a presentation package. Since there are really just two big TV shopping networks, QVC and the Home Shopping Network, you don't need to do much research, but this also limits your choices.

▶ *Mailing dates:* Catalogs typically only decide to buy products once or twice a year when they are laying out their new catalog. In many cases, this date could be four to five months (and sometimes longer) before the catalog is actually printed. You want to know when a catalog finalizes its product decisions, then mail to the catalog twice: once two months before the final date and then two weeks before the date. Mailing two months before will help get your product considered in the regular decision process. Mailing two weeks before the deadline puts you in front of catalog buyers right when they are trying to fill last-minute holes in the catalog.

▶ *Presentation package:* Typically, when they are considering new products, catalogs ask for only a sales flyer and a price schedule, while shopping networks also want to see a sample. But inventors find that they can improve their odds of success by including additional items in the initial mailing. Some inventors will actually lay out a sample catalog page with their product featured among complementary products already in the targeted catalog. You can also include videos—which are popular with shopping networks because they indicate how well a product can be demonstrated on TV—as well as testimonials, news articles, pictures of the product at trade shows, market research studies, and any other information that might be useful to the buyer. Here are the points to drive home: (1) The product appeals to the show's/catalog's target market; (2) the product has already been tested or sold; and (3) the product will fit in with other products in their catalog or shopping network.

▶ *Personal contact:* To give yourself the best chance of success, before sending your presentation package to a catalog, make sure you find out the name of the person who buys for your type of product. If you call and ask, most catalogs will tell you. If you don't know who the buyer is, you won't know if your information actually reaches the right person, and you won't know who to call when following up to get feedback on your product's potential in the catalog. However, the Home Shopping Network and QVC don't normally give out the buyer's name. One way around this is to buy products similar to theirs and then call the manufacturer (who's name will be on the package) and ask who the buyer was.

> ▶ MARKET **REALITY**
>
> First impressions are just as important selling to catalog and TV shopping network buyers as they are in other sales situations. As mentioned before, Tim Wilson of Jet Blast spends up to $5,000 on videos before approaching shopping network buyers. For catalogs, you want a great-looking picture of your product in use. If you can't do this yourself, hire a graphic artist to get a professional look.

▶ *Samples:* You need to send a sample of the product to shopping networks when submitting your product. Catalogs typically prefer to see a brochure first, and they will then request a sample if they are interested in the product. Catalogs want to check your product for durability, safety, and quality.

Off and Running

▶ *Wrap up catalogs:* As a rule, catalogs change a substantial number of product offerings every printing. So unless your product is a top seller, you can expect to be dropped from a catalog every now and then. You can minimize the roller coaster effect of catalog sales by creating a strong relationship with the buyers. The best way to do that is by trying to help the buyers create the catalog they want. Ask buyers what they are trying to do for the next issue and what you could do with your product to help them meet their objectives. Also ask the buyers how you could change your product so it will sell better in the catalog.

▶ *Wrap up shopping networks:* Networks will keep carrying your product as long as it sells. You can extend your run if you keep coming up with new demonstrations that present your product in new ways.

▶ *Create variety:* Catalogs don't like to have the very same products as other catalogs, so you should offer your product with several variations for catalogs to choose from. You can offer different colors or a few new features, or you can pair the product with different complementary items. A painting tool, for example, might come with a paint-can opener one season and a masking aid the next year.

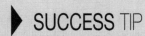

SUCCESS TIP

Chris McKay, the inventor of the Magnawatch, sends catalog buyers a chart showing the potential features of his invention, and then lets them decide what they want. Even if he hasn't ever made a particular Magnawatch configuration before, McKay presents the buyer with all the options that are possible. He's learned that buyers prefer to pick and choose what they feel will sell best.

▶ *Add catalog customers.* You may have offered an exclusive contract to a catalog for the first year of catalog sales, but you can only grow your business by adding catalogs on a regular basis. Use the catalog directory resources in Chapter 6 (page 80–81) to find

---

▶ INSIGHT

Comparison Shoppers

TV shopping networks and catalog buyers are an image-conscious bunch: They can be more competitive and catty than a host of Houston debutantes at high-society soiree. As I mentioned earlier, TV shopping networks don't like to carry the same products as other networks, and you are better off approaching only one network at a time. Catalog buyers are even more difficult to deal with because they also follow a pecking order. Catalogs with premium items do not want to carry product lines that also carry lower-priced products. They often will not buy from you if you haven't been selling to catalogs that are as prestigious—or if you've been selling to those that are more prestigious.

When you talk to buyers, ask them which other catalogs they feel they are competitive with, and which ones they feel appeal to a more cost-conscious market. Tell the buyers you are asking this question because you want to sell your product as a premium performing line, and you want to be sure that the consumer doesn't get mixed messages about just who the product is targeted at. You'll do far better with catalogs if the buyers know you are not offering your product to every catalog in the market. Also be careful when you tell buyers what catalogs you have been sold through. Only list catalogs that sell at the same price point or higher than the catalog you are talking to.

You also need to be careful in mentioning your TV shopping network sales to catalogs. Some catalogs, like Taylor Gifts, like to carry products that have been on TV, and they will even post an "As Seen On TV" label on your product in the catalog. Other catalogs feel that TV shopping networks don't appeal to their premium customers, and they may

new target catalogs, and then keep going after them. While you want to show catalogs that you've been in other catalogs, be careful not to give the impression that the new catalogs should buy your product just because others have done so. Catalog buyers get upset if you act as if another catalog is more important than theirs.

▶ *Approach new markets:* Normally, when you start out selling a product, you'll approach a single specific market that's right for your product. However, catalogs are the one area where marketers can do better trying to sell to everyone. A kitchen-organizing product might, with just a few small variations, sell well to hobby shops. A product for runners might be easily adapted to the hiking market, or even the bike market. Look at as many catalogs as you can to see if your product will fit in with a few changes. You might be able to find additional markets that will keep your sales moving up.

Building a Business

▶ *Hire helpers:* Marketing to catalogs and TV shopping networks entails three time-consuming tasks. One is to keep in touch with a core of current customers. The second is to continually add product updates or new variations to keep sales strong in both catalogs and TV shows. The last task is to search out new catalog customers, either in your current market or new markets. I've found that inventors enjoy coming up with new variations of their product, but that they don't do a good job searching out new catalog opportunities. Inventors can usually grow their catalog business best by hiring someone to take on the third task of finding new customers.

▶ *Secure key supporters:* You need several supportive catalog buyers to succeed. But you also need a manufacturer who is willing to turn out variations of your product for different buyers, and you need a model builder, or a prototype builder, who can help you prepare the different samples catalogs want to see before they order.

▶ *Write a marketing plan:* TV shopping network marketing is different than traditional marketing because you are trying to appeal to a broad range of customers rather than a narrow range. For TV, your product's branding is most important, as it makes your product memorable to consumers, a sales benefit prized by the shopping networks. Your marketing plan should concentrate on creating a strong brand through publicity, personal appearances, and the use of a distinctive name or logo.

> ▶ MARKET REALITY
>
> Over the last 20 years, one comment I have heard often from inventors is that they love to invent but that they aren't very good at sales and marketing. They are always hoping they can hire someone else to do that. This attitude is a sure sign that an inventor will fail to commercialize his or her idea. Inventors have to do everything, and if you convince yourself you can't or don't want to do sales and marketing, the end result will be that you accomplish neither one well.

Catalogs require the more traditional niche marketing. List all the catalogs that are appropriate for your product, and note when they publish their catalogs, when they make their buying decisions, and what their desired price points are. Then select your top-priority catalogs and approach them first.

▶ *Support the product:* Your value to catalogs and TV shopping networks declines rapidly if you have quality or return problems. Most companies try to overcome this by directing product returns directly to themselves. Make sure you give consumers an 800 number to call for questions and problems, and provide instructions on returning a product to you. You want to clear up every problem on your own to avoid conflicts with the catalog or network.

Are You Making Money?

▶ *Profit check:* One of the biggest advantages of catalog and TV shopping marketing is that you have few expenses other than manufacturing costs. There are also minimal sales and marketing expenses, which in most other marketing channels consume 20 to 40 percent of your sales dollars. You will probably be able to make money as long as you can sell your product for 50 percent more than your manufacturing cost. If you are using catalog sales as a springboard to other markets, you need to price your product at double your manufacturing cost, as that is the price you will need to charge in other markets.

The only major expense in catalog sales is that catalogs will frequently ask you to pay part of the printing cost. Those costs should be no more than 15 percent of your projected sales volume.

▶ *Corrective measures:* If profits aren't up to snuff, catalog marketers can either cut manufacturing costs (if they are too high) or negotiate a different arrangement for paying the printing cost of catalogs. Since

▶ **BUZZ** WORD

Branding is a marketing term that simply means establishing your name with customers, though this also extends to establishing attributes to that name. Sears, for instance, is a strong brand name: First, it is recognized by almost everyone, and second, people associate it with a dependable midpriced store. Orville Redenbacher used his name to create a distinctive, memorable brand for his popcorn, while Jolly Time microwave popcorn has a much weaker brand because its generic name just isn't as memorable.

TV shopping networks don't require an up-front fee, your only choice there is to trim your own costs. If you have a manufacturing problem, be honest with all your vendors. Tell them you need to cut costs by a certain percentage or you won't be able to continue production. Ask them for help and suggestions in getting your costs down. Vendors may be able to suggest lower-cost materials, different manufacturing techniques, or other ways to cut costs. If the printing costs a catalog is charging you are too high, you can frequently negotiate a better deal. You can tell the catalog you'll pay with free goods. For example, tell them you'll include 15 percent extra merchandise with each shipment to pay for printing. Or that you'll include X amount of free goods provided the catalog orders five times that amount in billable merchandise. Catalogs will negotiate this fee, so don't just accept their initial request.

▶ *Cutting costs:* One other tactic for cutting costs is to evaluate each product feature to see if it produces enough perceived value to justify the price. I recommend you include warranty cards with your products so you can get the names of actual users. You can then call them up and ask them how they like the product, what features they value most, and which features are unimportant to them. Consider eliminating any feature that people consistently mention is unimportant.

Internet Sales–
The Inside Scoop

The Basics

At one time, people thought all you had to do was put up a Web page and the people would come, browse, and buy. Another tactic was to sign on for a Web page at an online shopping mall, which supposedly would draw people to the site. Both of those tactics flopped pretty badly, as they just didn't build enough traffic. But after some stumbling around, inventors have learned two ways to build a successful business based on the Internet. One strategy is to link their site with other sites, to learn how to work the search engines, to build portal sites, and to offer free information to lure visitors to their site. The other strategy is to sell products to Internet merchants with active sites already drawing plenty of visitors.

In many ways, Internet merchants are the ideal customers for inventors. Internet merchants have only a small risk with a new product. They can buy only six or a dozen products, put the product up on the site, and then

MARKET **REALITY**

Many people will offer to host your site and even build your Web page. But those two steps won't bring traffic to your site, so you will probably lose your money unless you can spend four to eight hours a day building traffic. If you don't have time to promote your site, concentrate on selling to Internet merchants.

see how it sells. If it doesn't sell, their only costs are the purchase price of a half dozen or so units and the effort to add the product to the site. On the other hand, setting up and developing your own site is expensive because you need to work virtually full time to pull in traffic. It can be even more expensive if you need to hire someone to do the programming for you.

Perfect Products

The Internet is the ideal marketplace for a product that isn't widely sold but yet has a core of dedicated consumers who will look for the product. For example, most people don't buy replicas of air force bomber jackets, but there is a small group of people who do. When those people go on the Internet and search for "bomber jackets," the few sites that sell them come up as a match on search engines. A product like inventors' notebooks might also do well on the Internet because inventors look for that product, it is not widely available, and only a few sites sell it. If your product is widely available, people may not find you in an Internet search, they might be able to easily find the product in a store, and you might have to compete with discount merchants.

Other perfect products are those that relate to areas where there is already a large amount of Internet community activity. For example, singles and people getting married have many sites that cater to them and with which inventors can form links. A tactic to generate

Internet visitors is to offer giveaways that can be promoted on other Internet sites. You'll attract visitors especially if your promotional product has broad appeal. For example, if you have a product for engaged couples, you could bring them to your site by offering free downloads of an information booklet entitled "Ten Things to Avoid on Your Wedding Day." Your free offer can also be used on your banner ads to attract people to your site.

You should also have a relatively easy-to-produce product for an Internet program. Sales may be modest, and you'll probably need to bear all the set-up, production, and patenting costs on your own.

INVENTOR'S STORY

Adding Punch to Good-Bye

We meet, fall in love, and sigh. We're puppy-dog happy, until one day we just aren't anymore. Something happens, and eventually we break up, but rarely do we get to say that snappy rejoinder that tells the other person just how it feels or what we think. Jeff DeLong capitalizes on this need with his line of Internet greeting cards, called C-Ya, which is also the phrase that ends every card. DeLong was able to create traffic to his site first by offering free downloaded cards, and second by establishing connections with the thriving Internet community of young singles and couples. Some of those sites include

studentbodies.com	divorcesource.com
cupid.net	datingabout.com
singlescoach.com	singlescafe.com
getwild.com	singlesmall.com

DeLong offered visitors their choice of one of three downloadable cards, a freebie that really didn't cost DeLong anything. He used his links to build traffic, but he also took advantage of four main Internet tactics.

▸ He was associated with a major Internet search term, *closure*. DeLong called his cards "closure cards," playing off the popularity of that term. People searching the Web with the word "closure" came quickly to DeLong's site.

▸ DeLong captured the e-mail address of everyone who downloaded a free card. He was able to create a mailing list of potential customers, which he would e-mail to every time he had a new card.

▸ He utilized places that advertise "what's new" on Web sites, such as www.whatsnew.com and www.newtoo.manifest.com, to promote the fact he had new cards.

▸ He promoted his free cards and changed them frequently to capitalize on the high number of visitors to sites that promote free items, such as www.freestuff2000.com.

DeLong was able to quickly generate 3,000 to 4,000 downloads per day for his free cards, and his company, C-Ya Greeting Cards, based in Klamath Falls, Oregon, was able to sell over 10,000 cards per month within a year. But it didn't happen without a tremendous effort on DeLong's part. He spent six to eight hours per day checking for new sites, establishing banner ad exchange programs, adding new cards, and following up on retail contacts.

Your Goals

When selling on the Internet, your goals should be modest. Here are some of the things you could focus on:

▸ Initiating sales of your product so you can eventually introduce it to broader markets.

▸ Establishing a base for a line of specialized sales to a certain market. For example, you might want a Web page that was a central spot for an extensive line of horse-grooming products.

▶ Creating a sales channel to produce a modest level of sales. Some inventors might be happy with producing an extra $30,000 to $40,000 of income per year. Since Internet sales come from a wide variety of people, they aren't usually subject to the large swings of catalog sales.

▶ Generating testing data from customers that you can use in future promotions when you sell your product.

 MARKET REALITY

Internet-click through rates average between 0.5 to 2 percent. Typically less than 1 percent of the people who visit your site are likely to buy. Having free and new items you can list on free and what's new sites is crucial if you want to build the traffic you need to succeed.

Other Choices

Internet sales are ideal for building a modest level of sales that can support a home-based business. You can also do this by selling at fairs and shows (chapters 2 and 3), selling in a local market (chapters 4 and 5), and selling through catalogs and TV shopping networks (chapters 6 and 7).

Money Matters

You probably will have to pay for your initial production yourself. Manufacturers will be reluctant to give you extended terms, since Internet sales are typically modest and not a predictor of eventual success. If you sell to Internet retailers, you won't have Web page design and maintenance costs. But if you set up your own site, you'll be looking at set-up costs of $2,000 to $10,000 and monthly charges of $100 and up. You'll also have to plan

SUCCESS TIP

Internet sales can pay unexpected dividends. For example, retailers approached DeLong about carrying his C-Ya line of cards after visiting his Internet site. Other inventors/manufacturers have been approached by foreign distributors or alliance partners for foreign markets as well as distributors and manufacturers' sales agents.

on spending at least four hours a day keeping traffic coming to your site.

Protection

The one-year sales period for patenting your idea starts when you offer your product for sale. An Internet site starts the clock running. The type of protection you obtain really depends on your long-term plans. You may want to bypass patent protection if you have a product for a small niche market, and you only plan on selling on the Internet. Or you may want to apply for just a design patent or provisional patent to discourage competitors. You are unlikely to get too many competitors if your target market is small. You probably want to apply for more comprehensive patent coverage if you are looking to use the Internet as a stepping stone for a large market launch.

Prototypes

Some inventors will produce a prototype and then put that onto the Internet to see if it will sell. They only move forward to produce the product after they have received enough orders to justify production costs. Inventors also will let people test their prototypes through the Internet to make sure the product works right and to get testimonials about the product from well-known people or just everyday end users. Often, inventors selling exclusively on the Internet make their products at home, and typically it's easy for them to make as many prototypes as they need.

Research

Being able to bring people to your Web site is more important for your success than having the right product for the market. Before moving ahead with your product, go to the Internet and put in search terms that might lead people to your site. What type of sites come up? Your site is not going to get many visitors if the search produces a large number of frequently visited sites. Keep using as many search terms as you can think of and see if there are any terms that pull up a limited number of matches.

MARKET REALITY

Always make a prototype to be sure your product will both work and sell. Hundreds of inventors have assured me that they didn't need a prototype because they knew their product would work, and then they moved straight into production. Well, sometimes the product doesn't work, and even when it works, sometimes it doesn't sell. You build a prototype and run it by potential customers as an insurance policy to make sure you don't lose all your money.

Also make a list of the domain names that come up, so you can see what names you could create that aren't already taken. Come up with several names that are somehow connected to a search term a prospect might use. Then go to a domain registration site, such as www.embark.com, and see if the name is registered. Don't go ahead with your site until you have a distinctive name that ties in with your product and the type of Internet search terms people are likely to use.

Manufacturing

The uncertain sales potential of Internet products gives inventors very little leverage in negotiating for favorable terms with a manufacturer. You need to either finance production or create a low-cost production method you can do yourself. One other choice is to sell both to catalogs and on the Internet when you start out. If you can land that first catalog order, you should be able to arrange favorable terms from a manufacturer, including having the manufacturer pick up tooling and operating capital costs.

Key Contacts

If you are going to sell through Internet retailers, your key contacts are the buyers for those Internet retailers. You should treat them just like you would a catalog buyer, which is discussed in chapters 6 and 7. If you are going to set up your own Web site for selling, your key contacts are the people who control the sites that attract your target customers. You want to develop strong links with these sites: They can feature articles by you, prominently display your offers, and run contests featuring your products as prizes. Other Web site developers can also give you insight into what tactics you can use to create more traffic to your site. In the world of the Internet, people never meet other people, they just correspond through e-mail, so e-mail portal site developers and work with them to promote your site.

> ▶ **BUZZ** WORD
>
> *Portal sites* on the Internet are sites that try to be all-encompassing information sites for a certain topic. For instance, www.ivillage.com is a portal site for women. It has articles about issues that concern women, links to other women-oriented sites, and chat rooms and discussion rooms where women can offer their opinions on a variety of topics. Perhaps most important, these sites provide new information and updates every day.

Pros and Cons

Pros

▶ Doesn't require selling to the distribution channel (stores, distributors, or dealers), who are always the most difficult sale.

▸ Is the best way to sell to a niche market where customers are hard to find any other way.

▸ Is effective selling products that have too small a market for most stores or catalogs.

▸ Occasionally, Web sites will attract potential retailers or foreign distributors that will sell your product.

▸ Allows inventors to explore their market potential without making an extensive investment in inventory.

▸ Can help gather testimonials and actual end-user support that inventors can use when they expand into other distribution channels.

▸ Ideal sales channels for inventors who want a home-based business with a minimum amount of distribution work.

Cons

▸ Internet retailers like to carry unusual products that attract people to their site. That doesn't mean, however, that they will sell a large number of units.

▸ Working a Web site so it attracts a large number of visitors is lots of work.

▸ There is no guarantee that anyone will end up visiting your site.

▸ An Internet site doesn't have enough sales potential to justify a large investment in tooling or production.

▸ Products are exposed to everyone. It is possible that people might copy well-designed products sold on the Internet and introduce them to other distribution channels.

▸ Internet sales don't prove a product will sell in a store or in a catalog. Internet sales are not nearly as effective as selling in a small, local market if your goal is to prove your product will sell.

INSIGHT

So What's a Web Site Good For, Anyway?

As you may have gathered, I think Web sites have many limitations for making new sales and attracting potential customers. Does that mean you shouldn't bother with the Internet? No way. Rather than a way to start sales, Web sites have tremendous potential to support the sales you've already made. They can provide all kinds of product information, and they are an excellent buying source for your current customers and your distribution network—those people who already know where to look for you. Internet sites are ideal for the following:

▶ They can provide detailed technical or application information. This is a great way to cut your mailing costs to overseas customers. Just have them go to your Web site and download the information they need.

▶ You can take orders on accessory products. For example, when I bought an outdoor fireplace, the store didn't carry the cover. But I could buy it on the fireplace company's Web page.

▶ You can offer buyers downloadable versions of manuals that explain different ways to use a product. You can build an e-mail list of customers for announcing new products, events, and seminars.

▶ You can let customers post suggestions on how people can solve common problems or improve whatever they are doing. Some model railroad sites have customer postings, and those sites get a tremendous number of visitors. You can also let customers post their own questions and then let other users answer the questions.

▶ They are great for closing a long-distance sale. I once received a call from Switzerland regarding products for a company I was then working for. I had the prospect open up our Web site, and I walked him through the technical information he needed to know. He then gave me a $22,000 order that we shipped the next week.

▶ You can also give your distributors code numbers so they can check on any orders they have with you; they can find out when the product is expected to ship and when they can expect delivery.

Up, Up, and Away

Some inventors, such as Jeff DeLong and his C-Ya greeting cards, have gained retail distribution from an Internet site, but for the most part inventors have not moved off the Internet into major distribution. People are not sure that a product that sells on the Internet will sell elsewhere. If you want your company to have the option for future retail sales, you should combine the tactics of selling to catalogs and selling locally with your Internet sales strategy.

Key Resources

▶ *Increase Your Web Traffic in a Weekend* by William R. Stanek (Prima Tech). This is by far the best book I've seen on promoting a Web site.

▶ www.ideavillage.com. This site was founded by Andy Kubani, former president of Telebrands and the person who pioneered the "As Seen On TV" product category. You can post your invention for sale on the site and receive both orders and feedback. Ideavillage.com will take the best-selling inventions and put them on a weekly TV show featuring new products. Finally, the company will take the products that sell best on TV and promote them through mass merchants.

▶ There are Web guides and directories that claim to feature only the "Best of the Web," and people increasingly use them to cut through the clutter on

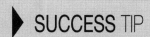

▶ SUCCESS TIP

Learn to do your own search-engine submissions. Many businesses on the Web offer a service to list your Web site on all the major directories. Eventually, you'll need to learn all the tricks for getting your site listed early by search engines, so you might as well start doing it yourself. There are many current books that cover this topic.

the Internet. All of the big search engines like Yahoo have guides you should submit to for review. Go to the submission page on the guides to learn how to get your page considered. These guide directories are also the place to go when you look for the portal sites for your target customer group, or when you look for Web retailers that might sell your product. Major guides include:

www.centraldrive.com	galaxy.einet.net
www.hitsgalore.com	www.infospace.com
www.linkcentre.com	www.linkmoster.com
www.peekaboo.net	www.questfinder.cim
www.scrubtheweb.com	

▸ www.virtualpromote.com is an excellent e-newsletter that is loaded with tips on promoting your Web site. Many developers of successful sites have told me they relied heavily on this site for information when starting out.

▸ www.tvpress.com/promote/yellp.htm is another site with plenty of information on how to promote your site.

▸ www.555-1212.com is an information source for businesses and individuals. A good spot to list your business especially if you are selling to businesses.

▸ Yellow pages and other similar directories include:

www.superpages.com	www.pronett.com
www.usyellow.com	www.where2go.com
www.yellowweb.com	

▸ Freebie directories can really boost you traffic. They include.

www.freestuff2000.com	www.free-n-cool.com
www.contestguide.com	www.contestworld.com

▸ Banner exchange programs are agreements where Web pages barter advertising with each other. You agree to display other people's banner ads on your site in return for your banner ad being displayed on other sites. Some of the sites that sponsor banner exchange programs are:

www.adnetwork.linkexchange.com
www.smartclicks.com   www.bannerswap.com
www.linktrader.com   www.net-on.com/banner

What to Expect

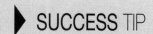
▶ **SUCCESS** TIP

▸ Only a small percentage of people who visit your site will buy, and only a small percentage of people who see your banner ad will click through to your site. Buying and click-through rates of less than 1 percent are

Spend your money on promoting your site and not on designing a "super cool" Web site. If you look at the Web directories, you'll find that many of the best sites are primarily text with a basic graphic design. Sites are judged by their content and how helpful they are rather than by how creative they are. Being creative with your site design doesn't hurt, but concentrate on promotion.

common. You need lots of visitors and contacts to have a chance of success.

▸ Offering free items, especially ones that can be downloaded, will dramatically increase traffic to your site.

▸ It may take two months or longer to start attracting a significant number of visitors. Don't get discouraged by a slow start as long as you have aggressively promoted your site.

▸ People will buy extra products if you offer them when you ship your product.

▸ You will get orders from around the world. You may get overseas distributors requesting your product.

▸ It may take a while to recoup your start-up expenses. Try to produce the product yourself.

▶ Selling through Internet retail sites is a low-maintenance operation you can run from your home.

▶ Expect small orders at first from Internet retailers.

▶ You will get a number of questions and inquiries from e-mail. You should answer them within 24 hours or you will lose sales.

9

Internet Sales—
Making It Happen

Keys to Success

▶ *Visitors all the time:* Don't underestimate the number of visitors you need. Tim Carter hosts the radio talk show *Ask the Builder* and writes a syndicated newspaper column with the same name. He attracts 12,000 people per month to his site, which sells a variety of products. Carter brings in several hundred thousand in revenue per year, most of which is from selling banner advertising. Indeed, 12,000 visitors is a lot, and without similar volume you are not going to succeed. Don't think that you will build that volume using just banner ads. Click-through rates for banner ads are at best 2 to 3 percent—which means you would need 500,000 exposures to bring 10,000 people to your site—and lower than 1 percent is common. You need a comprehensive and creative Web site marketing program that brings people to your site all the time to be successful.

➤ *Content over commerce:* You want every person who comes to your site to learn something useful. Most inventor sites are oriented solely toward selling a product. Instead, have your site address the problem or situation that brought visitors to your site. For example, if your site sells a product that keeps leaves from clogging up rain gutters, you could assume people coming to your site have tree problems. You could include information on how to keep trees pruned so they don't harm a house, how to help trees grow away from a house, proper fertilization of trees, and how to compost leaves to help your lawn grow. Two advantages of posting helpful information are that people will always get something of value when they visit your site, and you'll have more keywords and metatags on your site for search engines to find.

➤ *Connections that count:* I personally don't believe any Web site can succeed if it depends on creating traffic through search engines. Sites have to be so well known and attractive that people put the Web site address into their browser and then go right to the site. Many dot.coms have tried to do this with TV advertising, but advertising isn't remembered for long and is terribly expensive. To get people to enter your site directly, you have to have your site listed both on and off the Web by newsletters, associations,

---

➤ **BUZZ** WORDS

The Internet has spawned many new marketing terms. Here are a few of the more common ones:

Exposures refers to any time someone opens a page with your banner ad on it.

Metatags refers to text a search engine reads but Web readers don't see.

Keywords refers to the words you place in a metatag so search engines know what a page is about.

related businesses, end-user groups, schools, experts in the field, and any other group you can possibly think of. You only get these connections by having a high-content site.

Your other option, which is easier to execute, is to have your product sold by affiliated sites and Internet retailers as well as your own site. Affiliate agreements will cost you 20 to 50 percent in discounts and commissions. Internet retailers typically buy your product for a discount of 50 to 60 percent off suggested retail.

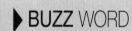 **BUZZ** WORD

Affiliate agreements on the Internet let other sites sell your product or refer people to you to buy your product. If the affiliate sells and collects for the product, they generally buy at a 40 to 50 percent discount off suggested retail. Sites referring customers to you receive a 15 to 20 percent commission for generating the order.

➤ *Not a waiting game:* People will simply not wait for your site to download and give them information. Make sure to slim down the data for pictures and graphics and have them load in as short a time as possible. The two other key elements of Web design are, first, that the variety of information you have on your site must be immediately obvious, and second, that your site doesn't appear boring. Buttons on the side with classifications—like products, markets, dealers, technical information, and so on—look and usually are extremely boring. They display a variety of resources, but they also display a lack of creativity. Make your opening page exciting and one that will make people want to keep going. The Web site for Rumpus Toys, www.rumpus.com, is great because it has interesting visuals, loads quickly, and looks like fun.

Learn to Play the E-Game

A native of Dallas, Texas, Craig Winchell thought he was off and running after the 1998 New York Toy Fair. He had just received glowing praise for his board game Conscience, an interactive game for children and their parents that helps children understand the difference between right and wrong in the real world. He was sure orders were soon to follow, but unfortunately he only picked up orders from a few small toy stores across the country. Toy retailers were unwilling to take a chance on an unproven product without any major advertising support.

But retailers with active Web sites took a much different view of Conscience, primarily because their situation is so much different. For one, a Web retailer—or e-tailer—doesn't need to stock much inventory and therefore has only a small risk with a new product. E-Toys was Winchell's first customer, and they bought only six units. Also, e-tailers like to have products that aren't available anywhere else. Finally, traditional retailers have a limited amount of shelf space and need to pick and choose the number of products they carry, while Web retailers can carry as many items as they want.

Winchell decided to sell his game through e-tailers, including Amazon.com, e-Toys.com, and toysmart.com. He researched a bunch of sites and then submitted his idea to the e-tailers where he felt his game would fit best. In many cases, he also called the e-tailer and found the name of the buyer, so he could follow up with phone calls. While Winchell isn't raking in millions, his company, GoRu (Golden Rule) Products, did sell 5,000 games his first complete year in the market through Internet e-tailers. This was far more than Winchell could have sold on his own Web site, primarily because he didn't have the money or expertise to properly promote a Web page that only sold his game.

Momentum Makers

▶ *Creating a buzz:* One of the great features of the Internet is how fast word of mouth travels. People can find something great on the Web, pass it on to their e-mail list, and the simplest joke can be heard around the world in just a few hours—or minutes. That instant communication by the masses can be the inventor's ticket to success. The greatest example of this phenomena is the "Dancing Baby." A small software firm, Kinetix, created a computer-generated clip of a dancing baby and put it out on the Internet without much hype. It was picked up by the *Ally McBeal* TV show and was soon found everywhere you looked—on Web sites, in e-mails, and on what seemed like everyone's computer screen. Only after the product was everywhere did Kinetix take credit and start generating orders for its animated technology. The secret to creating that buzz is to have something that is fun and free and that hopefully has a little bit of mystery and intrigue. You can also create a noticeable Web presence with funny or irreverent lists, stories, or cartoons. You want something people can send to whomever they want for free, listing your site as the source. This is a far better tactic than e-mail lists.

▶ *Portal sites:* These sites are typically free information sites that are loaded with content about a particular topic. They have constant updates, provide

MARKET REALITY

The Internet began as sort of an underground method of communication by computer geeks. The users had a certain disdain for corporate America, and to this day irreverence is a prized commodity on the Web. One of the top financial Web sites is www.doh.com, which is named after Homer Simpson's infamous exclamation. You'll find that the sites that create action are the ones that don't take themselves too seriously.

plenty of information, and are designed to be book-marked sites that people return to regularly. Companies with portal sites make money from the advertising of other companies. But they also make money by linking prominently to their own separate retail sites. For example, a portal site for home decorating might have a link to wallpaper suppliers. The owner of the portal site would have the first wallpaper supplier link be to its own site. Some of these portal sites, such as www.ivillage.com, would be expensive to run for an inventor. But other sites are more modest and could be run by an individual. Some portal sites will even allow you to be the site manager for a specific topic. The site provides all the programming tools needed, and the manager controls the content. Those managers direct visitors to key links that can include their own site. For example, www.miningcompany.com allows individuals with a special interest to be the site manager for a site on that interest, which becomes a portal site for that topic.

▶ *Words count:* You have a greater chance of success if your target customer group uses specialized terms that will lead them to your site. Jeff DeLong of C-Ya greeting cards took advantage of the popularity of the search word "closure," calling his cards "closure cards" to improve traffic to the site. You want to look as closely as possible at what words your customers might use when looking for information on a topic related to your product. The more technical or specific the term, the better chance you have of attracting visitors.

Before You Start

▶ *Identify the target:* For most marketing tactics, you need to identify a target customer and figure out how to reach them. On the Internet, people need to find you. The most successful Web marketers target a Web community. Communities are important because they frequently have one or more pages where you can establish a link to your site. You'll need to identify one and possibly more communities to target in order to generate a steady stream of visitors to your site. This is also why your site should offer something valuable to that community. E-Bay, the well-known auction Web site, offers community rooms for special interest groups as a major way of promoting its site. It has, for instance, a chat and trading room for Beanie Baby collectors. People can buy or trade with other collectors on the site without paying E-Bay a dime. The community room doesn't generate revenue, but it does keep people coming back to E-Bay's auction site, where I'm sure they also look to see what Beanie Babies are being auctioned off.

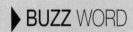

BUZZ WORD

A *Web community* is any group of people with a Web site dedicated to their specific interest. This includes portal sites, chat rooms, newsrooms, community update sites, and interview sites with key members of the community. For instance, fans of the Back Street Boys, the popular teen singing group, make up a Web community, as they have multiple sites dedicated to the band— where they can read reviews of concerts, chat with fellow fans, and win prizes.

▶ *Visit community sites:* Your goal is to be part of one if not more communities. Your site needs to offer something new to the community as well as offering your product, which should clearly satisfy one of the community's needs. In fact, treat your Web site just like another product, one that, in itself, meets your customers' needs. Visit all the community's various sites and start a chart that lists how each group or site serves the community.

Site	Major Emphasis	Community Rooms	Barter Rooms	Types of Updates	Major Attractions

Establish how your site will be meaningfully different from the other community sites, and then look at what type of link and affiliate programs the sites have. You need to fit into the community and have your site work well with the others. Talk to the other site managers through e-mail, explain what your product does and how it will fit in with their visitors, and get their input regarding how to establish links and affiliate programs. Do his before you go to the major expense of developing your site.

▶ *Off-line promotion:* You don't want to overlook the off-line promotional possibilities for your community. There may be magazines, newsletters, trade shows, cable TV programs, and other information sources that your community frequents. You want to send press releases to every source you can find announcing your site and explaining its distinctive features.

▶ *Pricing:* When you decide to serve a community, you are either "in" or "out." "In" sites are ones the community likes because they look out for the community. Your pricing policy is extremely important in deciding how the community looks at your product and site. That doesn't mean that your prices have to be low, but just that they have to be consistent with the policies of other community sites. You want your pricing to seem fair, and Internet sites often offer lots of freebies along with a purchase to make prices appear reasonable. The key to your success is that you are perceived as being a supporter of, and contributor to, the communities you've chosen to target.

▶ *Create a plan:* Creating a Web site and hoping people will come simply isn't going to cut it in the Internet marketing world. You won't get enough visitors even if you get exposure through all the different search engines, yellow page directories, and other Web guides and directories. Your plan should include:

- The communities you are targeting;
- What new things your site will offer to the community;
- A list of key contacts at different sites where your targeted community visits;
- A specific strategy on how your site will change to keep visitors returning;
- A list of how visitors will interact on your site, that is, through chat rooms, community updates, and so on;
- A program that details how you will be linked to other sites;
- A sales strategy that includes your own site, online retailers, and affiliate programs;
- An offline promotional program;
- A list of each revenue-generating program, including products you will sell as an affiliate;
- The banner-exchange programs you will participate in; and finally,
- Your site maintenance schedule, which includes who will do it, how much they will cost, and the time you personally will devote to the site.

First Steps

▶ *Develop the site:* There are dozens of books on how to create your Web page and set it up using a wide variety of programs, or you can hire an outside firm to design your Web page. But don't be fooled into the importance of the page's design. What you need is a site people want to visit, and one where you are linked to a variety of other community-oriented sites. That is what will make you successful. Most small businesses and especially inventors tend to concentrate on making their product more attractive to buy. But that is the wrong approach. Concentrate first and foremost on creating a site that is interesting to your community, one they might even feel compelled to visit to stay in touch. That is what will make your site work. Fancy graphics are nice, fun and excitement help, but none of that matters if your site is not community oriented.

▶ **MARKET REALITY**

www.tshirtcentral.com is a great name for a site, as it comes up quickly as a match when people enter "T-shirt" as the Web search term. The site has hundreds of varieties of T-shirts at competitive prices. While the site attracts a stream of visitors, it's not enough to produce substantial sales. The Web page owner doesn't have the time to work his site, and his sales reflect that.

▶ *Affiliate programs:* You may not have the time, energy, or resources to put together a community-oriented site. Your next option is to create a series of affiliate agreements where you let other sites sell your product for a 20 to 40 percent commission, or you can sell your product to other sites, who then resell your product. With a concerted effort, you may be able to generate hundreds of affiliate agreements that will keep sales growing. Other Web pages are often willing to strike affiliate agreements because they have the same problems you do—creating a site with enough

variety to keep people coming back, and creating
enough revenue sources to make the site pay for itself.

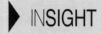 INSIGHT

The Straw that Stirs the Drink

It's daunting, no? Ultimately, your goal is to become, not just a vital member of your targeted Internet community, but its main focal point, the leader and center. If you can do that, customers will be easy to find. You can even team up with several other small companies serving your target community to fund the site, or you can hire a Web site developer to run the site. You may be able to get the developer to work for 50 to 75 percent of the advertising revenue.

But how do you do that? For starters, you have to put your product aside and think about your customers. What's important to them? How many ways does their special interest intersect with their lives? There are many features you can have on your site to make it a focal point, such as

▶ Calendars of upcoming events;

▶ Listings of local organizations and clubs;

▶ Chat rooms where people can debate controversial issues;

▶ Product or service business directories;

▶ Interviews with experts or with users trying out new techniques;

▶ Surveys of visitors about interesting topics (a common tactic of radio stations);

▶ Industry information;

▶ Reprints of relevant news and magazines articles; and

▶ Reprints of technical speeches given at recent meetings.

If you develop a portal site where a target customer comes, you can sign affiliate agreements with other Web businesses, sell space in product directories, or sell banner advertising space to generate revenue. And to help you out, you should be able to find a young, computer-school student willing to work on commission.

▶ *Major shopping site sales:* Affiliate agreements also take time and effort to set up, maintain, and nurture. If you don't have time to do that, you can offer your products through major online stores and catalogs. These stores like to carry products that aren't readily available elsewhere, so they may not like it if you have a major affiliate program. This strategy takes the lowest level of effort on your part, and it is the best tactic to use if you can't commit the time and resources needed to make your site work.

▶ *E-mail lists:* In the last chapter, I mentioned developing an e-mail list. But that list won't be worth the trouble if all you do is mail product offerings to past visitors. You need to build a community. Offer information about something of interest to your target group, and then give them a chance to order from your site as they are learning something they want to know.

> ▶ MARKET **REALITY**
>
> Many, many marketers have made the major mistake of treating the Internet like a typical offline retail location. It is not. People may go to major online shopping sites to shop, especially if the site already has an offline marketing presence. But they won't be coming to your site because they are on a shopping expedition. They come for the community.

Off and Running

▶ *Build a base:* You can build a base in several ways: by becoming a valued member of your Web community, by having an established number of selling affiliates, or by having a network of online retailers that sell your product. You will create the best ongoing business by becoming a key member of a Web community. That will allow you to introduce many products, sell a wide variety of other goods and services, and even establish a presence in offline locations where your community visits—where you can expand sales further. Affiliate agreements help create a sales base but don't have the same impact on long-term sales success. They are a starting point, however, in becoming a member of the community. This is a viable strategy if you don't have the resources to create a full community-oriented Web site now, but want to work toward that goal in the future. Selling through catalogs can provide a base for future business if the product takes off and establishes your brand name.

▶ *Online events:* Contests, promotions, special interviews, guests, and chat rooms on hot topics are all ways to create a little excitement and pull people to your site. Try to schedule some sort of event at least once a quarter so people won't forget about you. You should visit all the community-oriented sites directed at your target customers once a week to see what contests and other online events they offer. You can also get lots of ideas for promotions by visiting sites geared to helping Web site owners promote their sites. I prefer www.virtualpromote.com.

▶ *Publicity:* Your promotions will be more valuable, naturally, if you promote them. Set up a database of all the online and offline sites, magazines, newsletters, and other media outlets that your community visits, reads, watches, and hears.

Becoming a Business

▶ *Become a resource:* Your stock in the online world goes up when you become an authority on a topic of interest to your community. Offer to write articles, do surveys, and answer user questions, or frequently contribute to chat rooms to establish your expertise. You can also have a network of expert advisers on your site who frequently contribute information or answer questions to make your site a resource for your targeted Web community.

▶ *Brand the name:* People have to remember exactly who you are if they are to keep returning to your Web site, and they should remember your name in the offline world, too. That means you must brand your name, which simply means creating a memorable identity in your customers' mind. I also recommend that inventors put their own picture and history on their Web page. People like to know about the inventor, and it gives them an extra reason to remember your site.

> ▶ **SUCCESS** TIP
>
> Inventors don't have the resources to establish a name with repetitive advertising, and so they must create a distinctive name that is memorable the first time you hear it. A good example is David Lawrence, a toy inventor who sells primarily over the Internet. He called his company Rumpus Toys, and his toys have names like Gus Gutz and Harry Hairball.

▶ *Create a network:* As I've said, long-term success on the Web depends on creating a community-oriented Web site, which is expensive and difficult, or by creating strong relationships with other site developers that serve the same community. Either way, you must network even more so than in the offline world. Then again, one great feature of the Internet is that people do everything by e-mail. You don't actually have to meet anyone to develop a relationship. The key step for developing a network is to be very aware of the Internet rule "content over commerce." Focus on helping your potential customers meet their goals and you will succeed in becoming a vital part of the community's network—and in generating business.

▶ *New products:* The Internet is a fast-changing environment that seems to spawn new products and ideas at least once every six months. You can't expect to rest on you laurels at any point. People will be coming after you, and you need to constantly add new features and benefits to keep fresh in the market and to keep the interest of your targeted Web community.

▶ MARKET **REALITY**

The fact that so many inventors simply put their products on the Web and expect them to sell can be an asset for you. It allows the dedicated Web entrepreneur to be a product scout and to keep on the lookout for new products created by other people. You can add these products to your site on an affiliate basis, or you can just buy out the product from the inventor.

Are You Making Money?

▶ *Profit check:* Add up the following:

1. Your monthly expenses for being on a Web server, which run from $20 to $200 per month depending on the size of your Web site and the amount of time people are connected to your site.

2. Your monthly expenses for retaining a Web host, which run from $50 to several thousand dollars per month depending on the number of changes you have and the complexity of your site.

3. A salary for your time on the Web supporting your business.

4. Other expenses, such as telephone, mailing costs, the monthly charge for being able to take credit cards, and any other routine expenses.

5. Each month, 10 percent of the cost of creating your Web page, which can run from $1,000 to $50,000.

Your sales need to be at least three to four times this monthly cost for you to have a chance of making money. Promoting a site effectively into a community-oriented portal site is quite expensive. If you can't do that, switch to an affiliate or online retailer sales strategy.

▶ *Corrective measures:* The number-one reason inventors lose money on their sites is that they don't have any type of promotional strategy. (Incidentally, this problem applies to many more potential "Web millionaires" than just inventors.) The number-one corrective measure is to simply develop a Web marketing plan that will work. Then start executing it. Another major problem is when Web sites don't target a community to network with. You can't succeed unless you are connected with at least one, and preferably three or four, Web communities. You should find those communities, create a network of contacts, and start by signing affiliate agreements with important Web sites.

▶ *Cutting costs:* The number one, and virtually only, tactic for cutting costs is to learn to do everything yourself. Web developers, promoters, and other experts can help you create a site that works technically, but I've found that only the tireless efforts of the inventor are what turn a site into a valuable member of the Web community.

Selling on Commission–
The Inside Scoop

The Basics

Inventors often have great ideas they don't have the money to introduce effectively. One problem is that potential retail and distribution customers consider inventors with a new product to be unreliable suppliers, and a second problem is that inventors don't have the money to fund manufacturing start-up costs for their product. The traditional way of addressing this problem is to find a manufacturer willing to license the idea. Licensing has its own problems, the primary one being that manufacturers are often reluctant to take on all the risks of manufacturing and selling a new product.

Selling on commission is a tactic for getting around the fact that an inventor can't afford to create the new product. The inventor changes his or her approach from one of having a new product to one of having a new business opportunity. The manufacturer can tap into this

MARKET **REALITY**

Small to midsize manufacturers are always looking for new sales opportunities, especially if they are risk-free and without a lot of hassles. Companies will often build a product for sale if a customer wants it. An inventor offering to sell a product for a manufacturer is an even better deal if the company doesn't have a strong sales force, or if the inventor's product is going into a new market.

opportunity simply by hiring the person who understands it best—and who is willing to sell the product on commission. Manufacturers will respond favorably to this if the product fits in well with their manufacturing capability and if they feel the person is well connected to the target market and will be able to generate sales.

The same approach can work with companies in the distribution channel, either a distributor or wholesaler that is interested in expanding into a new market. The benefit to the inventor is that he or she is selling the product with the backing of an established company. That backing both enhances the inventor's credibility and provides the funding needed to launch the product. The biggest benefit versus licensing for the inventor is that he or she is still involved with the company and often has input into virtually all the decisions related to the product.

Selling on commission is also an ideal approach for individuals who spot a market opportunity they want to exploit but don't have the expertise to actually develop the product. This tactic lets the manufacturer worry about product design and engineering while the inventor/entrepreneur worries about exploiting the market.

Perfect Products

This tactic works best when the manufacturer has to make only minimal changes to its manufacturing process to produce the product. To arrange a selling-on-commission deal, the product itself, its benefits, and how important

INVENTOR'S STORY

No Money—No Problem

David Weisman of Minneapolis, Minnesota, observed that teenage girls had problems with broken mirrors. He thought a perfect solution would be to have an unbreakable mirror consisting of a piece of silver mylar film on a thin film of plastic. He envisioned his product, the Mirror Mate, being used for mirrors in school lockers, as premium or promotional items, as a mirror that could be sold at low-cost mall jewelry stores, and as stickers with designs that could be sold in sticker-dispensing machines. Weisman had just one problem—no money.

Weisman decided first to pursue markets where the mirror acted as a decal, attaching to a surface. He found the cheapest way to produce his product was to buy 5-mil.-thick mylar and then place double-sided adhesive tape on the back. The mylar could be attached to any surface and become a mirror. Weisman next located a decal manufacturer with the equipment needed to attach the tape to the mylar. Unfortunately, without any money, Weisman's idea appeared to have a limited future. But Weisman approached the company with an offer to sell the Mirror Mate for a 10 percent commission. The benefit he proposed for the manufacturer was that the product could have a huge impact on the company's sales levels and that Weisman knew and understood the market and could fast-track the company's sales.

The manufacturer didn't bite for that offer, but they did offer to give Weisman $1,500 of product that he could pay for once he sold it. They also left the door open for Weisman's commission offer if the product sold. Weisman then turned to the distribution channel. He found an advertising specialty products distributor who was willing to add Mirror Mate products to its line and who was willing to have Weisman work on commission to sell his and other products. As I'm writing this book, Weisman has started generating sales for his product, and he hopes eventually to form his own company, but his ultimate success is as yet undetermined.

those benefits are to the consumer aren't nearly as significant as the manufacturing costs involved in making it. In addition, it helps if the target market has a small distribution network. The manufacturer will be more apt to believe you can achieve sales success if only a few companies control product distribution and you have already established a relationship with those people.

Your Goals

▶ *Quick market entry:* Underfinanced inventors often struggle two to three years to get their product out in a major way. Having the product financed by an established company gets the product out quickly and provides the funding needed to expand sales.

▶ *Get established in the market:* You want to develop market connections if you plan on introducing a series of products. You'll develop more connections faster if you have the backing of a larger company.

▶ *Faster income:* You start collecting commissions as soon as you start selling products. On your own, you'd have to pay back start-up and cash-flow loans before you'd start taking home any cash. On your own, you'd also run the risk of spending more than you receive for a year or two before your invention produced income.

▶ *Proceed with limited patent protection:* Some product ideas can't get significant patent protection because of earlier

▶ MARKET **REALITY**

Inventors/entrepreneurs who get off to a fast start typically have great connections to the distribution channel of their target market. Often they get these contacts by working for a larger company. Buyers will almost always see a salesperson for an established company if he or she has a new product. You won't get that same reception as an underfinanced inventor.

patents obtained by other people or companies. This problem typically kills a licensing agreement, where the scope of protection your product can obtain is important. But it doesn't mean as much for selling on commission, where the company is just looking to add extra sales revenue.

Other Choices

If you are looking for quick income, the only tactic that works as well as selling on commission is private label marketing (chapters 14 and 15). If your goal is an alliance with a major company to give your product credibility, your other choice would be a joint-venture arrangement (chapters 12 and 13).

Money Matters

The beauty of selling on commission is that the inventor typically doesn't have to put up any money. The manufacturer will pay for the patent application, start-up costs, and operating capital required to launch the product. The inventor's only expenses are defining the product, possibly making a model or prototype, and the cost of making his or her early market connections.

Protection

Manufacturers interested in having you sell on commission also typically interested in turning a quick profit. They may not be concerned with going through the entire patenting process. They are also happy to pay you a commission if you are producing sales for them. You do, however, run the risk of the manufacturer trying to steal your

SUCCESS TIP

Manufacturers will often readily agree to give you in-kind services for free to build a prototype for a promising idea, but they don't like to pay for out-of-pocket or extra expenses. In-kind services are ones that the manufacturer is already paying for, such as the cost of machine time or the services of an in-house model builder. The manufacturer pays those expenses whether or not it works with you.

idea. Inventors can usually prevent this by simply applying for a provisional patent just before contacting potential manufacturers. That allows you to state that your patent is pending. You can then agree to assign the patent to the manufacturer if they agree to pay the full patent application and issue fees.

Prototypes

The manufacturer probably won't make an investment without at least some positive response from customers after seeing a prototype. You probably will be able to convince the manufacturer to pick up some, if not all, the expense of producing a prototype. This is especially true if the manufacturers you talk to are already producing similar products.

Research

The key to lining up a selling-on-commission agreement is to know who the key players in the distribution network are, and preferably to have their support for your product idea before you approach a manufacturer. That's the only way the manufacturer will be convinced that you can actually sell your product. Research trade magazines and attend trade shows to learn who the best contacts are. Then talk to those contacts to see if they believe your idea will sell. You should be able to get a selling-on-commission agreement if you get these contacts to endorse your product idea, or better yet, if they let you know they will buy the product if and when it becomes available.

Manufacturing

If your agreement is with a manufacturer, you won't have to worry about how they will produce the product. If your

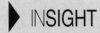

INSIGHT

How to Make Their Burden Lighter

So why is it that many manufacturers are so willing to negotiate with you for selling on commission? Why would the big boys care about a small fish like you? Because manufacturers make huge profits on incremental sales due to the impact of overhead absorption (which many companies also call burden). Overhead is the fixed costs of a plant, such as rent, utilities, plant management salaries, and other expenses. Companies divide this overhead by a number of methods and place an overhead burden on each product sold. A product's cost includes materials, labor, and overhead components, and overhead is often anywhere from 30 to 60 percent of a product's total cost. At the start of a year's budget, the company places an overhead burden on each product sold, so that it covers the total overhead. For example, if overhead is $1 million, and a company plans to produce 1 million units, a $1 overhead burden will be added to each unit.

Now, imagine that you approach that manufacturer with your selling-on-commission proposal. If the cost of materials for your product is $1.50 per unit, and the labor to build the product is 50¢ per unit, the manufacturer will add its $1 overhead burden for a total cost of $3.50. The manufacturer will then add a 20 percent profit margin, or 70¢, and charge you $4.20 a unit. But wait. Didn't the manufacturer already pay for its overhead with its 1 million units in sales? Yes. The real profit to the manufacture is $1.70. Manufacturers make huge profits when production levels exceed their budgeted levels. The result for inventors is that manufacturers will bend over backward to help inventors who could add 5 to 20 percent to their production volume.

agreement is with a distributor, you may need to locate a manufacturer. However, you should find several manufacturers who will offer favorable terms if you have a distributor lined up to provide the support you need to sell the product.

Key Contacts

Decision-makers at large distributors or customers are the key to enticing a manufacturer to take on your product and have you sell it. The manufacturer not only needs you but it wants you if you have established connections with important potential customers. You want to contact those people first and be sure they support your idea, and if possible, get a letter of support from them before approaching manufacturers. The letter of support just has to say that the person believes your idea has merit and that they would consider selling it when and if the product becomes available.

Pros and Cons

Pros

▶ Requires very little investment by the inventor.
▶ Can be the quickest route to full market penetration.
▶ Provides instant credibility to customers.
▶ Produces reasonably quick income.
▶ Establishes the inventor in the marketplace with key buyers.
▶ The inventor continues to have input into his or her product's success.

Cons

▶ Inventors don't always have control of their product.

▶ Doesn't establish an inventor's company or brand.

▶ Requires sales and marketing enthusiasm and expertise.

▶ Works best with products with large customers or a narrow distribution channel.

Up, Up, and Away

Selling on commission provides the contacts you need to branch out and start your own company, but it doesn't really provide a starting point for a new company. The product will always belong to the company you are selling the product through. It is an ideal tactic, however, for inventors who don't want the hassle of running or funding their own company. If your product is a winner, you should be able to continue to introduce new products through the manufacturer.

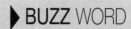

BUZZ WORD

A *narrow distribution channel* means there only a few key target customers who control most of the market. A *broad distribution channel* has many potential buyers. Products sold to tire dealers for changing tires is a narrow channel because there are only 50 distributors throughout the country selling these types of products. Day spas are also a narrow market because there are only about 10 major distributors in the market.

Key Resources

Your main resources are trade magazines, trade shows, and trade associations. You need to meet and know key people who distribute to your market. You also need to have a firm understanding of the market, how it works, what the pricing is, and how products are sold. The person who will be paying your commission will be paying for your contacts just as much as he or she is paying for your idea. *Gale's Encyclopedia of Publications and Broadcast Media, Gale's Source of Associations,* and several trade show directories are available at many larger libraries. One effective tactic is to contact the writers of articles in trade magazines and ask them who the key players are in a business. Often these articles are written by industry people, and they will provide you with names of key contacts and often even tell you who the best candidates are to buy your product.

What to Expect

▶ The manufacturer will expect quick results from you. Be sure to line up customers first before approaching the manufacturer to sell on commission.

▶ The manufacturer won't automatically print brochures, attend trade shows, or pay for a marketing program. Be sure to propose a marketing program and get the manufacturer's approval before signing a contractor agreement.

▶ You will only get paid commissions after customers pay for their product.

▶ You may go three to four months before sales are made. You can ask the manufacturer for an advance against commissions to cover those costs, but the manufacturer won't be obligated to offer an advance unless it is part of your agreement.

▶ The manufacturer might offer you its standard sales representative agreement, which pays a commission only on the products you sell. Insist on a commission on all your products, including an override (or commission payment) of several percent on any of your products sold by other salespeople or independent representatives.

➤ The manufacturer will want to produce the product as cheaply as possible and may compromise some of the product's features. You'll need to monitor closely the manufacturer's design to prevent this.

➤ The manufacturer will be reluctant to make immediate changes in the product once it starts production. Be sure to show a model or prototype to potential customers and get their approval before the manufacturer finalizes tooling and the manufacturing process.

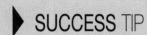 **SUCCESS** TIP

Most manufacturers will want you to be an independent contractor so they don't have to pay benefits or social security for the inventor. While some salespeople would prefer to be an employee to get those benefits, you are better off as an independent contractor because then you have the option of working on other projects and the manufacturer can't tell you what to do.

Selling on Commission–
Making It Happen

Keys to Success

▶ *Own the market:* The manufacturer or distributor who hires you on commission is really buying your ability to sell the product. You will improve your chances to land a deal with each additional person you know who is either in the distribution network or a major customer. Other tactics you can use to generate support include call reports, which you write after you interview key buyers; letters of endorsements from those same buyers, and provisional orders. You'll also have an easier time selling the concept of sales on commission if you have a sales and marketing background.

Sometimes You Need a Buddy to Light the Way

Cindy Jones's husband came home one Halloween with a cutout potato head riding on his car's antenna. Jones loved the idea and cut out a plastic pumpkin and put it on the antenna of her car. To add a little spice, Jones ran a light from the car battery to the inside of the pumpkin—and the Antenna Buddy was born. When people kept stopping her on the streets of her hometown, Oklahoma City, and asking where she got the product, Jones became convinced she had to move ahead with her idea.

But Jones didn't have money or manufacturing experience, and she knew she wanted to land a deal with a manufacturer. Her next step was to build a little momentum behind her product. First she applied for a patent, and then she approached MTV to see if they would use her Antenna Buddy on the travel trailer used in their popular show Road Rules. After considerable effort on Jones's part, MTV agreed to use the product on the show as long as it had a Southwestern theme. Jones created a cowboy hat for the antenna and a longhorn skull for the front of the vehicle, and her product appeared on every show.

Next, Jones lined up two big potential promotional-product customers, Radio Shack and Taco Bell. She wanted them to put their logo on an Antenna Buddy. The appeal was that the product would be cute and cool and, most of all, would be seen by thousands and thousands of people. Now Jones was ready, and she approached three manufacturers who produced specialty lighting products for automobiles. All three companies wanted the product. And all three made specific offers and virtually ended up in a bidding war. The company Jones chose not only offered her a commission on all products she sold, but they also agreed to distribute the product to auto specialty stores—and they agreed to pay Jones a royalty on every product sold, whether by Jones or the manufacturer. Jones's only big expense was the initial patent. All in all, it was a great deal for Jones and her company, Antenna Buddies, Inc.

▶ *Produce results:* The manufacturer or distributor will be watching your sales results to be sure you can back up your potential sales claims before investing significant amounts of money. You should have one or two customers presold before approaching a manufacturer. That way you can produce immediate results.

▶ *Act big:* One of the reasons you decide to go with a manufacturer or distributor is that you want to use their size to build credibility. Take advantage of that. Have your business card state the company's name, always mention the company's name when you call, and be sure to have first-class brochures, marketing materials, and trade show booths that clearly call out the company's name.

Momentum Makers

▶ *The monster account:* Nothing succeeds like having a big account in hand to land a selling-on-commission deal. Cindy Jones had strong interest in her Antenna Buddies from both Radio Shack and Taco Bell. Both of

▶ **BUZZ** WORD

For Cindy Jones, Radio Shack and Taco Bell represented what is typically referred to as a *promotional product* sale. They are buying the product to promote their business just as if they were buying a free calendar to give away. You can sell promotional products to smaller customers through advertising specialties distributors, who are listed in the Yellow Pages. This is an attractive market because you can often land big orders.

those firms could order millions of the product, and the lure of those big orders landed Jones three offers.

▸ *Orders first, production second:* You want the credibility of the manufacturer, and the manufacturer wants the extra business. But the manufacturer doesn't want to spend a ton of money on the product before it knows whether or not the product will sell. One solution to this concern is to have the manufacturer agree to let you represent it while obtaining orders. The manufacturer will go into production after you produce enough orders. This is a win-win situation for everyone. You will get the credibility of the manufacturer to help sell the product, and the manufacturer minimizes its risk.

Before You Start

▸ *Identify the market:* Your job is to identify the key customer groups who will buy your product, the distribution channel that can be used to sell to that market, and the key players in that distribution channel. Then you need to uncover the industry's price structure, which includes discounts to wholesalers and retailers, packaging required, key buying periods, and important trade shows. Once you understand the market, your goal is to meet and nurture as many key contacts as you can, both explaining your product and asking for their sup-

▸ MARKET **REALITY**

Selling on commission recognizes a new reality in today's market. Many inventors today are not the nuts-and-bolts types who build new widgets. They don't have the in-depth mechanical ability to design the product, make the prototype, or produce the product. Instead, they are opportunity finders, people who spot unfilled needs or a different way of solving customer problems.

port so that you can convince the manufacturer to take on your product.

▶ *Customer-defined products:* The most successful products are typically ones based on actual customer desires. When you talk about your product to manufacturers, always start with a customer focus, detailing how you have surveyed customers and explaining how your product meets their expressed needs. Most business executives have had it driven into their heads that their business needs to be customer focused, and you want to be sure to present your product in that way.

The First Steps

▶ *A clear advantage:* You can achieve a clear market advantage in a number of ways. Your product may be markedly superior or markedly different from other products. The Antenna Buddies are clearly a different product. But you also gain a clear advantage if you are approaching a market the manufacturer doesn't sell to, or if your marketing campaign, name, or packaging stand out in the marketplace.

▶ *Work the manufacturer:* You will typically get better results with a manufacturer if you propose your arrangement in steps. This gives them a chance to warm up slowly to your idea. You might start by approaching them to

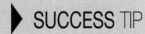

SUCCESS TIP

How do you know if your product has a clear advantage? Marketers use many phrases when they talk about a product advantage, such as a "forehead slapper," a "double wow" product, or a "Why didn't I think of that?" The point is, a product with a clear, substantial advantage will generate an excited reaction in potential customers.

see if they would make your product for you as a contract manufacturer. At a later meeting, you can then talk to the manufacturer about how the product's potential is larger than you expected and that you can't afford to proceed on your own.

➤ *Write an agreement:* You need a formal contract with the manufacturer that defines your relationship. The manufacturer will probably propose a standard manufacturers' representative agreement (which is available in virtually every book of legal forms in bookstores and libraries), but you need to add several additional clauses. One is that you receive a sales commission override on every sale of your product the company makes even if it's not made by you. The second clause states what happens to the overrides if you or the company decide to terminate the sales agreement. In most manufacturers' agent agreements, commissions stop three to six months after a salesperson leaves. You want the contract to state that your override continues for an extended period of at least two years after the agreement ends. You should also insist that the manufacturer sell you the product and all of its inventory and tooling if it should decide to discontinue the product. Finally, if the manufacturer decides to sell the product line to another company, the contract should state that the inventor gets a commission on that sale.

➤ BUZZ WORD

A *sales commission override* is a commission over and above what is paid to any other salespeople. In effect, the sales override acts as a royalty, since the inventor gets paid on everything sold. The override is a better arrangement for the inventor if a product doesn't have a patent or has a weak patent because it pays the inventor regardless of the product's patent status.

➤ *Connections:* Creating a network of influential contacts is a key step for every inventor no matter how he or she is introducing a product. It is even more important for inventors selling on commission. Keep a card file of every contact you make so you can go back to them when you are ready to sell the product.

Off and Running

▶ *Set up distribution:* There are usually plenty of sales opportunities for a product besides the big accounts you use to land your agreement. Your goal is to continue to increase sales, and you can do that by hiring manufacturers' sales agents to cover the country by adding distribution in new markets. You can advertise for sales representatives in trade magazines. Another tactic for finding them is to post an "agents wanted" or "representatives wanted" sign in your booth at trade shows. You will have to pay new representatives a commission, but you will still receive your override.

▶ *Develop a marketing calendar:* Sales and marketing professionals always feel that there is way too much to do in far too little time. You can overcome this problem to a degree by setting up a yearly calendar of all of your major marketing and sales events. Major trade shows, product introductions, calls on big customers, special events, and the timing for adding new representatives and distributors should all be listed on the calendar. Make sure the calendar demonstrates that you are earning your money.

▶ *Hire other salespeople:* Your long-term goal is to keep producing new products for this industry or for other industries. You can't do that if you have to handle all the sales activity on your own. Work with the company to hire new salespeople—accepting the fact that your only pay is your override. This will give the company better sales and allow you to branch out into new products.

Building a Business

▶ *Become a resource:* Your long-term success in commission sales depends either on your expertise at introducing a product into the market or on your creativity to continually come up with new product ideas. Both of these skills are ideal building blocks for going into business for yourself. You may not be able to reclaim your original product from the manufacturer, but you can move on to introduce a new product of your own or even products from other inventors.

 SUCCESS TIP

Many products have standards you must follow regarding product quality or use. In some industries, standards are created by the industry to make business easier to conduct. At one time, I was trying to sell a new testing process to IBM. I had no luck until I joined an American Society for Testing and Materials committee. IBM contacts on the committee gave me the opening I needed to present our product.

▶ *Create a key industry presence:* You can create an industry presence by being on industry committees, by volunteering for associations, and by serving on standards or trade show committees. You can also write articles for trade magazines, give speeches or presentations at meetings, and volunteer to help with any training meetings in the industry.

▶ *Take control:* There is an inevitable clash when you sell your product on a commission basis for a company. Inventors want to develop a network of contacts that (1) give them the ability to increase sales,

(2) make themselves important to manufacturers, and (3) set the stage for future sales growth. The manufacturer, on the other hand, will feel vulnerable if it doesn't have direct contact with customers and the distribution channel. The manufacturer will want to know, network, and develop a relationship with the inventor's contacts. The best path for inventors to follow is to introduce buyers and distribution channel contacts to the manufacturer when starting out, and then work to cut back the manufacturer's involvement as sales develop. This strategy helps land initial sales and then helps increase the inventor's control of market contacts.

▶ *New products:* Over the long term, your influence in the market depends on your ability to consistently introduce new products. The influence of a one-product inventor wanes considerably over time. The good news is that the market is predisposed to see you as someone who can spot new product opportunities and bring them to market. People in the market won't care that much if you invented the product or if you located a great product idea from another inventor. Your influence will be high, both in the market and with your manufacturer, if you can continually introduce winning products.

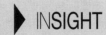

INSIGHT

Hooking the Big Fish

It's very possible for first-time anglers to catch the powerful marlins of retail: mass merchants like Wal-Mart, Target, and Kmart. But you need to have a strong line to

INSIGHT

reel them in. And in this case, I don't mean the product itself, which in this analogy is the bait that gets them to bite. The line is your sales pitch, and it must be top-notch. Mass merchants won't believe you are a reliable supplier if you can't master the details of the sales call, so here are some tips to prepare yourself for the big presentation.

▶ Know what season the buyer is buying for. Typically it's six to nine months away.

▶ Know what section of the store you want your product placed in, for example, housewares, automotive supplies, or sporting goods.

▶ Know exactly what part of that section you propose displaying the product in.

▶ Know what products you want your product placed next to based on what the store sold last year. Suggest that your product be placed near similarly priced products in the same product category.

▶ If possible, show sales results of your product against established products at other outlets.

▶ Show your product packaging and explain how it will fit into that section of the store. If all the products in the store are on hooks, make sure your package goes onto a hook.

▶ Know your pricing: your suggested retail price, the price smaller retailers are paying, and the price catalogs pay.

▶ Know all your incidental costs, such as freight, allowable returns, and warrantee repair policies.

▶ Be ready to explain your production capabilities and how fast you can respond to unexpected orders.

▶ Have a plan in place for handling electronic data interchange (EDI) order entry.

▶ Know exactly how your product will be boxed for shipment. Mass merchandisers expect different bar code numbers for the product, the case, and the master carton.

Are You Making Money?

▶ *Profit check:* When it comes to selling on commission, whether you make a profit or not depends mainly on two things: your ability to sell and the strength of your initial sales agreement with the manufacturer. I've already men-

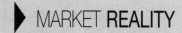

▶ MARKET REALITY

Big retailers don't like to mail purchase orders to vendors. Instead they send them electronically to a computer you specify (which is referred to as electronic data interchange, or EDI, order entry). This system was developed before the Internet became popular, and retailers may switch to sending orders over the Web in the future.

tioned several of the clauses you need to put into your sales agreement. Here are four important clauses I haven't yet mentioned:

1. You are an independent company or contractor.
2. You don't have a restriction on selling other products in the same industry for a specific time period.
3. You may develop products for the same industry that may not be offered to the manufacturer.
4. The customer list and networking contacts you make are not the exclusive rights of the manufacturer.

You need to stay independent of the manufacturer to keep your future options as broad as possible. If you are not careful, the manufacturer may end up with the rights to any product ideas you create while you work with it. Manufacturers also often want a clause restricting your activities in the same industry, such as a statement that you can't sell any product for another manufacturer to the same customers, or even an agreement that you will not work with another company for two years after your sales agreement is

> ## ▶ SUCCESS TIP
>
> Your contract with the manufacturer is crucial for your success. Unfortunately, most attorneys will look at the arrangement as a manufacturers' representative sales agreement. You will get the best contract, at the lowest price, if you do a rough draft before approaching the attorney using as your base a sales representative contract (available in most legal form books). Start with that agreement and add the clauses I mention in this chapter.

canceled. Manufacturers want this type of clause so you will offer all your ideas to them first, and you want to avoid it as it restricts your ability to sell further ideas to other companies. Customer lists are another major stumbling block for moving off on your own. Many contracts will state that customer lists and contacts are the exclusive property of the manufacturer even if you developed the list. The manufacturer can try to make it difficult for you to sell other products to these clients unless you include a specific clause in your contract giving you that right.

▶ *Corrective measures:* You can always renegotiate your contract if you sign a bad deal. The secret to doing that is to present your request in a period when the company really needs you. This could be right before a major product launch, before a buying season begins, or right before a major negotiation of a customer contract. Your only real negotiating power is to refuse to put in a full sales effort before the contract is changed. The manufacturer is unlikely to make any substantial changes if you continue to proceed with your efforts to sell the product. Ultimately, the power is in your hands because you can always walk away from the deal without losing much. The manufacturer will have much more to lose—including tooling, production equipment, and inventory as well as engineering and management time.

Matchmaker, Matchmaker, Find Me a Find

If you are going to find new products for your manufacturer, you won't be able to cut a deal to sell on commission because you also need to be sure the inventor or company you acquire the product from gets paid. Instead, you can negotiate a finder's fee for yourself, which could be a straight percentage of the sales price that the manufacturer would pay. This fee could vary from 2 to 10 percent of the sales price for an outright purchase. Or you could arrange to receive a sales override of 2 to 3 percent of future sales. The override might be your only option if you arrange for the company to license the product from another inventor.

The best new products to look for are ones that have been developed and have had some sales success. Since many inventors who start their own companies learn too late that they don't have the money or the expertise to sustain their company through the first lean year of sales, you can often find inventors who are happy to sell out and recoup their investment or get a royalty. When you find a product in your market that you feel will sell well, talk to the owner. If he or she isn't willing to sell, the inventor may be ready to sell in the future. You can look for small inventor-owned companies at trade shows and in the new product sections of major trade magazines.

One thing you don't want to do is to try and renegotiate the contract before the manufacturer has invested money in the project. The *manufacturer* might walk away from the deal if you do that. Wait until it has a substantial investment in place and then ask for a new contract.

12

Joint Ventures–
The Inside Scoop

The Basics

Technically, a joint venture for inventors is an agreement by two parties
to work together to design, promote, or manufacture a new product. The
parties split the work and split the profits. The split can be 50/50, or it can
be a different split depending on the work and resources each party contributes. The partnership could be a formal joint venture, or it could be a
more informal alliance or agreement. What distinguishes a joint venture is
that both parties contribute financial resources, and both share in the
profits. Inventors can form a wide variety of partnerships, including:

▶ A partnership with a manufacturer who will help design the new
product, build prototypes, and eventually produce the product. The
inventor would be responsible for all sales and marketing activities
and might also pay for the patent and some other tooling expenses.

▶ A contract with a sales and marketing group that agrees to market the product for an inventor.

▶ An agreement with an expert in the field—such as a pro golfer or a well-known doctor—to present the product to consumers.

▶ An alliance with an engineer or industrial designer who will be responsible for finalizing the design of the product.

▶ A joint venture with another marketing company to exploit a different market than the one you originally targeted.

▶ An agreement with an overseas manufacturer in which it makes your product for a reduced price and extended terms in exchange for overseas marketing rights.

> ▶ MARKET **REALITY**
>
> Inventors make one consistent mistake when trying to strike an alliance—they try for too high a percentage of the profits. Other companies are not going to work hard to make you rich. You won't get any deal if you ask for more than 50 percent of the profits. Remember that without you the company will continue in business, while you might not get into business at all without the help of an alliance partner.

Inventors form alliances for two reasons. One is that they don't have enough money and need to get a partner to help foot the bill. The second is that they need to offer an extra enticement to get help from key people in the market. An inventor, for example, who wants to penetrate the hardware store market may want to team up with a top manufacturers' sales representatives agency. Agencies might not be all that interested in taking on a product for a standard commission from a small company that can't afford advertising or promotion. But they might be willing to take the product on and pay for promotion if they were receiving 50 percent of the profits instead of a 10 percent commission. The agency would also help set up a complete distribution network across the country.

INVENTOR'S STORY

Could You Play That Song Again?

When Nathaniel Weiss was a musician in his early 20s growing up in Philadelphia, Pennsylvania, he noticed an interesting phenomenon: When guitar players practiced, they constantly came up with great-sounding riffs, but if they stopped to write the notes down, they seemed to lose the groove and the riff died. Weiss created a pickup device that attached to a guitar and connected to a computer. Weiss's software program then transcribed the notes played into sheet music. The result: Guitar players could play away knowing that their creativity was being preserved.

Weiss named his hardware/software product the G-Vox, but he knew he wasn't ready to go to market because he didn't have a distribution network set up, and he didn't have much credibility in the guitar community. Weiss's first step was to form a partnership with the Fender Guitar Company, a leading guitar manufacturer. Fender offered the G-Vox as an option on its guitars, and Weiss also sold the product to guitar stores.

The market for writing aids for guitar players was steady, but it didn't have much growth potential. While Weiss wasn't able to locate a large songwriting market, he did notice that there was a huge market for helping students learn to play an instrument. Weiss reconfigured his product for members of student bands and orchestras. The benefit now was that the G-Vox pickup allowed students to see exactly what they were playing while practicing at home or at school. The school market is big, has established sales channels, and typically only buys from a few well-known suppliers—it's a difficult market for any inventor to crack. So what did Weiss do? He formed another partnership, signing an alliance agreement with one of those major suppliers, McGraw-Hill. Together, the two companies proceeded to introduce new products created by Weiss's company, G-Vox Interactive Music.

Perfect Products

Alliance or joint-venture partners look for a significant business benefit when they decide to team up with an inventor. Typically, they are only interested if your product can increase their sales 15 to 25 percent, or if the product provides them with a significant market advantage over their competitors. The perfect product from their perspective is one that has significant market impact.

From the inventor's point of view, perfect products for an alliance partnership or joint venture are ones that the inventor doesn't have the financial, engineering, or manufacturing resources to produce, or that the inventor doesn't have the marketing network or credibility required to launch. The one feature of a perfect joint venture product is that the product provides customers a significant, important benefit.

▶ MARKET **REALITY**

Why should a manufacturer or distributor be interested in an alliance or joint venture? Sure, one reason is that they end up with an exciting product to sell, but that's not the real reason. It costs companies lots of money to introduce a new product. That financial risk is minimized in an alliance because the inventor is the one who does most of the legwork to get the product market ready.

I personally believe a joint-venture strategy should be used far more often than it is by inventors. It allows them to move their product to the market in a big hurry with much less financial risk. The trick to success is to find the right size companies to present your idea to. If your product can sell $1 to $2 million per year, there is no point in presenting it to a $100-million corporation. They won't be interested, since the product doesn't have enough potential for them. But a $5-million corporation might find that $1-million product perfect for their sales and manufacturing goals.

Your Goals

When forming joint ventures and alliances, you might be hoping to do any of the following:

▶ Introduce and penetrate the market as quickly as possible.

▶ Receive sufficient funding and support for a project that is beyond your resources and experience.

▶ Have more involvement in the ongoing success of the product than you would get in a licensing arrangement.

▶ Develop the product further before it can be licensed. An alliance can be a precursor of an eventual licensing agreement.

▶ Generate additional market information and distribution channel contacts that can be used for subsequent inventions.

▶ Obtain the management, administrative, and manufacturing support for a new product. A company with experienced personnel can do these tasks far better than most inventors.

Other Choices

Inventors have other choices depending on the skills they have. Inventors who are experienced in engineering and manufacturing might choose a private label strategy (chapters 14 and 15), or they may choose to try and license their

SUCCESS TIP

You need to bring something to the table to strike a joint-venture deal. You need to offer either (1) engineering know-how to create the final product, (2) key contacts with end users to create a product that best meets the needs of the market, or (3) numerous contacts in the distribution network to expedite sales.

idea (chapters 16 and 17). Inventors whose skill is in marketing, recognizing market opportunities, or in sales may choose to sell on a commission basis (chapters 10 and 11), or they may also pursue a private label strategy. Inventors might also decide to build their own company, raising funds from investors and/or banks and introducing their product on their own (chapters 18 and 19).

Money Matters

Typically, the main advantage of a joint-venture or alliance strategy is that you get funding from the potential partner. For example, an inventor may have identified a big market opportunity, but he or she doesn't have the money to create the prototypes. He or she then approaches a potential partner company and discusses a possible alliance *if* the product is successfully developed. The inventor can then ask for a sum of money to create the prototype or ask for engineering support to finish the prototype. One strategy is to ask for support only for accomplishing this first step, and then once it is finished, the two parties can decided together if they want to proceed further. This step-by-step process is frequently much easier to sell to a company than a license, where the company has to take on the entire burden of introducing the product.

Protection

Inventors don't really need a patent to strike a joint-venture or alliance agreement, but it does improve their negotiating position. It also helps ensure that the product's intellectual property rights belong to the inventor. In some cases, the inventor might apply for a provisional or design patent so he or she can say that a patent is applied for. This can create a dangerous situation, however. The provisional patent gives only one year for the inventor to apply for a utility patent. Your one year could easily run out before you have finalized your agreement and finished the product design. You are better off applying for a very broad patent, knowing that your initial application will be contested by the patent office. Then you can keep going back and forth with the patent office for several years before your claims are accepted. This tactic can keep your patent rights open for three to five years (see appendix A for more details).

Prototypes

One reason that inventors choose the alliance strategy is that they don't have the experience or money to finalize a "looks like, works like" prototype. But often a drawing just isn't enough to generate a positive response from a potential partner. If you want to strike up a joint-venture agreement, you'll find that having a prototype is an important tool. (Turn to appendix B for a complete discussion of creating prototypes.) However, you don't want to spend too much money creating a prototype. Just take the prototype far enough so the partner can see your

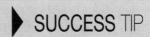

▶ SUCCESS TIP

Always approach a potential partner with several pieces of market research from target customers. Your position becomes much more favorable if you have survey results from at least 15 to 20 potential users. Your position is even stronger if you have survey results from 15 to 20 people in your potential distribution channel. You'll find that potential partners will feel you're a professional if you have survey results.

product's sales potential. More than likely your potential partner will want to make changes to better meet customer needs, to improve product quality, or to lower product costs.

Research

The last four tactics listed in this book, including this one, require you to know exactly what your target customer wants and the sales potential of your target market. You won't have any trouble finding a partner if you uncover a product that satisfies the needs of a large market. But it is up to you to prove the market is there. Your research should show that customers need and want your product and that they are willing to pay a reasonable price for it.

 INSIGHT

Research Report Basics: Replacing the Rolodex

▶ Start by clearly defining your target customer group. For example, the initial target group for the Palm Pilot, one of the hottest new products of the last 10 years, was businesspeople who spend a considerable amount of time out of the office. This included salespeople, executives, insurance people, and marketing managers.

▶ Define the size of the market. I like to do this in two ways, first by stating how many people are in the market, and second by listing the size of other products sold to that market. In the case of the Palm Pilot, the number of initial sales could be estimated by the early number of cellular phone sales.

▶ Explain why you feel the market needs the product. For the Palm Pilot, the reason would be that people are away from their computers for long stretches, and they want a truly mobile computer to take with them.

 **IN**SIGHT

▶ Verify your premise. Have actual interviews with both end users and dealers that show that they would indeed like the product you are proposing. For the Palm Pilot, you could interview 20 to 25 potential end users to clarify their need for a smaller mobile computer.

▶ List the customers' product requirements. You want to have survey information about what features potential users require. Inventors accomplish this task with six to eight in-depth interviews with potential users discussing what users would like to see and what they'd like to accomplish with the product.

▶ Establish how important this product would be to users. People typically buy functional products that solve their major priorities first. If you were pitching the Palm Pilot, you'd want to show that users would buy your product first before other time-saving, out-of-the-office products.

Manufacturing

Most of the time, inventors create an alliance or joint venture with a manufacturer that is capable of making the product. Then they don't have to worry about manufacturing the product. Most sales and marketing partners won't be willing to make an alliance with an inventor unless he or she has a manufacturing source. They won't trust the inventor, on his or her own, to make a quality product or deliver in quantities once orders develop.

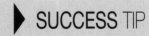 **SUCCESS** TIP

You must have a professional in charge of every phase of your operation if you want to get a joint-venture agreement. If you are going to handle sales and marketing and don't have marketing experience, be sure to have some advisors and helpers who do have experience. The same holds true for manufacturing. The partner won't count on you unless you're an expert yourself or have experts to call upon.

8

Remember that your partners are putting in a lot of effort on the product, and they don't want to see those efforts wasted because of lack of effort on your part.

Key Contacts

You have the best chance of striking an agreement when you can show you have unique insights into what your target customers really want—insights that allow you to develop the perfect product to meet those desires. Your key contacts then are people who have a very strong understanding of what your customers want. If you are introducing a home-decorating product, your key contacts are interior designers or architects who are recognized as having an uncanny ability to understand your target customers. If you were introducing the Palm Pilot, you would want contacts who have introduced other products to the same target customer group, or you would want people from that customer group who have always been early adapters of new technology. For a medical product, your key contacts would be doctors or hospitals that are influential in your product's field.

Pros and Cons

Pros

▶ Allows the inventor to introduce new products that are beyond his or her reach in terms of either resources or experience.

▶ Helps the inventor gain tremendous production experience that he or she can use later.

▶ Speeds up the introduction and market penetration of a new product.

▶ Offers the inventor much more control of the product and its subsequent development than a licensing agreement.

▶ Is a much easier sell than a licensing agreement.

▶ Allows the inventor to introduce new products when he or she can't afford to produce a "looks like, works like" prototype.

Cons

▶ Doesn't provide the inventor with total control of the product.

▶ Depends on another party to do their job effectively for the product to succeed.

▶ Doesn't allow the inventor to withdraw the product to start a company on his or her own.

▶ May not establish the inventor as a force in the market in order to launch his or her own company.

▶ May create stress for an inventor who's input is overridden by the joint-venture partner.

Up, Up, and Away

A successful first invention is often the launching point for a successful company. But a joint venture or alliance may actually leave the inventor's partner in a stronger position, especially if the alliance uses the partner's name or brand to build credibility. On the other hand, the inventor learns about the product introduction process and develops contacts that should be helpful in his or her next product. The best part about a joint venture is that often it places the inventor in big powerful markets where there is a lot of interest from investors. A success in a joint venture or alliance should help

MARKET **REALITY**

Inventors succeed because of their ability to produce and market a product, skills that count more than the particular merits of any one invention. I believe inventors in joint ventures have a 10 to 20 times better chance of success than an inventor going it alone. Inventors need the joint-venture partner's money and expertise. Inventors will be in a better position to succeed on their own once they've survived a partnership.

the inventor launch a full-fledged company on his or her own if the next idea is in the same market. Realistically, most inventors who use a joint-venture strategy would not have been able to launch their products otherwise. Also, if your eventual goal is to start your own company, the joint venture is a much better first step than selling on commission or selling through a private label because you maintain some ownership of the product (which doesn't happen when an inventor sells on commission), and you are also making contacts with distributors, end users, and key industry people (which doesn't happen when the inventor sells on a private label basis).

Key Resources

The key to success is knowing what your target customer wants, so your key resources are knowledgeable people in the market you are targeting. Here are some tips for finding those key resources:

▶ Meet people in the target market, as many as you can, and start identifying "early adapters," people who buy products before anyone else.

▶ Meet as many people as you can in the distribution channel and get their input.

▶ Read trade magazines and find out who are the key players in the market. Become familiar with your market's most influential people.

▶ Go to any local association meetings of your target customer to find new contacts and to get a better understanding of what people want.

▶ Learn from your contacts which manufacturers in the industry are strong in marketing and which are strong in manufacturing. Your best bet for a good joint-venture partner is a company that has strong manufacturing but weak marketing capabilities.

▶ Develop a relationship with a regional manager or marketing person at a company you have targeted as a potential partner. In order to succeed, you need someone on the inside of the potential partner pushing for an agreement.

What to Expect

▶ Potential partners will not be easily convinced that you have a unique, profitable opportunity.

▶ You will have trouble getting an appointment if you don't find a company contact who will recommend that the company look at your offer.

▶ You will have to push for a formal agreement to establish your rights in the relationship.

▶ The partner will try to keep the agreement on a more informal basis.

▶ You will have to convince the partner that you can do your part in the promotion.

▶ The company will want to proceed slowly

 ▶ MARKET REALITY

I've found that companies won't proceed with a joint venture, no matter how great the opportunity, if the inventor or entrepreneur appears difficult to work with. Don't call the potential partner constantly with questions, revisions, or suggestions. Limit your contacts to just one or two per week where you mention major concerns or suggested actions.

to ensure your idea has potential and to be sure they can count on you as a partner.

▶ You will be responsible for keeping the momentum going on the agreement.

▶ You will have to take charge of finalizing the product design, even if the partner does most of the work.

▶ Sales for most partners take three to four months to ramp up throughout the distribution network. Don't be alarmed if it takes six months for the product to show true sales potential.

Joint Ventures–
Making it Happen

Keys to Success

▶ *Big potential:* Most companies have plenty of projects they can work
on. Your project has to have significantly more potential than anything else the company is currently considering. Potential can be
understood in terms of market size, market opportunity, or the
strength of your product. The ideal opportunity for most companies
is one that has the potential of increasing sales by 40 to 100 percent,
and one with compelling reasons for success. For instance, Stephanie
Heroff's product, proper bra support for summer tops with spaghet-
ti straps (see "When Support Is Attractive" page 168), is targeted at
a huge market and offers a unique and better-performing solution.

When Support Is Attractive

On hot summer days, Stephanie Heroff enjoyed wearing spaghetti-strap tops, but she never felt comfortable in them. She didn't like the way her bra strap showed, and she was convinced the one-size-fits-all shelf bras sold to go with summer tops were only comfortable for ultra thin women. Her idea was to create a series of spaghetti-strap tops with soft hooks along with a series of detachable bras. Customers could then get one or more tops along with a correctly-size bra that was made to fit the garment, and they would never have to worry about their bra straps showing.

Heroff's problem was that her product—actually two products made to go together—was difficult for an inventor to manufacturer. The idea of soft hooks for a bra inside a strap was unknown, and Heroff needed over 80 prototypes to finalize her design. Apparel design is also full of technical details, including the "hand" (the texture and feel) of the fabric, what colors to offer, and how much extra fabric is needed to get the right product appearance.

Rather than try to negotiate these hurdles herself, Heroff decided to partner with three people. First she found a manufacturer who was willing to build prototypes and finalize the product design in return for a share of Heroff's company. She also found an experienced clothing designer who was also willing to accept equity instead of cash for her work. Finally, she found an investor who could help pay the start-up cost. Heroff gave up quite a bit of equity to the new alliance, but she was able to introduce her product. Heroff received two benefits: First, the manufacturer was able to fund product development, which ended up costing over $10,000; and second, she had experts as partners who were able to resolve thorny problems as they developed. The joint venture or partnership provided all the tools Heroff needed for her company, Heroff Group, LLC, based in Minneapolis, Minnesota, to launch her product in the summer of 2000. Since she had also done a good job preselling, she had over 30 retailers on board to take her product immediately, and within 30 days of her product introduction, sales had exceeded $25,000.

▶ *Something special:* Companies like joint ventures when they see that the inventor, or the inventor's product, offers a sustainable advantage, one that will last at least several years. This advantage can be the product itself, the inventor's support from leading experts in the field, the inventor's head start in product testing, or the inventor's special connections with the distribution channel. In Stephanie Heroff's case, her bra design was unique and difficult to replicate, both because of her patent and because of the difficulty in making the product.

▶ *Can see the end:* People in general don't start projects where they can't quite see how the whole project will pay off. In Heroff's case, she worked with a small manufacturer and a product designer. They probably wouldn't have signed up if Heroff wanted to sell to mass merchandisers. They would have worried about whether or not the price could be low enough, whether or not Heroff and the partners could raise enough money to build sufficient inventory, and whether or not Heroff could find someone who could make the sale. But Heroff's planned approach—selling mainly to high-end women's boutiques and stores—was one where the partners could visualize success. Boutiques will pay more for quality products, sales growth in this market can be coordinated with a limited budget by simply limiting the geographic area the company sells to, and there are plenty of sales representatives available to handle a new product line.

▶ *High margins:* Companies generally want their distributor price to be at least twice its manufacturing cost, and their final end user price to be at least four times its manufacturing cost. Companies simply won't make much money if the margins are smaller than that. Your potential partners won't expect your margins to be this high in trial production runs, but they will want to know that the profits will be there when the partnership begins actual production.

▶ **SUCCESS** TIP

Unless you have a manufacturing background, don't ever throw around cost numbers without some documentation. Manufacturing cost accounting incorporates overhead that you will either not include or badly underestimate. Tell companies what the models you've made cost, and you can tell them quotes you've received from contract manufacturers. If you offer a price on your own that's way off, you'll look unprofessional and you'll lose credibility in the company's eyes.

Momentum Makers

▶ *Early success:* Companies watch a new investment closely to be sure the product succeeds. Distribution channels and retailers also watch new products to see if they are going to be "the next hot item." Your product's start will probably determine how it will be perceived in the market forever. Early success doesn't just happen. It happens because you've presold the market and have customers ready to go. Heroff, for example, had 30 shops ready to take her product the first week it was available, even though the product was introduced out of the stores' normal buying season. That was a fast start, and it happened because she and her representatives built those orders over several months.

▶ *Easy entry:* Target companies should be able to participate with your joint venture without too much trouble. Heroff's main partner was the clothing manufacturer that specialized in sewing products that required special techniques. That partner was not willing to go forward with Heroff until she took on a second alliance partner, the fashion designer. The clothing company didn't have a designer on staff and didn't want to add an extra employee. The company was willing to move ahead once Heroff filled in the missing link.

▶ *New opportunities:* Companies want to grow, and they often are pigeonholed into a certain market or category that restricts their growth. For example, a plastic toy manufacturer who is considered a low-cost supplier for convenience stores might have trouble breaking into new and different but still related markets—like high-end toys or promotional products. Companies can be receptive to joint ventures that allow them to move into a new market opportunity that ties into its manufacturing expertise, since most companies will feel that, once they've gotten their

 MARKET REALITY

Inventors can become discouraged when a company turns down a partnership proposal that seems perfect in every way. But often companies pass on proposals because they simply don't have time. You'll probably have an underperforming partner if you form an alliance with a company that's too busy. Don't worry if a company turns you down; just go to the next one, where your timing might be right.

initial opportunity, they can sell subsequent products to that market on their own.

Before You Start

▶ *Take the leading edge:* The company that takes control of a new product category first typically holds that share for a long time. Companies that enter the market later often languish forever with a minor market share. That's the reason you want a partner, to accelerate your market penetration. And it is the main reason that companies form partnerships, to cut their time to market so they can be first. You want to point out how a partnership with you gives the company a better chance of grabbing a leading market position. Product testing, support from experts, and a fully designed product are all great sales points when you are targeting a new market trend or opportunity.

▶ *Key alliances:* You are trying to convince a partner that together you can create a dominating market presence. Your product may be great, but what will really get people excited is when you have some sort of relationship with key people in the market. Having an advisory board with key end users and distributors is a common tactic for showing that you are connected to the market.

> ▶ **BUZZ** WORD
>
> An *advisory board* is a group of experienced businesspeople that an inventor relies on for advice. The boards are often unpaid, though sometimes they are paid a small amount in stock options for helping out. People are much more willing to serve on an advisory board than on a board of directors because they are committing less time and because they are not responsible for the company's performance.

▶ *Clear market need:* When customers need a product, sales and profits typically follow. If the need is also well known by the distribution channel, the product will sell well. For instance, the Palm Pilot has been one of the fastest-selling new electronic products of all time. Companies kept making laptops lighter and smaller, but people were still looking for an even smaller computer they could hold in one hand. The Clean Shower, a product you spray onto shower walls to eliminate scaling and mildew, went from production in a garage to over $100 million in sales in less than three years because customers recognized they needed the product.

▶ *Target market perceptions:* The market has many perceptions about what types of products will and won't do well. While this perception shifts over time, it is a smart strategy to tie your presentation into what the market already believes. For example, in the last three years, the United States has had warm winters. Retailers have started to perceive that winter outerwear is a dangerous product to carry. There is no point trying to combat that perception. Companies are starting to introduce fall wear that can double as winter wear with an extra sweater. The Clean Shower is really a concentrated solution that easily mixes with water. But the market has the perception that concentrates don't sell, and so the product was initially sold in its diluted version, even though it added greatly to shipping costs.

First Steps

▶ *A sizzling presentation:* The potential partner doesn't know you, doesn't know if you have a great product, and doesn't know if you will be a reliable partner. You want your first in-depth exposure to the company to be positive. Don't be afraid to spend $1,000 to $2,000 to make a good impression so you can close the deal.

 INSIGHT

Take a Tip from P. T. Barnum

Inventors making their first presentation often assume that businesspeople like nuts-and-bolts demonstrations that focus only on the facts. They couldn't be more wrong. Managers and executives get just as bored as anyone else with a dry presentation. Put a little showmanship and excitement into your pitch to whip up some enthusiasm in the crowd. Once they are excited, they will look for reasons to move ahead.

▶ *The opening*: Knock the socks off your audience right off the bat. The best way to do that is to show actual end users excited by your product. For instance, Heroff could have gone to a park and taken a video of women with their bra straps showing, and then of women wearing her product and giving their first impressions. The Clean Shower could have shown before-and-after pictures. One time I had my product and the two top competitive products draped at the start of a presentation. A little mystery always gets people excited. I started by uncovering with great fanfare the first competitive product and made comments about its problems. Then I did the same with the second product. By the time I unveiled my product, my potential partners were primed and ready. A great opening also shows that you too are excited by the product.

▶ *The details*: Once you have the excitement level high, move smoothly but as quickly as possible through the rest of the presentation. Cover these points:

- target customer
- market size
- distribution channel
- profitability
- fit with company's other products
- why you're presenting to this company

▶ The proposal: Explain the type of venture you'd like to set up, who would be responsible for which tasks, and how you'd like to proceed. Don't list specifics—

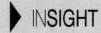

INSIGHT

such as how much of the venture that partner would own, how much the partner would have to contribute, or what commitments you are looking for. You just want the company to agree to move forward with some type of arrangement. You can negotiate further details at the next meeting.

▶ *Fair agreements:* The biggest killer of all joint ventures is when one side feels the other side is getting a better deal. I've found that even when a deal is very profitable for one party, they still won't sign if they feel the other partner benefits more than they do. That's one reason I like to make only a vague proposal at first. If the partner agrees to move ahead, you can ask for suggestions about how the deal should be structured. That input will help you create a deal that will be perceived as fair.

▶ *Introduction timetable:* Any project, even one within a single company, tends to fall apart unless it has a timetable that everyone can follow. This applies even more so to a partnership or joint venture. A timetable is just a list of the tasks that have to take place, when they will be accomplished, who is responsible for getting which ones done, and who will pay the associated costs. If you don't have a timetable,

SUCCESS TIP

When I ask partners on a project what percentage of the project's success they were responsible for, the total, when I add up the percentages, almost always comes to 150 to 300 percent. Which means that almost everyone thinks they contribute more to a partnership than they really do. So be flexible when negotiating, and don't try to get every last penny you think you deserve.

I can guarantee that people won't keep to the schedule you envision. Propose a tentative timetable to your partners, and then work with them to be sure the schedule is agreeable to all.

▶ *Connections:* You have established connections, but remember that your partner does, too. One of the benefits of working with a partner is that you get to meet and use their connections, so be sure to do so, meeting and utilizing your partner's contacts as you promote the product.

Building a Business

▶ *Take market control:* Products that move to the forefront of the market, even those that come from the very largest companies, usually have just one or two people who are aggressively promoting the product. The same situation evolves in most partnerships. One party takes the initiative and continually comes up with new ideas on how to get the product extra exposure and extra sales. If one party doesn't take the initiative, the project may not live up to its potential. Your should strive to be the partner with the initiative. Suggest new ways to do things, but more important, set things up on your own. Conduct seminars with experts on your product, work editors of key magazines for interviews, travel with salespeople, or

 MARKET REALITY

You read all the time about great marketing programs, innovative products, or customer-focused strategies. These are important, but they greatly minimize the value of a well-networked person. I was a marketing manager of a company where one product manager continually outperformed all others. The manager was always out in the market, meeting people, which demonstrates again that initiative and hustle can outsell the greatest marketing program.

set up a demonstration of the product at a store or site. Taking the initiative puts you in control of the product and guarantees that you will continue to be regarded as a valuable partner.

➤ *Add new products:* Every marketer, manufacturer, and distributor has become very aware that new products are the lifeblood of a business. If you can keep coming up with new products, you will cement your relationship with your partner—or you can eventually move on to launch your own products without the partner. Joint ventures are often based on new market opportunities, where a steady stream of new products will be introduced over a two- to three-year period. To maximize the benefits of your partnership, you and your partner need to be a leader in as many of the new product categories as possible.

➤ *Expand distribution:* Your goal is, in effect, to become the indispensable partner. One way you do that is to take the initiative on promoting the product. Another effective way is to find new distribution channels. Look for new ways to sell the product, either through different distribution networks to the same target customer group or to new customer groups. For example, Stephanie Heroff first sold her new tops and bras to boutiques through manufacturers' sales representatives, but she also could have

 SUCCESS TIP

Trade magazines, those magazines written for manufacturers, distributors, and retailers, are a great source of news regarding new sales outlets. They often contain success stories of companies trying new tactics. Each industry has several magazines, and you should subscribe to all of them. You can get their names in *Gale's Source of Publications* (available at larger libraries). Most of the magazines are free if you are a potential advertiser.

developed new distribution channels through catalog sales, Internet sales, TV shopping network sales, or direct sales to department stores. Also, she initially targeted customers who purchase premium clothes, but Heroff might also eventually go after a different target market, such as midrange-priced clothing stores.

Are You Making Money?

▶ *Profit check:* The main reason you create a joint venture is to push your product into the market more quickly than you could on your own. To generate a fast start, you need to spend money on marketing, and you will have lots of operating cash tied up in inventory and accounts receivable. As a result, you may have trouble evaluating how you are doing financially. There are four factors you should monitor constantly when you are beginning a high-growth structure.

1. The manufacturing cost. Make sure your cost is less than 50 percent of your wholesale price, or less than 25 percent of your end-user price. Costs can get out of line quickly, and you may need immediate adjustments.

2. Distribution discounts and sales commissions. You may have planned on selling to distributors at 40 percent off the retail price and then find out you need to offer a 50 percent discount. You might also pay more in sales commissions than expected. Since many products make only a 5 to 10 percent profit on sales, slight changes in commissions or distributor discounts can eliminate a company's profits.

3. Extra discounts to generate sales. You might run special pricing programs to generate sales, but you

need to keep these under control or again you could lose money. Set a total target for discounts, and stay within them.

4. Sales goals. Your venture needs to have a break-even sales target that it will hit in six months or less. Check to be sure that you are tracking on your sales levels. If not, you could be in real trouble.

▶ *Market share:* You may not be the market leader right away, but you do want to be the talk of the market, or the "market buzz," for at least the first six months of your intro-duction. Being the buzz guarantees you'll have a major market share over the long term. If you can't cre-ate a buzz, you're unlikely to ever have a major position. If you

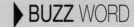

▶ **BUZZ** WORD

Break-even sales is the point at which profits from sales equal your expenses. In the case of a new product, this means when the profit per sale (sales price less the manufacturing cost) times the num-ber of units sold equals the combined costs of marketing, commissions, extra discounts, financ-ing, depreciation, and administrative salaries.

are not getting the respect your product deserves, you need to take corrective actions quickly, certainly within six months.

▶ *Distribution control:* When you are the buzz, you are the product that distribution wants. This is also the time when you can secure control of the channel. Control means being able to institute any require-ments you have, such as requiring the distribution channel to stock spare parts, hold training sessions, sponsor seminars, have a demonstration area, or do other activities that benefit the manufacturer.

▶ *Corrective measures:* You simply have to control your manufacturing costs, discounts, and commissions. Take immediate action if your costs are slipping. If you are not getting off to a great start selling in the market, think big, very big. You need to host a contest or a big event at a convention. Another option is to host high-profile receptions in various cities for key users or distributors. The best course of action to be sure you get off to a strong start is to have big events built into your introduction program and to presell your product to key contacts before it is introduced.

14

Private Label Marketing—
The Inside Scoop

The Basics

Private label manufacturers make products for other companies to be sold under the buying company's name. J.C. Penney, for instance, has lines of private label clothes sold under the J.C. Penney name. A private label manufacturer produces those products. Inventors frequently pursue this strategy in order to build a quick sales base or when the market resists a one-line company. For example, most inventors won't have much luck selling a painting accessory to mass merchants such as Wal-Mart. Mass merchants don't want to buy from small companies who may be unreliable suppliers. Rather than accept defeat, inventors often find another company that does sell to mass merchants. They then offer their product to that company to sell under the selling company's name. The mass merchants may then be willing to buy your product. Private label manufacturers cut into an inventor's profits, as they sell the product at 20 to 40

▶ **BUZZ** WORDS

Pricing discount variations can be confusing. Some of the more common discounts are:

Wholesale price—40 to 60 percent off suggested retail.

Full-service distributor price—40 to 50 percent off suggested retail when sales aren't through wholesalers.

Dealer (who sells to businesses) or retailer price—25 to 35 percent off suggested retail when through a wholesaler or distributor; 40 to 50 percent off suggested retail when they buy direct from the manufacturer.

percent below what distributors pay to the other company, but in return inventors have an established sales base. Since inventors can sell both on a private label basis and under their own name at the same time, a private label contract can provide the volume inventors need to successfully launch their own business.

Inventors can also sell on a private label basis to a retailer. For example, Sears Craftsman products aren't made by Sears. They are made by other companies that sell to Sears on a private label basis. You need to offer 50 to 60 percent off suggested retail pricing when selling on a private label basis to a retailer, but that is a much better deal for inventors than having to offer a 30 to 50 percent discount off the wholesale or distributor price when selling on a private label basis to a manufacturer.

Perfect Products

Products that are natural extensions of other product lines are ideal private label products. For example, your product might be a rack that allows people to bake four sheets of cookies at a time instead of just two sheets. This product may not have enough appeal to get mass merchants to carry it from a separate company. But the product is an ideal complement for a company selling other, similar baking products, such as cookie trays, spatulas, and cooling racks. The baking product company will be receptive to an offer to sell a product on a private label basis because it enhances its line and gives the company a better chance to secure shelf space in major retailers. The same situation applies to private label agreements with retailers. They look to add products that complement other products in their private label line. Private label marketing is often the best tactic for inventors with small accessory products that are helpful in completing a task the customer is already doing.

Private label marketing is also an ideal solution for inventors who would prefer to get a license, but who are unable to get a broad patent. In a licensing negotiation, companies look very closely at how strong a product's patent is because they are going to have to make an investment in the product to produce income—and they don't want immediate and strong competition. Companies are much less interested in patents for a private label agreement because they are only selling the product for supplemental income. Their investment is low, their risk is low, and they aren't overly concerned if the product attracts competition.

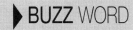
BUZZ WORD

Inventors also sell products on an *original equipment manufacturer,* or OEM, basis. An OEM manufacturer sells products that are used on another manufacturer's products. For example, if you sold bike seats to bike manufacturers, your sales would be considered an OEM sale. OEM and private label marketing strategies are the same. An accessory part manufacturer (like a bike seat) might have both private label and OEM customers.

Private label marketing is a strategy that gets inventors shelf space, but that doesn't mean that the product will be supported by an advertising campaign. Products that can sell themselves on the store shelf do best in a private label program, and you'll have difficulty finding a private label agreement if your product requires advertising. One last consideration is that you need a product that will sell at five to six times its manufacturing cost in order to have room for the extra discounts required. Most ideal private label products are easy to produce in volume and inexpensive to manufacturer.

INVENTOR'S STORY

Seeing Is Believing

Daniel Henry worked in an optical shop in Long Beach, California, where one of his jobs was fixing scratched lenses. Then one day a friend was about to toss a scratched CD, and Henry decided to take a look at it. What he saw surprised him. Unlike a vinyl record and its grooves, a CD has a clear protective layer over its actual digital data. A scratched CD actually has just a scratched protective coating, a defect Henry was sure he could repair. And Henry was right. After trying a few formulas, Henry found one that could quickly repair any CD—whether for music, computers, or games—that had previously been considered beyond repair.

Unfortunately for Henry, his product was so miraculous that people refused to believe it actually worked the way he said. Sales were very tough for Henry's company, Esprit Development Corp., as stores just wouldn't carry the product. Henry's sales were limited to a few music retailers and a small level of Internet sales. Then Henry struck a private label agreement with Radio Shack. The chain of electronic part stores started to sell Henry's products under its own name, and Henry's sales shot up to $400,000 per year.

With a little momentum and instant credibility, Henry was able to get industry magazines to test his product. The reviewers were skeptical, since they couldn't believe Henry could replace computer information (which, of course, he can't). But as the tests came back, reviewers swooned over the product. Once end users understood that CDs had a protective layer that was easily repaired by Henry's product, Wipe-Out, Henry was able to get retail distribution in computer stores. But there is no doubt that Henry's success was dependent on his initial private label deal with Radio Shack. As I'm writing this, Henry is working on a new private label agreement with a company that sells accessories to music stores. Henry has learned an important lesson: Private label agreements are an ideal way to crack into competitive consumer markets.

Your Goals

For inventors interested in forming their own business, common goals are:

▶ Entering competitive markets where one-line companies are at a marked disadvantage.

▶ Developing sales for a product that helps consumers in a small way and for products that don't have the potential of being a major factor in the market.

▶ Creating a sales base that will help support sales under an inventor's own brand name.

▶ Securing a distribution contract so that an inventor can secure the financing he or she needs to begin production.

For inventors interested in making money on their invention with a minimal effort, the goals are:

▶ Having just a few customers so that the inventor can operate his or her business on a part-time basis.

▶ Producing a steady income with very little effort.

▶ Avoiding investments in advertising and other promotions.

▶ Developing a relationship with a company that could eventually result in a licensing agreement.

Other Choices

For inventors interested in an ongoing business, the other choices are to sell at fairs (chapters 2 and 3), to sell locally to develop a sales base (chapters 4 and 5), or to create a joint-venture agreement (chapters 12 and 13). Private label agreements typically are the best choice for accessory and complementary products that by themselves don't provide consumers with a dramatic benefit. Stand-alone products, or products with a major impact, may work just as well in a joint venture.

Inventors who want a part-time business can also choose to sell through catalogs and TV shopping networks (chapter 6 and 7), or they can go straight to a licensing agreement (chapter 16 and 17). Private label agreements are typically easier to arrange than a licensing agreement because the other party doesn't have to worry about finalizing product design and producing the product.

 MARKET REALITY

One of the disadvantages of private labeling marketing is that you can become overdependent on one customer. If that customer decides to drop its agreement, you may not be able to recover. You can minimize this risk by asking the partner to invest and become a partner in your product. You should also keep in touch with other marketers in the industry, so you can strike a new deal if necessary.

Money Matters

One of the big advantages of a private label agreement is that you might be able to get a big order or a commitment before you actually have to produce a product. This could allow you to borrow money or possibly get extended terms from the manufacturer who will make your product. Another big benefit of private label marketing is that operating costs are low. You can make and ship all of your production to one customer. Your out-of-pocket expenses might be only for the prototype you use to land the private label agreement.

Your situation changes totally if your manufacturing costs don't leave you enough profit room to hire a contract manufacturer. Then you'll need to produce the product yourself, which can require tooling and manufacturing set-up costs. You might even have to hire workers. Unless you have an extensive manufacturing background, banks will be reluctant to lend you money to start your own plant. A positive fact for inventors is that they will do well if they can make just 10 percent on each sale. In a private label sale, inventors avoid sales and marketing costs and don't need to take a 30 to 50 percent markup in order to make money.

Protection

Companies buying private label products usually aren't overly concerned about your patent status. But you do run a risk that the company you approach might decide to produce the product themselves, or that a competitor might quickly introduce the same product. If you have enough money, you can apply for a utility patent before approaching the company. If your funds are limited, you may want to apply for a provisional patent, which gives you a one-year leeway until you have to apply for a utility patent (see appendix A for more on patents).

The one-year sales bar starts from the time you approach a company for a private label sales agreement. You need to be sure you are prepared to move rather quickly once you approach the manufacturer, or your one-year time could run out. Applying for a provisional patent

> ## ▶ SUCCESS TIP
>
> I've found that inventors are better off being able to say their product is patent pending, even if the product will only be able to get a narrow patent. People seem to take inventors just a little more seriously if they say they have applied for a patent. Companies are also much more reluctant to try and duplicate your idea if you say you've submitted a patent application.

after you've approached a company won't extend the time you have to apply for the patent. In any case, many times accessory or complementary products are not able to get a broad patent. You may prefer to apply for a provisional patent until you secure a private label agreement, and then let it expire if your product isn't eligible for broad claims.

Prototypes

Inventors need a "looks like, works like" prototype before landing a private label agreement. A company is going to want not only to see but also to test your product before deciding to go ahead. If you don't have the ability to make the prototype, you probably can get a contract manufacturer to make it for you at a low cost if you promise, or sign an agreement, to give them the business if you get the final agreement. You may need a letter from the potential customer saying they are interested in seeing a final prototype, or you may need to receive a provisional order if the prototype will be necessary to make. Finally, the potential private label may need to see a rough model or prototype before giving you such a letter.

Research

When you approach a company with a private label proposal, you want to show them that their target customers like your product and feel it helps them accomplish their goals. This can be shown by having surveys of potential customers, or by having interviews or supporting letters from influential users. The best research studies a group of the company's target customers actually using the product, with the results demonstrating that your product is a big benefit to them. In our cookie rack example, the results might be that 400 cookies were baked in half the normal time. Research for a paint accessory might demonstrate that it eliminated over 50 percent of the trim rework required for most interior jobs.

Another key piece of research that can help you secure an agreement is to compare the current product lines on the market, from a customer's perspective, and show how your product can place the company in a better market position. This research becomes even more valuable if you can show how the distribution network favors the new broader line and that the company will be able to secure more distribution outlets. I personally like to talk about competitors because it implies that you may go talk to every competitor until you land a deal.

Too often inventors try to get a company to enter a private label agreement without doing enough research. Typically, the person you sell to then has to go sell his or her management or sales force on the merits of adding this product. The more information you provide merely helps your contact sell the product within the company.

Manufacturing

You are responsible for providing the product in a private label agreement, either by making the product yourself or by having it made by a contract manufacturer. How you proceed depends on how well equipped you are to manufacture the product in quantity, and how much margin you

> ### ▶ INSIGHT
>
> **Margin Limbo: How Low Can You Go?**
>
> *Margin* is a common marketing and manufacturing term that refers to how much profit you are making on a product. The formula for margin is selling price minus manufacturing costs divided by selling price times 100 percent, or
>
> $$\frac{\text{selling price} - \text{manufacturing cost}}{\text{selling price}} \text{ X } 100\%$$
>
> If you sell a product for $100, and it costs you $60 to make (called *manufacturing cost or costs of goods sold*), your gross margin is $40, or 40 percent. If you sell to distributors, the price that matters when determining your margin is your distributor price. A 40 to 50 percent margin is typical for many manufacturers. Margins over 60 percent are considered high, and margins below 30 percent are considered low. You can also refer to *gross margins* and *net margins*. Gross margins only subtract the cost of manufacturing. Net margins also subtract out administrative, sales and marketing, and all other relevant costs. Most manufacturers have net margins of 5 to 10 percent, which are also called *profits before taxes*.

have to work with. If your gross margin is low, you will either have to accept a low net margin or make the product yourself. Inventors are typically better off using a contract manufacturer, as they are better able to deliver quality products in quantity. I recommend that inventors, no matter how low their margin is, start with a contract manufacturer to ensure the private label agreement gets off to a good start. They can then switch over to their own manufacturing operation once sales are secure.

Key Contacts

▶ You need to talk to the end users or target customers, the more influential the better, of the companies you will be approaching for a private label deal. You want to know influential people in the distribution channel. Their support for your product can play a major role in securing a private label agreement.

▶ Other key contacts include people who get you in the door of your target customers. Salespeople, marketing personnel, regional sales managers, or top executives are all people who can help you. You can meet these contacts by attending industry trade shows or association meetings. All you need to do is approach the people in the booth, explain that you have a new product, and ask if they'd share their opinion of it with you. If the people are positive about the idea, you can ask them if they feel the product would be a good fit in their product line. If they think it would, you can ask them whom you should talk to about a private label agreement.

Pros and Cons

Pros

▶ Doesn't require an ongoing sales and marketing effort.

▶ Negotiating an agreement is typically straightforward and brief.

▶ Offers a sales base to help finance the inventor's own brand.

▶ Can be executed with only a minimal effort by the inventor.

▶ Best method for introducing accessory products or products that aren't eligible for broad patents.

▶ Provides leverage for generating funding from a bank, investor, or contract manufacturer.

▶ Offers an extra incentive for retailers or distributors to buy your product.

Cons

▶ May require the inventor to come up with the money to manufacture the product.

▶ Reduced profitability due to the extra discounts that the private label partner receives.

▶ Doesn't help establish the inventor's brand name with either the end user or the distribution network.

▶ Minimal input in the sales program the private label company implements.

▶ Runs the risk of losing all sales if the private label company drops the deal.

Up, Up, and Away

Private label marketing can help you generate quick sales, but it does so at a price. First, the extra discounts cut into your profits. Second, you have your product promoted under someone else's name. Third, your agreement probably restricts the distribution outlets you can sell through. All of these factors work against you in launching your own larger business. One of the reasons most private label products are accessories or complementary products is that it is hard to build a powerful company out of those types of products. If

▶ MARKET **REALITY**

A very significant percentage of companies are selling at least one private label product, and in many cases they sell several private label products. This is a common business agreement, and you'll find virtually everyone you talk to will understand its benefits for both parties. You'll also find people feel a private label agreement has a much lower risk than a joint venture or licensing agreement.

your goal is to create a base to build from, use private label agreements sparingly. Often companies sell the product themselves in their major markets, and use private label sales in smaller markets.

Key Resources

▶ Well-known end users, or end users who buy lots of product.

▶ Important people in the distribution channel.

▶ Salespeople, a regional sales manager, or a marketing person at the companies you have targeted as potential partners.

▶ Trade magazines are a great source of information about what is happening in your target market. You can often glean tips from articles about what will be important to your target customer.

▶ Trade shows. At shows you can meet the key contacts you'll need to penetrate companies.

▶ The Private Label Manufacturers' Association, at w w w . p l m a . c o m , hosts trade shows and offers information for potential private label manufacturers.

▶ The Internet. Do a Web search for "private label," and you'll find hundreds of companies that private label their products in dozens of different ways. You might want

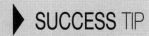

▶ SUCCESS TIP

One of the best ways to find out who would be a good private label customer is to walk into a small retailer and simply ask the owner what companies he or she feels would do a good job selling your product. He or she will probably know which companies already sell several other private label products. The retailers will probably also be willing to give you the names of their contacts at those companies.

to check out the agreements other companies are signing before finalizing your strategy.

What to Expect

▶ Companies will be willing to talk to you about private label agreements if you have a product they feel they can sell.

▶ Companies will sign a letter of intent or a private label agreement with you, but are unlikely to provide any funding.

▶ Private label marketing may produce a nice income, but it won't produce significant income because of the low margins.

▶ You may need engineering support to handle complaints and suggestions for improvement from customers and salespeople.

▶ Your private label customer may be picky about quality.

▶ Your sales could disappear overnight if sales aren't what the private label partner expects and they decide to drop the product.

▶ The sales forecast you receive from your private label customer will probably be way too high at first.

▶ Don't build your production level until you actually have orders for additional units.

▶ Your private label customer probably won't share much information about who they are selling to.

15

Private Label Marketing– Making It Happen

Keys to Success

▶ *Easy to implement:* The major appeal to a private label buyer is that they can generate a little extra profit without a lot of extra work. And if sales don't work out, the private label buyer just stops buying your product. You can make things easy by asking the buyer for a purchase order and stating

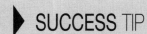 **SUCCESS** TIP

A private label agreement is only worthwhile if the product sells. Inventors' products will sell best if the buyer's sales force gets behind the product and promotes it. It is to your advantage to offer a sales contest or some other reward for salespeople who sell your product. A contest might wipe out your profits for the first six months, but the cost is worthwhile if it generates sales momentum.

that you'll supply the product in the buyer's package, or that you'll modify your package to the buyer's specification. If necessary, you can also offer training to the buyer's salespeople, and you can even offer to maintain a Web site for the product. If you are selling to a retailer, you might want to offer a display, and you also want to show a diagram of what complementary products your product should be displayed next to.

▶ *Customer approval:* Buyers will want your product only if it helps them meet their customers' needs. Make sure buyers understand the customer need that you are proposing to meet, and make sure your product is instantly convincing as the best way to do so. Your prospective private label buyer won't proceed without being convinced of these two things, so make them central in your first presentation.

▶ *Competitive market:* It is difficult to sell a private label agreement to a company that has the market locked up. After all, why should they rock a winning boat? Companies in competitive markets where they gain and lose customers all the time are much easier to sell a private label agreement to. They are always looking for ways to land more distributors that could lead to larger market share, and they are open to any agreement you might propose that will give them an edge. The same holds true for retailers. They are constantly looking for an advantage, and they will often ask for an exclusive agreement for a year or two in order to maintain that advantage.

▶ *Flexibility:* Rosanna Bowles of Seattle, Washington designs tableware and is an aggressive private label marketer. When she was showing her products to Target, the buyer asked if the patterns were available in melamine, a type of resin used in making plastics.

Well, that's all it took to start a private label negotiation. You really gain a leg up in your negotiations if your buyer suggests changes specifically for its customers. You can afford to make those changes when the buyer is a large customer, the changes more or less obligate the buyer to moving ahead with the purchase, and the changes still allow you to introduce your own version of the product independently.

▶ MARKET **REALITY**

When private label buyers evaluate an inventor's product, they don't judge it on its own merits; they evaluate it against the known needs of their customers. When they suggest a product change, it doesn't mean they don't like your product. It just means that they have particular market needs that your product could satisfy with a few revisions.

INVENTOR'S STORY

We Aim to Please

Dr. Edward Tarr, a dentist from Tulsa, Oklahoma, helped his son create an unusual bracelet out of an old toothbrush for a school project. To his surprise, kids at school loved the bracelet, and Tarr decided to start a business making them. Calling them Funky Brushlets, he created a variety of wild handle designs, which just need to be submerged in hot water for five minutes to be turned from a toothbrush into a fashion-only bracelet. He added a Funky Holder that attaches to a bathroom mirror, and his company, D JET Enterprises, LLC, was able to get his product placed at May's Drugstores, Drug Warehouse, and Med-X Drugstores.

Tarr loved the product, as it helped promote proper dental care for kids, but without a big advertising budget, he had a difficult time getting the word out and getting kids to buy them. Then along came a company that sold toothbrushes in bulk to dentists. Dentists have long liked to give patients a toothbrush on every visit, so Tarr struck a private label deal with the supplier, and soon kids everywhere were receiving a Funky Brushlet after their trips to the dentist. And what happened when their Brushlet wore out? They could march into their local drugstore, find "Dr. T's" product, and buy another. Tarr benefited from his private label agreement in two ways: First, he got a big sale, though it was at a reduced price, that helped fund his business. More important, the sale introduced more kids to the Funky Brushlet (which retained its name under the private label agreement), and when kids went looking for a new one, the "Dr. T's" brand was the only one available. Without the private label deal, Tarr might not have been able to generate enough sales volume to keep his product on drugstore shelves.

Momentum Makers

▶ *Helps entire line:* Companies are most interested in a private label deal when it helps them sell their other products. They might have a void in their line that hurts them, or a competitor might have one better product that helps it secure more distribution outlets. Stores and distributors can't carry everyone's product line, and often one or two products determine whose line the store will carry. If you are selling a private label agreement to a store, you are looking to help one of its departments either to provide a more complete solution to its customers' needs or to offer more variety.

▶ *Support from distribution:* Most companies consider a strong distribution network the most important asset they can have. Marketers and buyers are always interested in what the distribution network has to say, and they will typically take whatever steps are needed to keep its network happy.

▶ *The product sells itself:* Your private label buyer is probably not going to invest any money in marketing. So potential buyers need to see your product and immediately realize your product's benefit. If you have a consumer product, take the time to package your product so it sells itself. The packaging and design of a product is particularly important if your private label agreement is with a retailer.

▶ *Target key consumer desires:* End users worry first about their major desires or concerns, and they will often buy a product immediately if it addresses one of them. Customers might wait a long time before they buy a product that satisfies only a minor concern.

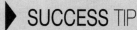

▶ **SUCCESS** TIP

Your job is to make the private label buyers decision as easy as possible. Having an ad, package, and brochure already prepared helps make the sale. But be sure your materials are crystal clear, and that your targeted end user will understand your product with just a quick glance.

Before You Start

▶ *The right target:* You have to pick carefully the companies you want to approach. The companies with the biggest market share typically are a more difficult sale because they are often complacent. Companies that have the second through fifth market share positions are usually easier to approach, and they are more willing to take a chance on a new product. You also want to see what companies your product will help the most. You have a good chance of signing an agreement with a company that doesn't have any products similar to yours. You also want to approach companies where your product is a good fit with their product line. You want the potential buyer's sales force to be already calling on or selling to your target customers. Potential buyers won't push your product into new markets. One way to find a good lead on a private label agreement is to read new product releases in trade magazines. Companies that don't have many new products coming out typically are more open. Be absolutely sure to attend industry trade shows to confirm your findings. Retailers also need to innovate and improve their stores, and many manufacturers will only sell to one or two retailers in an area. Retailers who don't get a manufacturer's new line are often receptive to a private label agreement.

▶ *Inside support:* When you are targeting a company or distributor, you need someone within the company to help promote your idea. Again, you can meet contacts at your target company at trade shows. Salespeople, regional sales managers, and marketing personnel all attend trade shows, and any of them can be the right one to push your product. Meet as many contacts as you can at the shows, and ask for help from contacts who like both you and your idea.

▶ *Know the competition:* Companies take on private label products primarily for competitive reasons. To sell the concept effectively, you need to know your target company's competition and how your product improves the company's position in regard to them. Knowing the competition is also important if retailers are the final stop in the targeted distribution channel.

▶ MARKET **REALITY**

Private label marketers like to keep selling to the same industry. Knowing the competition and what factors give a company a market advantage or disadvantage will help you discover what other types of products you could be offering. You could come out with one or two new products per year on a private label basis just by knowing the market's trend and what the competition is doing.

Potential buyers want to know how your product will help them compete for retail store space. Survey the products offered in all the stores to learn which companies need the most help in selling to retailers.

First Steps

▶ *Important and clear benefit:* Your company contacts who are helping support your product can also help you coordinate your presentation. You want to learn first what the company feels are important benefits for its customers, and then gear your presentation so that your product provides at least some of those benefits.

▶ *Cooperative marketing effort:* One of the dangers of private label marketing is that your product will be shuffled off to the corner. Offering your help for no charge ensures that the company will at least have a marketing plan in place for your product. Your company contact might also be willing to prepare a better package, brochure, or sales manual if you are doing most of the work. If you are selling to retailers, offer to work with the buyer to provide a display to help sell the product. This could be as simple as a small card that hangs on a pegboard or that attaches to the front of the shelf. The buyer may end up placing the product on the shelf without any support at all unless you offer to supply it.

▶ *Write an agreement:* If you are selling to distributors or retailers, all you really need is a purchase order. If they want an exclusive on your product, you can give them a letter saying that you will sell to them exclusively for a fixed period, usually one or two years as long as the company hits certain sales levels that you both agree to. You also have the buyer include exclusive language in its purchase order.

You need a more extensive agreement if you are selling to another company who is then marketing the product under its own name. The agreement can cover all or most of these points:

1. *Period of agreement:* You don't want the agreement to continue forever, as your business goals may change. Three years is the longest period you should agree to.

2. *General responsibilities of each party:* You want to be specific regarding who will pay for packaging, brochures, and other marketing materials.

3. *Conditions for terminating the agreement:* Typically, lack of performance by either party is cause for terminating the agreement.

4. *Price-increase protection:* The private label customer may want some protection that price increases will be limited to a certain percentage every year. The inventor may have a provision that increases can go above that limited percentage if its costs increase over a specified amount.

5. *Price-protection provision:* The customer may want to specify that you can't charge them more than you charge another private label customer.

6. *Exclusivity:* This could be by geographic market or territory or by market segment. Exclusivity clauses might also stop you from selling to other private label customers or prevent you from selling the product under your own name. You want to offer as little exclusivity as possible, while the private customer wants as much exclusivity as possible. If you offer exclusivity, you want strong performance clauses, that is, the company has to purchase a certain quantity of product.

7. *Product change provisions:* This clause should make it clear what type of changes you can and

cannot make with-out your customer's approval.

8. *Shipping and billing details:* Who will pay the freight, the minimum order quantities, how many free samples the customer will get, and the payment terms should all be included in the contract.

9. *Product ownership*: The product, and all its subsequent

▶ SUCCESS TIP

You'll save money if you prepare a rough draft of an agreement before seeing your attorney. Many books of legal contracts have samples for a private label agreement. You can also find information on drafting a legal contract at the following Web sites:

www.businesstown.com

www.legalissue.com

www.freelegalforms.com

www.rjsventures.com

www.digicontracts.com

---

variations, belongs to you and no one else—even if the customer requests extensive changes, provides engineering support, or helps get the product produced. Inventors might agree not to sell to anyone else a specific version of the product requested by the customer, but you want to make it clear that all variations of your initial product belong to you.

▶ A *first-year plan:* You can't afford to rest on your laurels after signing a deal. You need to write a first-year plan to get your product off and running. You should include in your plans sales promotions, sales materials, visits to customer locations, training as required, new product development, attending trade shows, market research for new products, an ongoing system of customer feedback, and quarterly reviews of sales status. Your goals in the first year are, one, to be sure the sales and marketing effort for your product is first

▶ MARKET **REALITY**

Private label agreements often involve products where broad patent protection isn't possible. Inventors should apply for a low-cost design patent or a trademark when they make product changes for customers. The patent may not offer much protection, but it does establish ownership. If you don't do that, you open yourself up to the possibility of the company claiming the product is really theirs.

class and, two, to network with company contacts and with influential end users. The success and staying power of your agreement will increase as you become better known to people involved with the product.

Building a Business

If you want to build a strong ongoing business, your private label sales should supplement sales through normal channels. This section addresses a variety of tactics companies use to expand sales in channels other than with a private label.

▶ *Address new markets:* Look for other markets where your product could be useful. These markets could be in different geographic areas, they could be for a different application, or they could be sold through a different sales channel. For example, an inventor might have a product that sprays a plastic coating on windows before a wall is painted with a spray gun. When the painting is over, the coating peels off, leaving a clean window—a much easier process than previous methods of masking windows. The inventor might first sign a private label agreement with a company that sells air sprayers to professional painters, but the inventor could still sell under his or her own brand name to hardware stores or to big home-improvement stores like Home Depot. The inventor could also sign another private label agreement with a manufacturer of industrial spray booths for farm equipment or trucks.

Now How Much Would You Pay?

The game show *The Price Is Right* plays off a universal consumer awareness: perceived value. Contestants are shown consumer items and asked to price them, and the contestant who is the most skilled at discerning the relative market value of products wins. As an inventor, you must understand intimately your product's perceived value in the market, and you must take particular care when your product is being sold as a private label by another manufacturer. The problem is that there is an extra company that needs to make money on the product, and that usually results in a higher end-user price. If the price slips out of line with the product's perceived value, there are several things an inventor can do.

▶ Add low-cost features that add value. Kids' eyeglasses can be purchased with a little spring that allows the bows (the part that goes to the ear) to spring outward. That feature probably raises manufacturing costs by a quarter, but it raises the perceived value by $10.

▶ Change materials to those with a better price/value relationship. A stainless-steel chrome tip for auto exhaust systems, for example, costs more to manufacture than a standard steel chrome tip, but the market values them about the same.

▶ Drop features that are unimportant to customers. Inventors often want to build a top-performing, high-quality product. But in doing so, they sometimes add features that customers don't especially want and aren't willing to pay for.

▶ Move your manufacturing to a lower cost foreign manufacturer.

▶ Improve the design or appearance of your product. Products with a "garage shop" look, like a typical toaster oven, have a much lower perceived value than products with a high-tech look, like a breadmaker.

▶ Change packaging. Packaging can be a major expense. You can opt for either a lower-priced packaging alternative or a more upscale package that raises your product's perceived value.

▶ *Change the price/value relationship:* An inventor might private label his or her product to a big mass merchandiser like Wal-Mart or Target. That product would be made inexpensively with a few functional features. The inventor could then build the same product out of better materials—or possibly add a bigger motor or a designer look—and sell the product to a higher-priced retailer. The inventor could target a midrange retailer like J.C. Penney or, if enough features were added, a department store like Macy's.

> ▶ MARKET **REALITY**
>
> Customers buying on a private label basis don't expect suppliers to sell only to them. Often they don't even request an exclusive arrangement. If they do, they are usually happy with an exclusive that's limited to their territory or market. They won't get upset if you change the product for another customer or if you sell to different markets. So remember to keep looking for new markets for your product.

▶ *Broaden performance:* If an inventor private labels a special weed remover for sidewalks to Sears, he or she could also sell a weed remover that also works in the yard and garden. A company selling an instant tire repair kit for flat tires might broaden the product's application so it could be used to prevent flat tires. The inventor could then sell that product to new customers.

▶ *New products:* Private label marketers often survive by introducing products that fill voids in the market. The products are not always innovative, but they are an item the company wants so their line is competitive.

Are You Making Money?

▶ *Sales agreements:* Your customers may not want a sales agreement unless it provides them benefits, which could include limited price increases, guaranteed lowest pricing, or some sort of exclusive agreement. You, however, want to have an agreement so that you can receive a notice if the customer is going to drop your product, but more importantly so that you put limits on the customer's ability to have your product made by someone else. You may also want a formal agreement to use as leverage for getting a loan, obtaining a lease, or negotiating payment terms to your manufacturer.

▶ *Level of service:* Customers will be reluctant to leave you if you provide marketing support, such as by attending trade shows, doing publicity releases, actively working a Web page, or offering layouts for ads or brochures. You can also offer to provide customer service for handling product problems, to take care of product returns, and to suggest product improvements. The customer will be reluctant to think about sourcing the product somewhere else if you provide plenty of service support.

▶ *Product ownership:* Appendix A discusses patents and outlines when a patent offers real protection and value to the inventor. In some cases, it is not worthwhile to have a patent. Patents are useful, even design patents or patents with very narrow claims, when you engage in private label marketing because they establish that the product is yours. As your product becomes more

 MARKET **REALITY**

Patent law requires that everyone who participates in the creation of an idea be listed as an inventor on the patent. You want a clause in your contract that specifies that patent rights for any new patents based on your original idea will be assigned to you. That protects you in case a buyer's employee contributes to a new patent and is listed as a coinventor on the patent.

successful, your customers may start to think about making the product on their own, and any patents you have will discourage them from doing that.

▶ *Corrective measures:* You need to be careful not to commit too many of your resources or markets to a private label customer unless you have an agreement. Simply tell the customer you are not willing to risk your markets and resources to any meaningful extent without a sales agreement, which means you will need to limit your commitment to exclusive terms, pricing protection, and product support. However, you should be able to get an agreement that benefits both companies as long as you don't overcommit to favorable customer terms too soon.

16

Licensing–
The Inside Scoop

The Basics

In simplest terms, a license means that someone is given the permission to do something. In terms of new products, a license means that the owner of intellectual property (which is a patent, trademark, copyright, or trade secret) gives someone else permission to produce the product related to the property. In return for granting permission, the inventor is paid a royalty, which is a percentage of sales. The royalty typically varies from 2 to 8 percent depending on the importance and profitability of the product.

Once inventors license a product, they in effect turn over all aspects of the invention to the licensee, which will manufacturer, promote, and sell the product. Inventors just collect royalties. The drawback to licensing is that inventors have no control over what the manufacturer decides to do with the product. The licensee may change the product, may not promote it very well, and may even decided to drop the product after a few years.

> ### ▶ BUZZ WORD
>
> A *license agreement* grants a licensee permission to produce something. The licensee doesn't need permission unless you have the right to exclude others from producing or using your idea, which requires the licensor to own intellectual property (such as a patent, trademark, or copyright). Without ownership, you can still receive a sales commission for your idea or sell future patent rights for a sales override (see chapters 10 and 11).

The inventor may get the product back after lack of performance on the licensee's part, but often by that time the market opportunity has been lost. The other drawback to licensing is the licensee typically investigates your idea thoroughly before signing a contract. This can delay the agreement. The manufacturer may also decide during its investigation that you have a weak patent, and instead it will design its own version of the product.

Most companies prefer licensing if they are convinced a product will sell, since then they have total control. A company that takes on an inventor as a commissioned salesperson or alliance partner, or who buys on a private label basis, will frequently switch to a license once it is convinced the product will succeed.

Perfect Products

Virtually any type of product can be licensed. What varies is the stage at which a company will license the product. You may be able to strike a quick licensing agreement if you are already successfully producing and selling the product. You may be able license a product with just a prototype if it meets a clear market need in a convincing way. You may be able to license an idea in the concept stage if the product has breakthrough potential in a major market. I use the word *may* here deliberately. Getting a license is a difficult process, and most larger companies rarely sign a license agreement.

Your Goals

▸ Invent and profit from new products without having to create an entire company to manufacturer and sell the products.

▸ Take advantage of the marketing power of a large company to penetrate the broadest market possible as quickly as possible.

▶ MARKET REALITY

Some novice inventors believe that to get a license all you need to do is come up with an idea, file for a patent, and maybe produce a prototype. Indeed, a few inventors get a license by doing just that. But over the last 10 years, I've talked with over 70 inventors who have received a license, and of those, over 50 had to actually produce and sell their product before finding a licensee.

▸ Concentrate more on creating new products than on marketing products.

▸ Once inventors are established, it's an ideal situation for those who want to offer "create to order" invention services.

▸ Ideal for inventors who don't have the personality and expertise to network in the market or to sell and market their product.

INVENTOR'S STORY

Momma's Gotta Brand New Bag

A native of Spokane, Washington, Cassie Quinn was a new mother who could never find things in her diaper bag when she needed them. The bag contents tended to get tumbled together, and Quinn, always fumbling for what she needed with a baby in one arm, began to feel there had to be a better way. So she created a diaper bag with lots of compartments so that everything had a place and she would know exactly where to find what she needed each

212 - THINK BIG

time. Quinn knew her product was a winner, but she also knew that she didn't have the time or money to finish the product's development or to take it to market. So she and her husband, Robie, decided to try to license the idea.

Quinn's first step was to research the market before making any presentations to potential manufacturers. With the help of a marketing consulting firm, Quinn's research report included the following information:

▶ A market analysis of the industry;

▶ An analysis of shelf space allocated to diaper bags at mass merchandisers, midrange department stores, drugstore chains, and juvenile products stores;

▶ A report on competitors, including the total number, their size, and their strengths and weaknesses;

▶ Total sales dollars of the market category;

▶ An analysis of how and why the three top firms attained their market success;

▶ A detailed explanation of how her product would be positioned in the market; and

▶ Research results from a focus group study Quinn did with parents and grandparents of young children.

Quinn had the marketing consultant take her research and a presentation package to the 1997 Juvenile Products Show in Dallas, Texas, to talk to potential licensees. The consultant made several contacts, but the one that turned out to be the key was Monica Kalozdi of Kalencom, a manufacturer of children's accessories. Kalencom was swayed by the research report and ended up licensing the product.

Other Choices

There are two basic reasons people license a product. The first is they don't have the expertise or money to properly introduce the product, and the second is they want to launch the product with enough money to establish a market share. Inventors can achieve similar results with private label sales (chapters 14 and 15), alliances or joint ventures (chapters 12 and 13), or by selling the product on commission (chapters 10 and 11). Private label and alliances both require more of an investment in time and money in order to launch the product, and selling on commission requires you to have sales and networking skills. Any of these three agreements is easier to strike than a licensing deal and can be used as precursor to a licensing arrangement.

One point to remember is that several of these tactics can be used together. You might form a partnership with a small company to develop technology that you eventually license. You might also partner with a distributor to get a sales-on-commission agreement, or you might use a private label sales agreement as a major sales point in negotiating a license agreement.

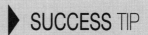 **SUCCESS** TIP

Many inventors take on an investor who supplies the $5,000 to $20,000 needed to get a patent and prototype in order to be ready for a license presentation. Don't give the investor a fixed percentage of the product. Say you offer an initial investor 25 percent. That could cause problems if and when you take on other investors, since your first investor will always feel he or she owns 25 percent. Always give an investor shares of stock in the company.

Money Matters

Licensing is not the low-cost option most people believe because typically you need, at minimum, a patent, a prototype, and research that shows your product is needed. You need to either put up the money yourself, get an investor partner, or have people who can assist you, such as a product designer or prototype engineer, who then may become partners in your invention. If your product idea is compelling enough, in some cases you might be able to get a small to midsize manufacturer to be your partner in finalizing the product design and producing prototypes. Another variation of this option is to be a partner with a smaller company and actually begin to sell your product to a market. Then after you have sales success, you can approach a major manufacturer in the market to obtain a license.

You can try and license your product with little development if you don't have enough money to proceed very far with your idea. But your odds for landing a license will not be good. The licensee has to see that the product has a good chance of success before proceeding. The more finalized your product, the better your chance that a company will believe it will succeed. Try to get money from an investor, or family and friends, or team up with a small company to take your product as far as you can before trying to license it.

Protection

You can't give someone permission to produce something if you don't own it. A strong, broad patent is an essential element of a licensing agreement. Companies generally don't investigate patents that thoroughly for private label agreements, or even for alliances, because they are looking for a one- to four-year opportunity. Typically, you can get by with a provisional patent in most of these agreements. But that tactic won't work in a license agreement. The company will want to carefully check your patent, and the stronger the patent, the better your chances of a licensing agreement.

Prototypes

A "looks like, works like" prototype is almost always necessary for a final licensing agreement. Inventors sometimes think a product is only licensed for its intrinsic value. Actually, that is not true at all. Companies most often license products because they don't have to spend time developing them. Developing a new product is time-consuming and expensive, and most companies are lucky to get one product to market for every five to ten they start development on. A license agreement looks inviting to a potential licensee when they have had all their R&D projects go bust. But a licensing opportunity is only inviting to the potential licensee if the inventor has taken the product to the point where it is close to being ready for production.

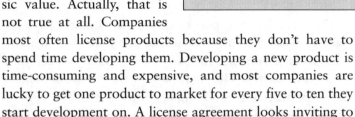

▶ MARKET **REALITY**

A danger of talking so distinctly about licensing contracts, joint ventures, private label agreements, and the like is that it implies that real-life agreements fall neatly into categories. In fact, agreements vary widely and contain an incredible number of different clauses to meet different needs. Use your creativity and search for the particular solution that satisfies everyone. Don't be constrained by terminology or what a certain type of agreement should be like.

Research

Companies license products when they are fairly confident that the product will be successful. Which means research is a key component. Cassie Quinn negotiated a license for her new diaper bag primarily because she had researched her market opportunity thoroughly. The research also gives your potential licensee the comforting feeling that you actually know what you are doing. Topics for a research report include:

Customer Information
    Number of customers
    Key buying influences
    How they buy
    Where they buy

Competitive Audit
    Market share
    Major strengths
    Major weaknesses
    Product opportunities

Industry Opportunities and Threats

Key Industry Trends

The second to last part of the report should be a summary of what the customer wants and needs and is motivated to buy. Your product, of course, exactly meets those needs and desires. The final part of the report should be your competitive positioning statement, which is the reason why customers should buy your product over others. Quinn's target customer group is high-income parents who are having their first child after they are 25. Her competitive positioning statement is that it is the one bag that lets you carry all the items you need and also find them when you want them.

Manufacturing

Inventors typically license their product because they don't want to be involved in manufacturing. Inventors who have to sell their product first under their own brand name or on a private label basis will usually use a contract manufacturer if they plan on eventually licensing their idea.

Ask Questions First, Invent Later

Licensing is traditionally thought of as the ultimate in pure invention: While musing dreamily in a dusty workshop, the inventor is struck by a brilliant idea, slaps together a prototype with duct tape and baling wire, and then presents it to a company, who licenses it immediately, giddy at their good fortune. Established inventors with a strong mechanical background, especially ones who have worked in the industry they are inventing products for, sometimes turn this scenario inside out. First, they talk to marketing and R&D people at various companies and ask what types of products they feel the market needs. When the inventor learns of a need for a new product concept, he or she will then agree to try and develop the product in return for expenses and a royalty.

This reversal of the normal approach to licensing is an intelligent response to the fact that companies license products to meet their goals and objectives. Most inventors present products to companies without really knowing their long-term strategies and plans. If the product happens to meet its goals, the company is interested; if it doesn't, the company will send the dreamy inventor back to the workshop no matter how nifty the invention.

I have occasionally used an option strategy to achieve the same goals. I once worked with a high-tech metallurgical invention that we thought would work well for a semiconductor manufacturer to reduce defects. We couldn't afford to finish the product without being sure we were giving potential licensees the product they really wanted. So we went to a manufacturer with a model and proof of the technology's potential. We had the manufacturer gives us $20,000 to develop and test a model for its needs in return for a six-month exclusive option on the technology. This helped us understand the potential licensee's needs and goals, and it raised $20,000 to help fund the product's development. The option tactic can also be used with potential private label customers and joint-venture products.

Key Contacts

You need two types of contacts. The first are people who will convince a potential licensee that your product is ideal for the market. These would be key users, key people in the distribution channel, or key retailers. The second type of contact is someone who can push your product inside the company toward a license agreement. This could be a company executive, a regional or national sales manager, a marketing person, or sometimes the R&D director.

Of the two, your most important contact is someone inside the company. This person can help you fine-tune your proposal, tell you whom you have to convince, and then after your presentation, offer you insights into what you need to do to get the deal done. To meet these contacts, you need to get out and attend trade shows, industry events, and association meetings. Making these contacts improves your chances of licensing a product at least 100 percent. Without a helpful contact, you may never make it past the company's invention submission policy to make a presentation.

 MARKET **REALITY**

Why do companies deliberately discourage inventors from approaching them? It's because most companies have been contacted by dozens, if not hundreds, of people looking to make a quick buck without really fully developing their idea. To improve your chances, you need to meet someone in the company who can attest that you are a serious inventor with a solid product opportunity.

Pros and Cons

Pros

Inventors can:

▸ Do what they do best, create new products.
▸ Avoid what they often do worst, manufacturing and marketing their products.

▶ Get their products onto the market with the backing
and promotion of a big company.

▶ Receive quick payments from an advance and guaranteed
minimum royalties.

▶ Have access to full design, engineering, and testing
capabilities.

▶ Make the most money possible on their invention
with very little personal risk.

Cons

▶ Inventors lose control of their product.

▶ Trying to license an idea is difficult unless a prototype
is available and possibly until the product has
already started to sell.

▶ Licensing doesn't help create a long-lasting business.

▶ Inventors could lose their opportunity if a company
sits on an idea for several years and never launches it
in the market.

Up, Up, and Away

Licensing is not typically the way you want to go if you
want to create a business. The only exception is when an
inventor is targeting one market that he or she will then
sell to on his or her own while licensing the product for
sales to another market. For example, an inventor could
have an adjustable sink that goes up and down and is helpful
to disabled people. The inventor might sell the product
through his or her own company to assisted-living facilities
and home contractors. The inventor might license the
product to another company for the beauty salon market
(to wash the hair of people in wheelchairs) and license it to
another company for sales to nursing homes.

MARKET **REALITY**

Royalty rates vary anywhere from 1 to 15 percent, but most fall in the 3 to 6 percent range. Typical royalty agreements call for advance royalties of from $5,000 to $ 40,000, with minimum royalties per year ranging from $5,000 to $50,000. You can find a standard licensing agreement in many books and in software on legal forms. One site that has licensing information is www.frompatent-toprofit.com.

Inventors who get one license have a much better chance to license subsequent projects to companies in the same market. You also shouldn't underestimate the potential of a license for even a minor product. One company I worked with signed a licensing agreement with the inventor of a vibrating dental scaler. The inventor took in an 8 percent royalty on sales that amounted to over $30 million in a ten-year period. That's not bad for a total investment of about $15,000 for a patent and a rough prototype.

Key Resources

Trade magazines, trade shows, and associations are key resources. Inventors who want to get a license need to learn an industry inside and out, and they need to learn who the major players in the market are and which companies are most likely to sign a license deal. You want to keep up on all the trade magazines and attend trade shows and association meetings. You also want to have a patent attorney who is familiar with licensing products. Here are some other resources:

▶ United Inventors Association of the United States of America, PO Box 23447, Rochester, NY 14692; 716-359-9310; www.uiausa.com. They offer information regarding local inventor groups that may be able to help you.

▸ *Thomas Register of American Manufacturers,* available at most libraries and at www.thomasregister.com. This contains a listing of manufacturers for many product categories.

▸ Licensing Executives Society, a network of licensing professionals. They also publish a magazine, a helpful newsletter, and other publications relating to license agreements. Call 703-836-3106, or visit their Web site at www.usa-canada.les.org.

What to Expect

▸ People may treat you like a crackpot inventor unless you have a product and a prototype.

▸ You'll probably get some resistance from R& D departments that suffer from "not invented here" syndrome.

▸ The licensing agreement the company offers will be unfavorable at first. You'll need an attorney to help you negotiate a fair deal.

▸ Once the deal is signed, you probably won't be kept well informed about the product's progress toward introduction.

▸ After the advance, you probably won't see your first royalty check for 18 to 24 months.

▸ The company may make substantial changes to the product before introduction.

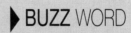

▶ BUZZ WORD

NIH syndrome—for "not invented here"—is a common inventor complaint. It stands for the resistance that R&D departments often exhibit toward outside inventions. Inventors theorize that R&D departments want their companies to introduce their own products first. This resistance was certainly strong in the past, but it is fading as companies cut R&D budgets while still wanting to introduce more products than ever.

▶ Most people will never know you are the inventor of the product. The company certainly won't tell anyone.

▶ If your product is a success, you can receive regular quarterly royalty payments for five to ten years.

▶ You'll need to keep active in the market if you plan on presenting additional products for licensing to industry companies.

▶ Your first presentation will be the determining factor on whether or not you'll get the company interested in your product idea.

Licensing–
Making It Happen

Keys to Success

▶ *Target the right companies:* Many inventors like to create a product based on their perceptions and then go out and try to license it. They are then surprised when companies don't immediately give positive response. Companies consider a number of factors when evaluating a potential license, such as: who is the target customer, what is the target customer trying to accomplish, how will your product help the target customer meet his or her goals, and do all these things match the company's own focus. They also are concerned with a product's price point, its look and quality compared to the rest of their product line, and the product's acceptance by the distribution channel. Your chances of meeting these concerns increases dramatically if you target the companies you hope to license to before you start creating your product idea.

> ▶ MARKET **REALITY**
>
> Companies license inventions for three reasons, and each is considerably different:
>
> 1. The inventor has innovative technology with enormous market potential.
> 2. The product is "ready to go": The inventor has manufactured and marketed the product, even if only in a limited way.
> 3. The product meets the needs of a company, such as filling a hole in the product line.

You want to choose companies that already sell similar products to your same target customer. For example, if your product helps food-processing companies package products so they look better in a store, you'll want to sell to companies selling products that package food for consumers. Then evaluate the price of the products companies sell, their image, their marketing positioning statement, and their distribution channel. Once you select the three or four companies you'll target, you can try and design the perfect product for those companies based on their existing strategies and capabilities.

▶ *Early involvement:* Companies evaluate your product from their own point of view, not yours. Your best chance of success is to fine-tune your product as much as possible to the needs of the company. To do that, you need the help of some of the company's people early in your development cycle. By doing this, you'll get valuable input on your product, plus these same people can help you sell the company later. This is much easier to do than you might think, since sales and marketing people love to have input into new products. Simply approach sales or marketing personnel of the companies you are targeting at conventions or association meetings. Explain that you are developing a new product that you think would be an ideal licensing or private label product for their company, and then ask them if they would be willing to provide input to you during your product development cycle. Many people will help.

INVENTOR'S STORY

Persistence Pays Off

Ann and Bill Schlotter of Fredricksburg, Virginia, and Ann and Tom Coleman of Abingdon, Virginia, created a nifty little product, the Spin Pop, which is a holder for a lollipop that moves the lollipop all around—up, down, in, and out. The two couples eventually licensed their product to Cap Toys (a division of Hasbro) for a 5 percent royalty, but not before they struggled for seven years.

The couples came up with their first version of the idea while watching kids running through their neighborhood one Halloween in the late 1980s: Why not, they thought, make a lollipop with a light shining in it? The couples made rough prototypes of clear lollipops and a holder with a small light bulb, which they dubbed the Glow Pop (Cap Toys later renamed it the Laser Pop). They soon learned, however, that while the Glow Pop looked neat at night, it was nothing special in the light of day. Thus was born the Spin Pop, which looks great day or night, inside or out.

After the couples received their first patent, they started approaching candy companies—who all said thanks, but no thanks. Believing their idea would generate interest if only people could see it, the couples attended an invention convention in Pittsburgh, Pennsylvania, where they made contact with Cap Toys. After a few months of negotiating, they signed a licensing agreement with the company, but that didn't mean success was around the corner.

Cap Toys initial sales efforts were rebuffed. Stores didn't believe that the holder would sell for $4.50. Cap Tops was willing to do whatever necessary to succeed, and finally ended up putting display units into stores on a consignment basis. Eventually, the tables turned, and the Revco Drug chain signed on and, after that initial success, K-Mart followed.

▶ *Remove the obstacles:* Only occasionally do inventors have that earth-shattering invention that companies are ready to pour more money into. In most cases, the number of obstacles in the way, or the resources needed to finalize the product, play a big role in a company's decision whether or not to license your idea. Take the Spin Pop: The inventors were committed to designing any needed product changes so the product would sell. They removed obstacles, and that was one reason they got the contract signed. The main reason that companies prefer to license a product that is already selling over one that is only in the concept stage is that they don't have to do nearly as much work.

▶ **SUCCESS** TIP

Always ask for money when a potential licensee asks you to complete some additional work. For example, if a company says they'd like your product if it had an additional feature, offer to make a new prototype with that feature, but then tell the company you'll need expense money to do that. Companies interested in your product will often pay for changes if the cost is reasonable.

There are many other ways inventors can make a license transition easier for the company. You can offer to make a prototype, work with engineers, do market testing, conduct consumer surveys, visit an overseas production facility, arrange to have experts attend a product-introduction open house, help produce marketing materials, or even arrange for a contract manufacture to make the first production runs. Typically the potential licensee will pay to get these things done, they just need a competent person to do them.

▶ *Customer focus:* When you are selling a license to a company, the company is the customer—and you need to focus on the customer's needs, perceptions, and desires. Don't focus your sales presentation exclusively on your product. Focus the presentation on how the product helps the potential licensee meet its goals and needs.

Momentum Makers

▶ *New market trends:* The manufacturer who gets into a new market area first is typically the manufacturer who holds onto a leading market share for the long term. This is why bigger companies buy so many small companies; the big company wants to have a position in the new market. Companies are anxious to talk to you when you can position them in a major way in a new market. The problem with developing a product for new market trends is that the company may already have a product in development to meet the same need your

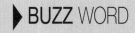

BUZZ WORD

Competitor is a frequently used word that everyone supposedly understands. But I've learned that inventors look at competitors much more broadly than companies. For example, who competes with a paint roller manufacturer? Most inventors would say other paint roller companies. But that is not who the manufacturer would consider its competitors. They'd only count competitors that sold with similar features, at the same price point, to the same distribution channel.

product meets, and if so, they are unlikely to license your idea. That's one reason you want early involvement from company people, to help you create a product that isn't already on the company's drawing board.

▶ *Competitive threats:* Companies always have their antennas up regarding what competitors are doing and what impact it could have on them. Inventors have great luck licensing an idea when they position their product as the one that can capitalize on a competitor's problem, or as the product that can counter a strong market move by a competitor.

▶ *The leading edge:* In the competitive marketing world of today, companies want to create a sustainable advantage, some feature of their business that gives them a significant edge for an extended period of time. New innovative technology is one way to achieve that edge. Most markets have at least one company that wants to be the innovator, and those are the companies to target if you have a breakthrough product design or new technology.

Before You Start

▶ *Appear competent:* Companies have seen dozens if not hundreds of poorly prepared inventors, and not surprisingly, they are highly skeptical when yet another inventor approaches them. You have to appear businesslike. The best way to do that is to have made earlier contacts with people in the company, as well as with key experts, distributors, and other knowledgeable people in the trade. The company will assume you are competent if you've dealt with many industry personnel. If you are a first-time or previously unsuccessful inventor, include a list of your advisors and the people you've interviewed every time you contact a company. That list more than anything else will show that you've done your homework, that you know what has to be done to sell your product, and most important, that you'll be a reliable partner.

▶ *Find opportunity seekers:* Within every company there are certain people who look for new opportunities, while most people accept the status quo until disaster strikes. You want to be sure to present your idea to people looking to expand their company's market share, whether your product is a simple one that's already selling or a complex one that needs further development. You can find the opportunity seekers first by talking to various people in the industry. Find the last three or four new industry products and then ask who was responsible for bringing the product to market. Also read trade magazines and watch for stories of people doing new things in the industry or who are making presentations at trade show association meetings.

▶ *Make the decision easy:* Companies first decide if your product has potential and whether it is something they want to license. Once they answer yes to that question for themselves, they start looking at any reasons they still might not want to go ahead. They might decide

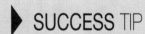
▶ SUCCESS TIP

Inventors are often told they can find manufacturers to license their product by looking up their product category in the *Thomas Register of American Manufacturers*. That is an approach with two problems. First, companies with complementary, not competitive, products are more likely to license your product. Second, the name of the company isn't what is most important; it's finding the right contact in the company.

they don't have enough engineering time, might be worried if the product hasn't had enough testing, or might be concerned the product isn't going to be perceived as significantly better than the competition. Companies rarely resolve these issues themselves, even when they say they will at your initial meeting. They will say they need to check whether they have enough engineering time, but time will slip away, and instead of just admitting they didn't follow through, they'll say they aren't interested. You need to listen to any objections and then suggest solutions. Not enough engineering time? Tell them you can line up an outside engineering firm to finish the job. To put yourself in a position to troubleshoot problems become well connected with as many sources as possible before you begin formally presenting your idea. Attend inventor club meetings, entrepreneur clubs, and every industry event you can to meet the people you'll need to solve any problem.

First Steps

▶ *Select the targets:* Companies respond better if they feel an idea is not being shopped around. Your best bet is to select one or two companies your product is ideal for and concentrate on one of them at a time. That way you can target your product from the beginning of your product development. Here are my criteria for choosing the best target customer:

- Market share: The top two companies in the market are often complacent. The next three or four companies are usually better targets.
- Age of the company: Old companies sometimes keep their market share because of a product they intro-

duced 10 or 20 years ago, and they typically won't take on new products. Newer companies, with frequent product introductions, are a better choice.

- Chief executives' backgrounds: Companies run by sales and marketing companies are typically much easier to license a product to than companies run by engineers or finance companies.

- People in the market: There is a big difference in the number of people companies send to trade shows or association meetings. Companies that work hard to have a market presence are easier to license to.

- R&D capabilities: Companies with small R&D staffs are more open to a license agreement.

- Inside contacts: You need a company insider to promote your product. Don't use this is as a sole criteria, but don't target a company till you have a contact.

▶ *A big bang presentation:* Your job at any presentation to a company, whether it is to a contract manufacturer, a private label customer, a joint-venture partner, or a potential licensee is to make a powerful first impression. See Chapter 13, pages 173–174, for more on how to do this. The main thing to remember is that businesspeople respond emotionally just like anyone else. Wow them with a great start and they will be on your side.

> ▶ **BUZZ** WORD
>
> When you present your product to many companies at once, the companies will say you *shopped the product around.* Inventors think shopping a product builds up competition and helps them get a bigger deal. Sometimes that happens. But more often this tactic is a big negative for most potential licensees. It detracts from your sales point that the product was created to help the company meet its specific needs.

▶ *The initial offer:* Don't make a formal offer on your initial visit. It is too soon to be positive what the company wants, and in reality, all you want is the company's support to introduce the product. I believe your offer should be along these lines: "Obviously, this opportunity is far too big for me to exploit on my own. I'm here today because I feel you are by far the best company to promote my idea. I'm really open to any type of partnership deal that might work for you—from buying the product for a private label sale to signing a license." The company won't be able to respond immediately, but you have let them know that you are open to anything.

What happens after the initial meeting? I feel the best result is when the company approaches you and wants something else done, such as a prototype for a new feature, a product test by potential end users, or perhaps interviews with key distributors. You can volunteer to do the work yourself or offer to help someone else do it, and you can ask the company to help pay to get the task done. Your deal is on the way once the company gives you money for a specific task related to the invention.

If the company doesn't have a suggested course of action, you should suggest that you work with someone in the company to come up with a proposal for the next steps that the company should take in evaluating your idea. Or you can tell the company that you'll submit a proposal for moving ahead if they indicate what direction they want to take.

Building a Business

Inventors rarely have just one idea. In fact, they often want to continue inventing products simply because they can't

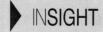

Keep Pounding the Pavement

Sometimes inventors have a product that their target manufacturers simply don't want. Don't let this discourage you. There are several other tactics you can use to find a licensee.

1. Approach manufacturers that actively seek inventor's ideas. These companies advertise in trade magazines directed at likely inventors of their type of product, or in inventor's magazines like *Inventor's Digest*, www.inventorsdigest.com. Lisle Manufacturing of Clarinda, Iowa (712-542-5101), makes tools for auto mechanics. Each year Lisle attracts 600 to 700 submissions and licenses six to ten new products from ads it runs in auto mechanic trade magazines.

2. Run a publicity program. Some inventors run their own publicity campaign directed at newspapers and magazines with the hope that a potential licensee will see the stories and contact the company. Ronald Demon of Boston, Massachusetts, invented a new type of running shoe that adjusts the sole's air pressure depending on the impact level of the user. The shoe raises air pressure as the user's shoe-to-surface impact increases. Demon's company, VectraSense Technologies, had a big publicity program released right after he received his patent. Both Nike and Reebok contacted him after reading the story to discuss the possibility of licensing the idea.

3. Every year several inventors make contacts that lead to licenses at invention trade shows. These shows allow inventors to set up a booth highlighting their product, where they hope to make contacts with marketers and manufacturers who are looking to license an idea. Here are some of the leading trade shows, with contact numbers:

   • Invention and New Product Exposition, or Inpex. It is held each year in May in Pittsburgh, Pennsylvania. Call 800-422-0872, or contact them at INPEX@/ix.NETCOM.com.

stop thinking of new ideas. Most inventors would like very much to become professional inventors, spending their days brainstorming one idea after another. That's the business I discuss building in this section: your business as a professional inventor.

▶ *Become a resource:* Inventors who turn their products over to a company on a license and consider their work done frequently become frustrated. Companies make changes inventors don't like, they may not promote the product, or they may drop the product after a short run. While companies don't like inventors who simply pester them, they do like inventors who help them succeed. One way to do that is to serve on industry committees in an effort to promote your product. You can also call on customers who are having service problems, suggest new product improvements, or help a company keep track of university research that might eventually impact their product line.

▶ *Write the agreement:* You will probably only negotiate a fair agreement if you have the negotiating help of a patent attorney experienced in licensing. The licensee's attorney will be involved, and he or she is not going to look out for your interests. The intricacies of negotiating a license are tricky, the clauses involved are many, and I don't think any inventor should try to strike his or her own deal. Licensing negotiations

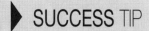

▶ SUCCESS TIP

Companies are usually worried about competition. An inventor I knew about ten years ago made a living analyzing competitive product introductions. When a new product came out, he prepared a report on the product's design and patent, and then he explained how he could get around the patent and improve the product. Often a company would ask him to pursue his suggestions, and then it would eventually license the final product.

can also get contentious. You want your attorney, and not yourself, to be the contentious party because, after all, your goal is to have a continuing relationship with the company.

Some smaller companies might ask you to provide the agreement. You might want to use a standard license agreement to start with, but still consult an attorney so you add other pertinent clauses. Some books and software on legal forms may contain a sample license agreement. Another good source of sample agreements is a resource guide published by IPT Co., which you can order by calling 1-888-53-PATENT or by visiting their Web site at www.frompatenttoprofit.com.

▶ *Create new product ideas:* Inventors typically create their most successful products when they truly understand what end users want. Once you've taken the time to get to know an industry, you might as well keep creating ideas to meet that industry's needs. Licensing will be much easier the second time around, and you'll find most product areas have plenty of problems a new product can solve. I worked with a dental company that licensed an inventor's air motor mechanism for their first high-speed drill. That inventor kept the company on the leading edge for over 15 years by continually creating faster and better motors, which the company was happy to license.

Are You Making Money?

▶ *Patent strategy:* As I've said above, you need a patent to get a license. But once you've got the license, unless your patent is very broad, you should also patent any other approaches to creating a product with a benefit similar to yours. Look at your patent and see how someone could design around it. Then patent the various ways of making your product so it will be more difficult for a company to introduce a variation of it. Some inventors wind up with ten more patents of design variations of their product idea.

> ▶ **BUZZ** WORD
>
> Engineers are frequently asked to design around competitors' patents, and it not surprising that a potential licensee may look at designing around your patent. *Design around* just means that you create a product that doesn't infringe on a patent. To infringe, a product has to read-on (or have) every feature listed in the original product's patent claim. See appendix A for a full description of patents.

▶ *Ongoing relationship:* You always want to be kept up-to-date on the company's latest thinking regarding your product—whether it's planning a big new promotion or it feels that a competitive product is superior to yours. You can't keep informed if you don't keep in touch with the company. Keeping informed also lets you continually present new ideas.

▶ *Corrective measures:* The two biggest failings of inventors in licensing agreements are (1) when they walk away and expect those checks to keep coming, and (2) when they don't have an active strategy to protect their patent from developments in the field. If your industry relationships have grown cold, you need to attend trade shows, visit the company, and reconnect with as many people as possible. Your goal is not to simply meet people; you want to sell them on your value as an asset and resource.

It's very tough to recover once you've let your patent slip away. You don't have a problem if you have a core technology that everyone needs to use to build a competitive product. An example would be if you patented the only known technology for recording digital music from the Internet onto a CD. Rarely do inventors have such a broad technology that prevents competitors from creating their own products. Instead, inventors have to keep filing new patents on variations of their product. That strategy will delay both your licensee and their competitors from introducing their own versions of your product. Most companies I've known are reluctant to tangle with inventors who have a comprehensive follow-up patent strategy.

18

Your Own Company—
The Inside Scoop

The Basics

Medtronics, the giant medical products company, was started by the inventor of the pacemaker, Earl Bakken, in a small building not far from my parent's home. He had a great idea, got a partner who handled marketing and fundraising, and in less than 20 years, Bakken was helming one of Minnesota's leading companies. This is the same path followed by leading companies like Hewlett-Packard, Microsoft, Gillette, and Estée Lauder. In reality, inventors who follow this course succeed because they become top-notch executives, and they often leave inventing behind to drive their company forward. But establishing an enduring legacy and forming a great company is still the dream of many inventors.

With the chance of greater reward also comes greater risk. Inventors stand to lose a lot more of their own money. One of the main reasons inventors pursue alliances or licensing is that it spreads the risk out among partner companies. Inventors who start their own companies have to learn how to actually run a company, raise money, handle employees, and develop a strategic plan. These are not easy tasks, and they can take an inventor's every waking hour. Probably the most difficult part of starting your own company is that you have to stand alone. Everyone looks to the inventor for decisions and action. Having partners, especially ones with experience and financial muscle, takes a tremendous burden off the inventor.

Inventors following any of the other eight tactics in this book might also form their own company. The difference is that the inventors following this tactic are not looking to form a small company or a company that shares profits with partner companies or a private label company. This tactic is for inventors who want to make every penny of profit they can from their idea and who want, eventually, to form a major powerhouse company like Hewlett-Packard.

INVENTOR'S STORY

The Proverbial Million-Dollar Idea

Mike Mogadam had a friend who was driven out of the bar business in large part because of employee theft. Mogadam's friend told him he'd have a million-dollar idea if he could solve that problem. An engineer and resident of San Francisco, Mogadam talked to owners of some of the city's biggest nightclubs, who confirmed that employee theft was one of their biggest problems. So he set to work developing a solution. His idea was to create a system that combined electronic liquor bottle spouts with wireless electronic communication technology and a back-of-the-bar computer. Every time the bartender would pour a drink, the spout would send a signal to the computer, which would then signal the cash register. Mogadam's product would eliminate three problems: first, bartenders giving away free drinks for bigger tips; second, bartenders pocketing the money for drinks; and third, bartenders ringing up lower-cost drinks on the register and pocketing the difference. Mogadam did a preliminary product specification and determined he could sell such a device for an estimated $10,000 to $20,000 apiece. Calling his proposed invention "the Barmate," Mogadam then wrote a financing plan to get his company up and running:

▶ Produce a working prototype. Estimated cost: $12,000 to $15,000. Funding source: credit cards.

▶ Attend a beverage and restaurant industry trade show to verify buyer interest. Estimated cost: $3,000 to $5,000. Funding source: credit cards.

▶ Finalize engineering design, documentation, and beta testing. Estimated cost: $80,000 to $120,000. Funding source: Relatives, investors, and friends.

▶ Produce the first run of 10 to 15 units. Estimated cost: $200,000 to $400,000. Funding source: Investors and SBA loans.

Mogadam's plan called for attending a trade show. His goal was not to gain market input as much as it was to invite investors to attend the show with him. He knew the $80,000 to $120,000 he needed to finalize and test his design was a lot of money, and he was only going to get it if investors could see firsthand how the Barmate could excite potential customers. Mogadam contacted family, friends, businesspeople he knew, and people in his neighborhood to help find potential investors. With a solid product, a ready market, and a clear, realistic financial plan, Mogadam was able to raise the necessary funds and launch his company. And his friend was right: Just five years after starting out, Mogadam's company passed the $1 million sales mark.

Perfect Products

▶ *Products targeted at narrow markets:* An inventor's biggest problem in starting his or her own company is distribution of the product. Some markets with broad distribution, such as the hardware store market, are difficult to penetrate without a large, expensive-to-set up distribution network. A second problem is that broad markets have thousands of products to choose from, and inventors can have trouble getting customers to try a new product. Small markets, on the other hand, usually have a small distribution network that's easier to penetrate. For example, uniform products sold to police officers are sold through uniform shops and specialty catalogs. Those outlets are easy to find, and they are easier to sell to, as customers have a limited number of products to choose from.

▶ *Products that don't fit well with established companies:* Mike Mogadam's Barmate is an expensive product that provides a unique benefit. While that uniqueness limits the number of companies with which the inventor could try to form a partnership or try to sign a licensing agreement, the upside of products like the Barmate is that you don't have to stand out in a cluttered market. Customers will notice your unique product immediately if it solves one of their major problems.

> ▶ **SUCCESS** TIP
>
> The best product introductions create demand among end users as well as create a push for the product with distribution. Inventors have limited budgets. They create end-user demand most easily when their target customers are easy to find. Police officers are a good target group because they read a couple of police-oriented magazines, and you can buy their names from the publications.

▶ *Low start-up and prototype costs:* Inventors are in the best position when they can handle most of the initial prototype and product costs themselves. These costs can rapidly escalate on even the simplest products if you need to make product changes. I've talked to many, many inventors who have simply run out of money before they could get a prototype made to present to investors. If possible, focus on a product for which you can make a great model or prototype using your own money, or by borrowing money from family and friends. Mike Mogadam, the Barmate's inventor, went ahead with a complicated product, but at least he was an engineer and was able to do most of the costly engineering work himself.

▶ *Long product life*: The Barmate is the type of product that might sell well for ten years. The product is complicated and difficult to duplicate, and the market is not large enough to encourage dozens of competitors. You should look for a product with the same extended "shelf life," since inventors starting their own company often encounter initial funding delays or problems setting up manufacturing. They can't afford to compete in fast-changing markets because the market might change before their product is released.

Your Goals

People who decide to develop their own company usually have two goals. One is to be in charge of everything that happens with their product, and the second is to build a high-value company. These inventors aren't interested in making $25,000 to $100,000 per year selling on TV shopping networks or in catalogs, or earning a smaller sum on a licensing agreement. They want to maximize their return on their invention, and they are willing to put

244 - THINK BIG

> ▶ MARKET **REALITY**
>
> Over the last 20 years, I've found that inventors who succeed have seven distinctive traits:
>
> 1. A firm belief in their products
> 2. Infectious enthusiasm
> 3. Bulldog determination
> 4. Persistence in the face of constant rejection
> 5. Continual creativity with all aspects of new product introductions
> 6. A willingness to seek help
> 7. And they ain't too proud to beg

in whatever work is necessary to make that happen. These inventors eventually want a company of substance that will last 20 to 40 years and produce significant income.

Other Choices

This is really the only viable option for inventors seeking control, growth, and maximum profits—along with the ability to become a large company with long-term viability.

Money Matters

Money is a major, ongoing concern for inventors looking to build a major company. They have to fund the beginning stages of the company themselves or with the help of investors or possibly a contract manufacturer, and then they usually need to fund operating capital and initial start-up marketing and manufacturing costs. Appendix C covers financing more thoroughly. Inventors starting their own company need to use all of the tactics listed there to make their companies go. Basically, inventors have to cover four stages of development.

1. The concept stage. This includes developing the idea and its market potential, and preferably building models or prototypes. Funding source: the inventor himself or herself, family and friends, a contract manufacturer, or a person in the industry.

2. Verification stage. Preferably, this includes selling preproduction or pilot plant production runs to real customers in a small market. If that is cost prohibitive, it should include either trade show attendance or interviews with 10 to 15 potential users and potential customers in the distribution network. Funding source: the inventor him- or herself, family and friends, a contract manufacturer, or a person in the industry.

3. Initial production runs. Typically, new companies are more worried about losing a lot of money on their product than they are about having a low profit margin on their initial production run. Frequently, they will run with low-cost temporary tooling for an initial run. The tooling will cost 15 to 20 percent of permanent tooling, and it might only last one or two runs, but it will let the company determine without a doubt that the product will sell. Funding source: outside or industry investors, contract manufacturers, or possibly eventual distributors of your product. You might also get investments from family and friends, although they need to have significant financial resources to afford this period of growth.

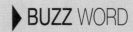

▶ BUZZ WORD

Preproduction models are products that look and work exactly like an actual production unit. A *prototype*, in contrast, might use different components or work differently than the final product. A *pilot run* is an initial production run typically with temporary tooling to produce a small quantity of units. Pilot plant-run parts are costly because they are done in small volume, typically with a lot of handwork.

4. Full-scale production. Once you've proven through four or five steps or trials that the product will sell, you

SUCCESS TIP

The best early investor for an inventor is someone in the industry, preferably either a potential end user or someone in the product's eventual distribution network. These investors can give you helpful advice, but more important, having industry investors onboard impresses outside investors. Even though it might be easier to use your own money or money from your family, try to get an investment from one or more people in your industry.

can now get more traditional funding for full-scale production. Funding sources: bank and SBA loans, venture capitalists, larger investors, and contract manufacturers.

Inventors stage their growth through these four periods for two reasons. One is that it is easier to get investments in small chunks while you prove conclusively how your product will sell. The other reason is that it allows inventors to keep a controlling interest in their company. Your company becomes much more valuable as you complete each step. Investors are going to demand a substantial portion of the company if you ask for money before you have made any discernible market progress.

Protection

Inventors building a company are probably investing three or four years of their lives and much, if not all, of their personal worth in their product. They would be foolish not to get every ounce of patent, trademark, and copyright protection they can afford. Before proceeding very far, inventors need to investigate carefully the type of protection they will be able to obtain. Investors frequently get a patent attorney's opinion about the strength of a patent before investing, and inventors contemplating starting their own company should also get an opinion from a patent attorney about just how strong their patent protection may be. If the attorney feels that you'll only be able to get narrow protection, consider falling back to either a private label sales agreement or a joint-venture introduction to cut your risks. Your other choice would be to come up with another product where broader patent protection could be obtained.

Prototypes

You need to make a prototype both for mechanical testing and for market research. You need to do this step no matter how sure you are that the product will sell. My experience is that most inventions need three to four prototypes before they are perfected from both a manufacturing and a marketing point of view. In the long run, making those prototypes saves you tons of money and allows you to produce the best possible product for the market.

▶ MARKET **REALITY**

Patent attorneys have an interest in selling you patent services. They may also have a different view of what constitutes a strong patent than you do. Ask these specific questions of your attorney:

1. What chances do I have of obtaining a patent with broad coverage?

2. What types of product variations by competitors will infringe on the potential patent claims?

3. What type of product variations won't infringe on the potential patent claims?

Research

You want to conduct thorough research the entire time that you are working on your project to ensure that you are not wasting your time or money, and so that you can make a strong case to your investors. Research should start before you spend any money, and it should continue until the product is introduced.

➤ *Initial research*: Before starting out, you need to validate your premise and check that you are meeting a primary customer need. People express many desires, but they generally won't buy something unless it is important to them.

➤ *Prototype research*: You need to be sure the product does what people want, and that it performs well enough for people to buy it. You also want to check that your product has all the features end users feel

---

➤ **BUZZ** WORD

Your *premise* is the reason that you feel people want your new product. The Clean Shower is an after-shower spray that eliminates scaling and mildew. The product's premise is that people get tired of having to scrub their shower. Some products have a less functional premise. The premise of a new hair accessory might be that teenage girls are looking for a funky new style.

---

are necessary. Consider the string-type edge trimmers people use on their lawns. When the product was introduced, the premise was that people weren't happy about the products available, especially little clippers, to trim around trees and buildings. Several other products were introduced before the string-type trimmers, but none of them did the job well enough and they just didn't sell. How do you know when your product is good enough to inspire people to buy it? Only by letting them try out the product out and getting their reactions.

➤ *Preproduction model testing*: You want to verify again that the product works well enough for people to buy it, and you want to verify that people agree that your product is worth the money you are charging. Be sure to do this even if you had successful research results with your prototype. You may have made changes that seem inconsequential to you but that are important to the end user.

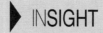

INSIGHT

It's No Longer a Game: Is the Price Right?

Pricing is extremely important for every new product, and every company struggles with getting the right price point. You have two goals when setting your price: You want end users to feel the product offers good value for the money, and you also want to be sure your price is high enough so that you can make a profit. For most products, your end-user selling price needs to be four to five times your manufacturing cost.

Inventors usually overvalue what their product can sell for. To avoid this mistake, conduct your own version of The Price Is Right game show, but with real consumers and your own product. For example, if you have a hardware product, pick out five to eight other products sold in hardware stores, and make sure the prices extend from 50 to 200 percent of the price you think you can charge for your product. Try to find products where the price difference between each one is only 15 to 25 percent, and make sure the prices are evenly divided along the price range. The other products don't have to be the same as yours; they just have to be products that are sold in the same market. Depending on what your product is, you can use either actual products, including your product or prototype, or brochures.

Then ask 10 to 20 end users to rank the products by their value, with the highest-value product first. If you find your product consistently ranked between one costing $4.95 and one costing $6.49, you'll know your perceived value is somewhere in that range. If your product's perceived value is not four times your manufacturing cost, you need to either add features or cut costs. If you do that, repeat your survey to be sure the revised product has the right perceived value. It is also useful to repeat this survey with people in the distribution channel.

Manufacturing

I believe most inventors, when starting out, should use a contract manufacturer and focus their energies on marketing their product. Tooling and other start-up manufacturing costs are very high, and manufacturing can be a complex process. You don't want to dilute your efforts as you start to sell your product. After you get sales going, you can take over manufacturing if you choose.

Key Contacts

Unless you are really well funded, your most important contact is probably someone who can help you raise money. Your second most important contacts are industry insiders who are in the distribution channel and can help you launch the product. Your third most important contacts are end users or distributors who can give you, or help you make, a big sale.

Most companies get initial funding from "angel investors"—people who might invest $25,000 to $50,000 to help get a product off the ground. "Angels" are usually more interested in helping out new businesses than in making tons of money for themselves. Some of these investors, especially ones who are retired, are also willing to mentor young inventors through the new product introduction process. Make contacts with people in the industry first, and find one or two people who will help you learn the market. Then look for an angel investor to join your team.

 SUCCESS TIP

Most inventors don't have to go far to find their mentors and early investors. You can find mentors with extensive business experience by being active in your church, chamber of commerce, and other local groups. Your friends and family may also have contacts that can help you. Make a list of the people you learn of and start calling them, explaining what you are doing and asking for their help.

Pros and Cons

Pros

▶ Inventor has the most control over the product's success and has the potential of making the most money.

▶ The best tactic for building a sustainable company that can introduce a series of products.

▶ Inventors can respond to market changes much more quickly than they can with partners.

▶ Allows the inventor to fully utilize his or her creativity in all aspects of the business. Partnership ventures require inventors to get approval from their partners—before making key decisions.

Cons

▶ Most expensive route for an inventor to take, and it usually requires taking on, and dealing with, investors.

▶ Requires inventors to learn all the skills of running a company.

▶ Often takes an inventor three to four years to produce a living income, as all the money he or she earns typically needs to be plowed back into the company to fuel its growth.

Up, Up, and Away

In all the other tactics, "up, up, and away" means arriving at this stage with your own company that you control and that you can use as a base for your future inventions. In this tactic, you start the company from the beginning. Your goal is to start with the first invention and then keep

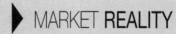 MARKET REALITY

Inventors like to believe that investors are primarily concerned about the product. Unfortunately, that's not true. Investors are just as concerned about your abilities as a manager. Many investors believe a good manager can make almost any product go, while a bad manager will botch every product, no matter how good it is. If your experience is limited, expand your mentor and advisor network to reassure investors.

252 — THINK BIG

developing the company by expanding your distribution and product line. You'll be able to add personnel and funding once you've proven you can manage a company and its products.

Key Resources

▶ One or two experienced mentors to help you.

▶ The local Small Business Development Center (SBDC). They offer a wide variety of seminars and one-on-one counseling. Call the Small Business Administration office in your phone book for the SBDC office nearest you. Or go to www.sbaonline.gov for an up-to-date listing, or contact www.asbdc-us.org.

▶ Entrepreneurial courses at local colleges. Don't try to start a business without taking at least one of these courses. They will introduce you to all the legal requirements and ramifications, and they will help you set up your administrative functions. Many colleges have special entrepreneurial programs for people in business who aren't going to college. Your SBDC office will know about courses in your area.

▶ The local inventors club. Go to www.uiausa.com for a club in your area. The club will have lists of local engineers, industrial designers, and prototype builders who will help inventors for below-market rates.

▶ *Gale's Source of Publications and Broadcast Media* is a source of trade magazines. *Trade Shows World Wide* lists trade shows, and *Packaging Marketplace* is a source of packaging manufacturers. All are published by Gale Research, 835 Penobscot Building, Detroit, MI 48226; 313-961-6082.

▶ Manufacturers' Agents National Association (MANA) is a source of manufacturers' sales representatives who may carry your product. Contact them at P.O. Box 3467, Laguna Hills, CA 92654, or call 714-859-4040.

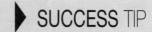 **SUCCESS** TIP

Product design in today's market is upscale, and people aren't willing to buy products that don't have an attractive, complete look. Industrial designers are skilled at making products simpler and more efficient as well as modern and up-to-date. You can find industrial designers in your phone book or by contacting the Industrial Designers Society of America, 1142 East Walker Road, Great Falls, VA 22066; 703-759-0100; e-mail: idsanhq@aol.com.

▶ Office of the Indepen-dent Inventor at the Patent and Trademark Office. They publish information that helps individual inventors better understand and access the patent office. They can be reached through the patent office's Web site, www.uspto.gov.

What to Expect

▶ Lots of hard work.

▶ Difficulty in raising all the money you need.

▶ Resistance from the distribution network and investors unless you have an experienced management team.

▶ More time than expected before you start earning money.

▶ Potentially great rewards after you succeed.

▶ A quick transition from crackpot to genius once your product starts to sell.

▶ The pressures of being the boss may sometimes feel overwhelming.

▶ If you build early momentum, this tactic has the potential to produce a buzz in the market.

19

Your Own Company—
Making It Happen

Keys to Success

▶ *Easy starting point:* Inventors can't build the market momentum they need by just adding a few new stores per month. They need to generate real excitement and momentum. Inventors might do this with catalog or TV shopping network sales, by attending a major trade show or a big event aimed at their target customers, or they might do it by preselling a few accounts that will help get the product off to a quick start. You won't succeed if you spend six months trying to find your winning strategy.

▶ *Clear-cut customers:* Every smart businessperson targets a certain customer group. Inventors will have the best luck selling their product when their clear-cut customer group is the same as their target retailers or distributors. Tony Loiacono (see page 256) targeted young children and their daily bath. That's a customer group that

It's Not What You Make, It's Who You Know

For little kids, what's more fun than bath time? Not much (ice cream aside), except perhaps bath time with a bunch of fun toys. With this for his premise, Tony Loiacono of Bonsall, California, designed two products: Kid Soap, kid-friendly fun soap shaped like animals, and Kid Soap Plus, which is the soap and a background scene that wraps around the inside of the tub, creating a whole new colorful world for the child to play in.

Loiacono knew his product would be need broad distribution, and he couldn't afford a big advertising budget. He created models of both his products and first talked to other inventors and companies that had already sold products to the same mass merchandisers he was targeting. He showed them his products and explained why he wanted to see the retail buyers—to get input from the buyers regarding any changes they'd suggest. These contacts liked Loiacono and thought he had a promising product, so they helped him get his foot in the door by suggesting to the major retail buyers that they meet with him. The buyers agreed, and Loiacono substantially revised his product based on the input he received from them. At that point, his company, Heads and Tails, Inc., was able to place its products in Kmart, Wal-Mart, Hallmark, Toys 'R Us, and a number of gift shops just six months after Loiacono had come up with his product.

Loiacono's success was due partly to the fact that he was willing to change his idea for the buyers—knowing retailers will usually buy once you follow their suggestions. But more important, he understood that the difference between success and failure can often be the personal contacts an inventor has established within a distribution network. Those contacts can and do deliver sales.

mass merchandisers also target in their stores, and they were open to try Kid Soap.

▶ *Major product advantage:* Stores don't like one-product companies because it costs them extra money to do business with them. They much prefer buying from a company with a broader line.

▶ MARKET **REALITY**

Tony Loiacono had something else going for his product. He was offering a high-margin product in a stagnant product category. Stores were already selling soap for kids, bath mats so kids wouldn't slip, and a variety of bath toys and bath towels. But those products weren't changing much, and that leads to price competition. Retailers and distributors love to sell new products in stagnant categories because they can charge a higher price.

But that doesn't mean that they *won't* buy from a one-line company. They certainly are willing to do so if your product offers important benefits to end users. If retailers or distributors resist buying your product and claim it's because you are a one-line company, it's because they don't feel your product stands out enough in the market.

Momentum Makers

▶ *Major customer support:* Most inventors spend their time lining up small end users or retailers to carry their products. I feel this strategy is counterproductive. First, a series of small retailers won't get you anywhere. Second, selling small customers often will discourage a big customer from buying. You are much better off throwing all of your efforts at a major customer. Offer special promotions, exclusive agreements, special sale pricing, or a large co-op advertising program to try and sign the order. That first big order is worth it even if you don't make much money on it because it helps launch your product.

▶ *Industry buzz:* You'll know you've created buzz when everyone is talking about your product. Lots of publicity, big events, or dramatic research results are all ways of creating buzz. Another way to create momentum and buzz around a consumer product is to pass out mail-in rebates to end users. For example, an inventor of a new sports drink might pass out mail-in rebates for $5 for each six pack of sports drink purchased at local stores. The inventor can do this even if stores don't stock the product. The stores will wonder what the product is if people keep coming in and asking for it.

> ▶ **SUCCESS** TIP
>
> One great way to get a business-to-business product started is to host a free informational event. If your product is used to meet a customer goal, you can often set up a daylong seminar with other suppliers who target the same customer. If you're introducing an electronic computer organizer, you might line up three or four other companies to sponsor an event focusing on sales productivity.

▶ *Key alliances:* You might have an alliance with a large distributor or a manufacturers' representative group, or you might share a sales force with another inventor. Other alliances could be with a manufacturer for product testing or with a university professor or other respected researcher.

Before You Start

▶ *Know your customers:* Hopefully, you researched your customers' needs well before introducing your product. But a little extra work before you finalize your product package and marketing materials can pay big dividends. Answer the following questions:

1. Do customers buy your type of product for function or image?
2. Does your product address a major customer concern or desire?
3. What have customers told you is the major reason they will buy your product?

Your package and brochure should first catch customers' interest by highlighting their major concern, and then by stating clearly the major benefit customers feel your product has. If the product is bought for function, the package should be straightforward with lots of information. If the product is purchased for image, the package should be fancy, perhaps show a happy user, and contain a minimum amount of copy.

► MARKET REALITY

I've found that inventors treat packaging lightly—when in fact the package is often the determining factor in whether or not a product sells. Don't design your own package or have it designed by the packaging supplier. Hire a graphic artist or a packaging designer (both can be found in the Yellow Pages). Ask the designer for three or four package layouts, and then ask potential customers which ones they like best.

► *Sales help:* You need to have at least three to four salespeople, including yourself, making the prelaunch contacts you need. You want to hire highly qualified salespeople who have experience in your industry; focus especially on hiring any qualified industry contacts you made as you researched your product. This is not the time to hire a relative or friend. If you can't afford to pay your salespeople, offer stock incentives or big commissions. If you can't get the support you need, scale back your introduction plans.

► *Distribution counts:* The most important part of marketing is always distribution, which includes the sales

MARKET **REALITY**

I've found that nothing is more difficult in marketing than changing the way a sales channel works. Even big companies have trouble changing a channel. You need to learn the protocol of the channel and match your pricing, sales, and distribution policies to the way the channel operates. If you don't learn the rules first, you have an excellent chance of not even getting to first base with a marketable product.

channels you use to get the product from you to the end user. I recommend that inventors lay out every sales channel that takes products from manufacturers to customers. This could include sales to mass merchants, hardware stores, and catalogs. Sales to mass merchandisers can take two or three different channels. One could be directly from the manufacturer to the retailer, one could be through independent manufacturers' sales agents, and one through a distribution network. Learn how each channel works, who the key players are, and which one is most open to small one-line companies. That is the channel you want to use for your introduction.

▶ *Presell customers:* For most products, inventors require two or three months, and sometimes much longer, to visit all of their major potential customers. Those buyers then may take two to three more months each before deciding to buy. Not surprisingly, inventors experience slow introductions if they wait till they have products before they start selling. One of the reasons I chose to highlight Tony Loiacono's Kid Soap story is because he did such a great job preselling the distribution channel. Getting out early and talking about your product launch allows you to pinpoint the buyers most interested in your product; it can even uncover retailers or distributors willing to set up a joint introduction program.

▶ *Inventory needs:* You want to have at least three months of inventory on hand, and you want to be in a position to obtain more inventory quickly. The worst thing that can happen to an inventor is that he or she launches the product, gets immediate sales response, and then can't ship. Your buyers are already a little unsure that you as an inventor will be a reliable supplier, and not being able to ship will prove them right. When you presell, the buyers know you can't ship, but when you launch the product, they expect full product support, including shipments within a week. This is one reason I don't like inventors launching a product at a trade show when they don't have inventory in hand. They lose all their momentum—and many of their customers—when they can't deliver for three to four months.

▶ *Pricing:* As mentioned earlier, you set your end-user price based on a consumer evaluation of your price/value relationship to other products. But you also need to be sure that you are offering discounts to distributors, wholesalers, and retailers that are consistent with the market norms. Make sure to run your proposed pricing and discount structure by some of your industry contacts and have them confirm that it is in line with people's expectations.

First Steps

▶ *Small start—heavy promotion:* Most inventors can't afford to heavily promote their product to the entire market right away. Initially, inventors need to select a market that's small enough for their promotion to have an impact. Inventors start small by only selling to certain types of customers, only selling to a certain geographic area, or only selling to certain types of retailers. One of the purposes of a preselling period is that it allows you to recognize which small market offers you the best chance of a fast start.

▶ *Events and special promotions:* You are investing all of your time, energy, and possibly money into your product—so it must be a big deal to you. Don't slide out in the market and introduce the product like it's not important. Make sure everyone knows about your introduction. You should be willing to put 30 to 40 percent of your first year's projected sales into big promotions or special events—that should get your product established in the market quickly and hopefully set the stage for a successful future. Events can be contests, drawings, seminars, demonstrations, fairs (such as a book fair), classes, open houses, entertainment events at trade shows, or just about any other activity you can think of that draws a crowd.

▶ **SUCCESS** TIP

Events are a very cost-effective marketing tactic, and most retailers, manufacturers, and distributors know that. If you are having trouble getting support in the distribution network, consider offering a jointly sponsored event. Cosponsors, which include two or three other suppliers, often pick up the costs if you are willing to do most of the work. The more sponsors you recruit, the better your event will be.

▶ *Work industry supporters:* You hopefully have made many industry contacts during your pre-introduction period. Now is the time to contact those people, explain that you are introducing your product, and ask them if they have any suggestions for or can offer any assistance in obtaining orders. Also ask if them if they know any buyers that you can approach using their name to get in the door. You won't get their help if you don't ask for it. Also be sure to include your contacts in any of your event plans. Your contacts should be able to assist you in both the presell and introduction periods.

➤ *Every effort counts:* When you launch a new product, you can begin to feel like Sisyphus, eternally pushing a heavy stone up a hill only to have it roll back down. You push and push and push, not feeling as if you are making any progress, but if you keep at it, one day you will make it over the top and sales will pour in. Unfortunately, I don't know where the top of the hill is, but I do know that you will succeed if you keep calling prospects, running events, and offering innovative marketing solutions. You can't afford to run just one or two activities and then stop because sales didn't develop immediately. Many inventors don't succeed until their fifth, sixth, or seventh overture to customers and markets, so keep plugging away. You might think you are failing, but the market probably just wants to see that you have staying power.

Building a Business

➤ *Solidify distribution:* Distribution is the lifeline of every company, so make sure your distribution network is getting the product support it needs. Offer enough sales training, sales materials, and technical support to keep up momentum. I recommend you always have at least one knowledgeable employee available to field calls from distributor salespeople. It is not

➤ MARKET REALITY

Inventors frequently fail to understand the kind of sales and product support that's needed to keep customers. They will sell to a customer, expecting the customer to then keep buying. In reality, the customer expects to be contacted frequently by the supplier: to check that everything is working as expected, to see if they need to reorder, to offer additional promotions or sales training, and to keep tabs on the customer's new product requirements.

unusual for a salesperson to call a supplier to answer one of their customer's questions while the supplier is actually visiting the customer. You'll make the distributor happy, and possibly get the order, if you can provide top-notch sales and technical support.

▶ *Full sales effort:* Even an absolutely fabulous product won't sell without the proper sales and marketing effort. A new company needs to concentrate its resources on bringing salespeople on board to increase sales. One reason I recommend that inventors start production with a contract manufacturer is that they need to devote most of their attention to sales. If you sell directly to retail customers in an area where you don't have sales coverage, ask that customer for a recommendation about which distributors or manufactures' sales agents you should contact. Even though this means you have to pay commissions on orders you could sell direct, in the end a distributor or agent will give the customer the support it needs and pick up additional sales.

Don't keep sales agents, inside or outside salespeople, or distributors who aren't doing the job. Most companies need to hire and fire three agents or sales employees for every one they keep. Poor performers will drag your company down.

▶ *Customers as advisors:* I've found that it pays to have an advisory board composed of both end users and distribution personnel; they can offer suggestions of what a company can do better and what the company could do next to generate more business. These advisors are your customers, and they know what they want better than anyone else. Also don't be afraid to call people up and ask for their advice on a specific

Spurring Your Thoroughbred

One of the reasons you presell a product is to find out early if it will be difficult to sell. Still, even when it appears your product will fly out of the gate, it happens that sales won't take off the way you had hoped. If you are disappointed with your early sales results, start cracking the whip with these tactics.

▶ Talk to more industry people to see if they can help you figure out what's stopping sales and what can be done to turn the situation around. Don't be too proud to tell people that sales are slow and that you need help. More than half of the people I've met have gone way overboard to help a struggling inventor.

▶ Concentrate on a smaller market. Each initial sale takes a great deal of effort for most inventors. If sales haven't developed, try picking only 10 to 20 potential customers to focus on. Better yet, choose prospects that share a specific geographic market or are similar in some other way, such as by type of industry or category of store.

▶ Choose your two best prospects and offer a special promotion, such as co-op advertising or an exclusive sales agreement, or if necessary, guaranteed sales, which means you promise to take the product back if it doesn't sell. You might also offer a retailer an extra large discount for the first three to six months they sell the product.

▶ Switch to another sales channel: If you are unsuccessful selling directly to a distributor, retailer, or end user, ask them if you would have a better opportunity selling through a manufacturers' sales agent or a distributor. If they say yes, be sure to get their recommendation of whom you should approach to sell your product.

question. I personally like to run any new price or promotional strategy by customers, even if just quickly over the phone. I've found that customers are sympathetic to your problems and that they'll offer valuable input if you ask for their advice.

▶ *Meet every customer desire:* Customers and the distribution channel love suppliers who are responsive to their needs. While you can't always meet every customer need, you can take each one seriously. Every time customers express a need or desire, ask them why it's important to them and promise to consider it, asking them if you can get back to them later if you don't have an immediate solution. Obviously, it's best if you can meet their need. The next best course is to suggest an alternative solution. Even if you can't give a positive response, the customer will still appreciate that you didn't just dismiss his or her request.

> ▶ MARKET **REALITY**
>
> Remember that successful products are always customer focused. Inventors often succeed initially because they create a new product that meets the needs of a target customer group. Inventors often fail to realize the reason for their success and think instead that it is due to a nifty product design. These inventors often fail with their next niftily designed product because they lose the focus on customer needs.

▶ *New products:* Your long-term success depends on your ability to help customers better meet their goals and objectives. You can do this with a steady stream of new products, innovative variations of your current products, by private labeling or licensing other inventor products, by forming joint alliances with small manufacturers, or by building special products requested by distributors and end users. Your goal is to become an entrenched part of your customers' world, one they turn to and rely on.

Are You Making Money?

Whether or not you are making money is the most difficult question to answer for most inventors who are running their own company. But your investors, bankers, and partners will consider it the most important one. Cash flow is one of the main problems: You could be making plenty of money, but at the same time you are pouring out tons of cash for more raw materials and finished products while waiting for customer payments to come in. Companies also frequently have high, sometimes very high, sales and marketing expenses and administrative costs when they start to sell a new product. But don't let these problems keep you from checking your profit status, since it is very possible there are profits to be found.

▶ *Start-up expenses check:* You should have the funds in hand to cover a start-up budget that includes the following items.

1. Marketing introduction costs, including new brochures, trade show attendance, special events, new product promotions, sales training aids, special discounts, and any other planned marketing program.

2. Administrative costs, including computer purchases, setting up a phone system, financing or loan fees, setting up payroll and accounting, deposits for rent and utilities, alarm systems, state registration and license fees, product liability insurance, and other costs required to get your product on the market.

3. Manufacturing costs, including initial tooling, fixtures, manufacturing set up, and engineering documentation (the costs of preparing part drawings for

▶ BUZZ WORD

Many distributors and retailers will require you to have product liability insurance before they sell your product. *Product liability insurance* covers you in case your product injures someone in any way. You need this insurance even if you don't think there is any possibility your product could cause an injury. Insurance typically costs 2 to 8 percent of your sales revenue, which you pay up front based on your estimated sales.

vendors, assembly drawings, and final product specifications for quality control).

4. Operating capital, which should cover inventory purchases, labor, salaries, and any other operating costs until the company starts making a profit. Typically, your operating capital should equal to four to six months of sales.

Check to be sure that your start-up costs stay on budget, or else you'll end up spending your operating capital on them. This could spell disaster if it happens too quickly, forcing you to shut down before you make it through your first three months.

▶ *Profit check:* You should develop a net-margin-ratio financial chart that looks like this one:

Revenue	
Sales dollars	100%
Less discounts/allowances	(5)%
Net sales	95%
Costs	
Cost of goods sold	50%
Profit after deducting manufacturing costs	45%
Sales and marketing costs	20%
Includes salaries and commissions	
Administrative costs: Office personnel,	
financing, insurance	15%
Net Margin	10%
Your profit	10%

You need to be sure your month-to-month costs are staying within these boundaries. The biggest problems occur when production yield rates are too low (or scrap rate is too high), and/or when marketing administrative expenses are too high. You need to do a monthly financial statement to show you are on track.

➤ *Cash check:* Inventors typically put all their money in an account and just pay the bills from it. Inventors feel they don't have a problem unless they run out of money in the account. Instead, I feel they need to track it monthly against start-up expenses and operating capital. That way they make sure they are not overspending. Operating capital left on hand should always be greater than the dollar amount from this formula:

Formula	Example
Starting operating capital	$100,000
Less monthly operating budget times	$30,000
times the number of months operating	
(In this example the month's operating	
costs are $7,500 and four months have	
elapsed since product introduction.)	
Less current inventory levels	$10,000
Less current accounts receivables	$25,000
Equals minimum current level	
of operating capital	$35,000

Using this example, if you have less than $35,000 of operating capital left in your account, you are overspending somewhere. You need to find this out quickly so you can adjust your costs.

➤ *Corrective measures:* You need an accountant or bookkeeper who understands your budget and funding to approve your expenditures. Otherwise, I can guarantee you'll overspend. You should be cautious about spend-

 MARKET **REALITY**

Inventors are pie-in-the-sky optimists when it comes to their product's potential. Otherwise they wouldn't be launching their business. That also makes them the worst person to approve spending. It is hard to say no to reasonable spending requests when you are sure the money will soon come rolling in. I know inventor/entrepreneurs hate this, but they do need to give someone who is tightfisted approval rights over each expenditure.

ing every dollar because you can run out of cash quickly. Believe me when I say, you won't be able to generate sales fast enough to overcome overspending at the beginning of your product introduction. This tenuous financial situation is also why I keep emphasizing the importance of the presell period. The net-margin-ratio financial chart listed on page 268 contains general ratios (such as that discounts should average 5 percent) that apply to most companies. However, the *Prentice Hall Book of Business Ratios* (available in most libraries) lists the specific, standard ratios that apply to a wide variety of industries, including, most likely, yours. Use this book to create a more fine-tuned formula for financial health in your industry.

▶ *Cutting costs:* There are three distinct areas where costs can typically be cut.

1. Sales costs. Try to make each salesperson responsible for keeping his or her costs down to 10 percent of the sales he or she is generating. Also, don't run ads that don't produce immediate sales results. Focus on calling on the distribution network and running events that produce sales.

2. Scrap rate is too high. Inventors are usually picky— and rightfully so—about the quality of the products they ship out. However, if the scrap rate is too high, inventors need to evaluate if they are being too picky, or if there is a flaw in the manufacturing process.

3. Administrative costs are out of line. Often, the inventor hires too many office helpers before there is enough income to pay them. The inventor may also be taking out too much salary. Try to hold down these expenses as much as you can. Since it is difficult to fire someone, the best solution is to wait to hire people till you are absolutely sure you can afford them.

Patent Strategies

Acknowledgments

The vast majority of the information in this appendix was provided by Albert W. Davis and Don Flickinger of Phoenix. Al Davis is a retired patent agent who has worked both independently with inventors and as an examiner with the United States Patent Office. Don Flickinger has worked for over 30 years as a patent agent. Both are found in the list of registered patent agents found at www.uspto.gov. At the end of the appendix is a list of invention-related books, with additional resources regarding intellectual property.

Overview

As defined by U.S. law, trademarks, service marks, copyrights, and patents are "intellectual property." In contrast, a car is considered "personal property," and a house and its land are considered "real property." Unlike with real and personal property, there are no criminal penalties for stealing intellectual property.

Infringement Remedies

When a person or a company uses your trademark or service mark on their products or services, makes copies of your copyrighted work, or makes, sells, or uses your patented device or method, the only option to stop them provided by law is to sue them. The cost of a lawsuit is very high, and usually both sides understand this. As such, most businesspeople will settle a lawsuit without going to court if they believe that they will lose in court and if what you are asking them to do is reasonable. Many times, all that you— or your attorney—need to do is to write a letter to the offending party explaining the violation of your intellectual property right. If you are forced to go ahead with a civil suit, you may be able to find investors to fund an infringement case or a patent attorney to take the case on a contingency basis. To receive this funding, you need a strong case and a defendant (the person or company you are suing) with substantial assets.

Patent Law—Key Points

There are two patent laws that bar inventors from receiving patents on their inventions: one is the "on-sale bar," and the other is the "publication of public disclosure bar." These mean you have one year to file your patent application in the U.S. Patent and Trademark Office (USPTO) from the earliest date that you either showed your invention to someone who is not under a confidentiality relationship with you or offered your invention to the public for sale. You start the one-year clock ticking for the on-sale bar if you offer to sell your product in any way, including offering the product on a private label basis, offering your product to a retailer, having your product for sale at a flea market, or offering your product on a Web page. An offer to license or sell the future intellectual property rights in your invention, is not an offer to sell your invention.

You start the one-year clock ticking for the public disclosure bar anytime you show people your idea without a signed confidentiality agreement. This includes if you and the product are mentioned in a news story, if you show the product at a trade show, or if you do consumer market research. A signed confidentiality agreement can protect you from the publication bar, but it won't protect you from the on-sale bar. Filing a provisional or regular utility patent application will protect you from both of these bars. While the patent office won't know if you have violated these two bars, your patent can be challenged after it is issued if you have not patented your product in time. Your patent will be ruled invalid if the challenger can show you did not meet one of these two bars.

Another key point in U.S. patent law is that it is currently a first-to-invent system, which means the broadest claims will be granted to the inventor who can show he or she came up with the idea first. However, there are bills floating around Congress that would change it to a first-to-file system, meaning that the first to apply for a patent, not the first to invent, would get the broadest claim. The USPTO Internet site, www.uspto.gov, has information about the current legislation, as does the *Inventor's Digest* site, www.inventorsdigest.com.

Patent Agents Versus Patent Attorneys

Patent agents and patent attorneys are people who have passed the educational requirements and the examination of the USPTO. They are listed on the USPTO Web site by area of the country, along with their registration number. The higher the registration number, the more recently the agent or attorney was registered, usually indicating that the person has less experience; the number 38,700 was issued in 1994. The difference between the two is that patent agents can only write and prosecute the application (that is, deal with the patent examiner), while patent attorneys can write and prosecute applications and also go to court for you. Because of this, agents are usually less expensive than attorneys.

The advantages of using a patent agent or attorney are that they know how to deal with the examiner and the rules of the USPTO, and they can prepare a much better patent claim than an individual can on his or her own. The disadvantage is that they are both expensive. Also, if you have hired an agent or attorney, the patent examiner can only talk to the patent professional. If you are applying for you own patent, the patent examiner will not only talk to you but also will often offer you advice.

Interviewing an Agent or Attorney

An agent or attorney should give you an interview to see whether you truly need his or her services. The interview should last at least an hour. You need to find out whether the patent professional understands the technology or science of your invention, and you need to get a feel for how well you will work together. If the patent professional is not going to be the one to write your application, then you need to talk to the person who will.

The agent or attorney should also be asking you questions to find out about your situation and capabilities. Such as, Have you run a business? Do you know potential investors? What are your long-term goals? Then the person should be able to present you with several possible patent and protection strategies that *you* can pick from. Even if you have obtained "prior art" (such as an earlier patent or a publication based on your idea), you can take it to the interview and ask the agent or attorney what you could do to work around it. A good agent or attorney will offer you a number of strategies.

Types of Protection

Trademarks

Definition: Names, slogans, phrases, and images can be trademarked. For example, in the fast-food world, McDonald's Fish Filet® is an example of a word trademark, while its golden arches are a trademarked symbol. Burger King has trademarked its phrase "Have it your way."

Requirements: You need a word, phrase, symbol, design, or some combination of those that is distinctive and/or different. For instance, you can't trademark common words like *sky*, but you can trademark unusual spellings, like "Skyy" vodka.

Costs: A thorough search of registered federal and state trademarks costs $395, while the application fee per class—that is, by type of product or type of service—is $325. There are many classes of products and services, and you designate what product or service class your trademark is used with. You can apply for as many classes as you want.

Resources: The Trademark Office is part of the U.S. Patent and Trademark Office (USPTO) and is located in Washington, D.C. You can obtain information about trademarks, as well as the forms for filing, by calling them at 800-PTO-9199 or 703-308-9000; or log on to their Internet site at www.uspto.gov. The site has a FAQ (frequently asked questions) section that can usually answer your questions, or do the search at your local library, which can help you if you have trouble finding what you need.

Advantages/Disadvantages: The main advantages are that the trademark application is easy to file by yourself, and the trademark lasts for as long as the product or service is being offered by you. Because only you can use the trademark, others cannot label their products with similar trademarks. The main disadvantage is that if your application is rejected by the examiner, you may have to change your trademark or go to a trademark attorney for help. Before going to an attorney, first ask the examiner for help in solving the rejection; most examiners are very helpful. Usually your trademark only has value to you if you are able to create a trademark that is well known.

Search: A thorough trademark search should be obtained from a company that specializes in them and whose computer database covers federal, state, and common law trademarks. Thompson and Thompson of Boston, Massachusetts, is the leading trademark search firm. It charges $395 for a search and can be reached at 800-692-8833. You can also do the search yourself on the Internet at the USPTO Web site, and libraries will sometimes have books listing registered trademarks by class. These are not thorough searches, however, and you shouldn't invest heavily in establishing your trademark with customers until you've done one.

Marking: Place TM after your trademark and SM after your service mark. A trademark is used for a company name or product, and a service mark is used for a service feature. For example, an industrial design firm might use a service mark for MM$LOOK, a service that creates an innovative look for consumer products. After your trademark or service mark is registered by the USPTO, you use an ®.

Copyrights

Definition: Writings and other visual works can be copyrighted. Those works include instructions, sales literature, drawings, catalogs, directories, computer programs, books, pamphlets, photographs, and so on. You can also copyright the works that you create to sell your product or service, such as brochures or ads. You should copyright your works as soon as the final version has been decided on.

Requirements: The written or other visual work must be original.

Costs: A registered copyright costs $30 per work.

Resources: The Copyright Office is part of the Library of Congress and is located in Washington, D.C. You can obtain information and filing forms by calling 202-707-3000 or 202-707-9100 (forms only), or log on to www.loc.gov/copyright. Another copyright Web site is www.lcweb.loc.gov/copy right.

Advantages/Disadvantages: Copyrights are easy to file yourself, and no search is needed. The copyright lasts the life of the author plus 50 years. The main disadvantage is that your copyright only protects the form of your work and not the ideas contained in it.

Marking: Always mark your work. Place the mark or notice at the bottom of each page or at the end of the work. The following form should be used if you have not registered your copyright: "Copyright 2000 by Joe Jones. All rights reserved." You are not required to register your copyright at the Copyright Office, so this is all you need to do to have a valid copyright. If you have registered your product, mark it with a © followed by your name or your company name and the year it was registered.

Utility Patents

Definition: Utility patents cover new methods of doing something, new devices for doing something, and new chemical compositions. A method of advertising, a method of washing clothes, and a method of making a product can be patented—as can a device that holds advertising, a device that washes clothes, a machine for making a product, and equipment for producing a paint remover. Specific formulas can also be patented, such as a soft cookie mix or a headache medicine.

Costs: To start, there is a $345 filing fee for filing a Small Entity Statement at the USPTO. It will cost $2,000 or more for the drawings and the writing of the application by a patent agent or attorney registered to practice before the USPTO, and your patent attorney will charge $1,000 for each response you need to make to the patent office if (but more likely when) they dispute your claims (count on at least one response). There is a $605 USPTO issue fee when your patent is finally awarded, and your agent or attorney will charge another $1,000 to prepare the application for issue once it is awarded. In addition, you have to pay patent fees to keep your patent valid: a $415 USPTO maintenance fee at 3.5 years, $950 at 7.5 years, $1,455 at 11.5 years

Requirements: The invention must be novel (new) and unobvious (a new combination that a person skilled in the field would not have thought of). For example, a Post-It note has an adhesive that sticks to the note and not to the paper it is placed on. The paper for the Post-It note is specially designed to do this, and that paper formula would be nonobvious because that feature had never been seen before. However, if someone today invented a menu pad with the same type of paper that sticks to a refrigerator, it would be considered obvious based on the previous invention of the Post-It note.

Resources: The Patent Office is part of the USPTO and is located in Washington, D.C. You can obtain information and filing forms by calling 800-PTO-9199 or 703-308-HELP (a 24-hour help line); or log on to www.uspto.gov. The FAQ section at the site will answer many of your questions.

Advantages/Disadvantages: The main advantage is that you have an intellectual property right that can be enforced—if the claims are broad enough (see "Patent Claims," page 282–84)—to stop your competitors from copying your method or device and which can be licensed or sold to others. Many companies that license products require you to have a utility patent. A patent also offers benefits in the marketplace, as people in the distribution channel and end users tend to perceive patented products as having more value. Some disadvantages are that a patent may not prevent competition, it is expensive, and there is no one to enforce a patent except the patent holder. Stealing an idea is a subject for civil courts and not criminal prosecution.

Search: A "search" means looking at patents, magazines, product brochures, newspapers, and any written publication for information about what has already been thought of in the area or field of your invention. When these written publications are found, they are called the "prior art." Prior art can be in a foreign language, and it doesn't have to be found in

278 - THINK BIG

the United States or be easily available. Anything that is found may preclude getting a patent, and there is no differing level of importance among types of prior art; a magazine article can be just as meaningful as a prior patent. Any search that you do or that you hire others to do is called a preliminary search (the "final" search is done by the patent examiner). A preliminary search can be done on the Internet of U.S. patents from 1976 to the present. Search firms in Washington, D.C. can search all of the U.S. patents and some foreign patents (but they usually search very few foreign ones). If you hire a private searcher, you should have the searcher sign a confidentiality agreement. Inventors should know that prior art that is searched will be less than half of the worldwide prior art, and that the U.S. patent examiner will see less than half of the worldwide prior art. That means that any patent issued by the USPTO may be found invalid later if better prior art is found, or if a company looking to copy your product can find previously unfound prior art.

You can do an Internet search at your public library for free. A search done by a private Washington, D.C., search firm is $300 to $400. A search conducted by a patent agent or attorney typically costs a minimum of $500.

Marking: Patented products, and all accompanying literature, need to be clearly marked with the patent number. If a patent hasn't been issued, products and their literature need to be marked "patent pending."

Design Patents

Definition: The design of an object—its shape or ornamental look—can be patented. Some examples are a car fender, a soap holder, and a computer housing, such as the design of Apple's new iMac computer.

Costs: The USPTO application filing fee is $155, and a patent agent or attorney will charge $1,000 plus $70 per sheet of drawings to write an application. It will also cost you $1,000 for each response your attorney needs to make to the patent office. USPTO issuance fees are $215, and your agent or attorney will charge about $150 to prepare the application for issue.

Requirements: The design must be different from what has previously been done (as established by prior art). This can be a very arbitrary decision, but almost all design patents are approved.

Resources: See "Utility Patents" above for information.

Advantages/Disadvantages: The main advantage is that you now have an intellectual property right that you can enforce, license, or sell. You can place "patent pending" on the product as soon as your application is accepted, and you no longer need to have confidentiality agreements signed. The main disadvantage is that any minor changes in what is shown in the drawings of your patent may be enough to allow the competition to design around your patent monopoly.

Search: Preliminary searches are generally not done for design patents.

Marking: See "Utility Patents" above for information.

Provisional Patents

Definition: The "provisional application" is a new tool that has been provided to protect inventions. It is an application that is never examined, meaning that no one reads it, and it allows you one year to submit a regular utility patent. The provisional patent was originally created to protect U.S. inventors' foreign patent rights. U.S. patent law gives an inventor one year to apply for a patent after you start selling your idea, while foreign patent law requires that you obtain a patent before any sales efforts or any publicity is released.

Costs: Filing a Small Entity Statement costs $75, and if you have an agent or attorney prepare the patent, it's an additional $1,000 and up.

Requirements: The application must explain in words and drawings everything about your invention. Photographs can be photocopied onto paper and included; however, a drawing of what is shown in the photograph should be provided. The application must be submitted on 8½-by-11-inch paper only. You must explain your invention so completely that someone can make your invention without asking you any questions (which is called a "reduction to practice"). The application will be examined when you submit your official utility patent to make sure they are the same, and then the filing date of the provisional application will be used if there is a future patent dispute or if the patent office needs to decide who to give a patent to when two similar patents have been filed.

Resources: See "Utility Patents" above for a list of resources. The book *Patent It Yourself* by David Pressman (Nolo Press) is very helpful if you want to prepare your own application. See especially the section on "Drafting the Specification."

Advantages/Disadvantages: One main advantage is that you can do the provisional application yourself, and it is a very low cost alternative to a regular application. It is considered a reduction to practice because, similar to making a prototype, you have proven the invention will work; you no longer need to use confidentiality agreements; and you can place "patent pending" on the product or method. It is a useful tool even if you never intend to apply for a utility patent, as it offers patent pending status for one year, and this should allow you enough time to evaluate the commercial potential of your invention. The main disadvantage is that you are required to file a utility patent application within 12 months or forfeit your ability to patent the idea. That means that you have to go to a patent agent or attorney within nine months of filing your provisional patent, since creating the regular application will take three months. You must also file for foreign patents within 12 months.

Marking: Once you file a U.S. patent application (provisional or regular), you can mark your invention and its literature with the notice "patent pending" or "pat pend."

Other Tactics

Confidentiality Agreements and Nondisclosure Statements

Definition: This agreement goes by many names, but it is an agreement between you and another party (or person) not to disclose to a third party what you have shown them concerning your invention.

Costs: Free.

Requirements: Some type of signed written statement where the person receiving confidential information agrees not to disclose the information to others.

Resources: You can get copies of confidential agreement forms in many of the books listed in "Recommended Books" below. Most books of legal forms include a sample confidential statement.

Advantages/Disadvantages: The main advantage is that a confidentiality agreement makes the information you share with the other party a nonpublic disclosure under U.S. patent law, which in many cases protects your patent rights. Using such an agreement shows a very careful and businesslike approach to your dealings. The biggest disadvantage is that the agreement can't be enforced against a third party who learns from the signing party of your idea. Further, enforcement of the agreement against the signing party requires the filing of a lawsuit. Many of the people you will want to talk to concerning the commercial potential of your invention will not want to sign such an agreement. The use of these agreements can slow the process of finding out whether your invention is worth pursuing.

Inventor's Notebook

Definition: This is simply any kind of bound notebook—preferably one with numbered pages. If the pages are not numbered, number them yourself; this is done to show that no new pages were inserted at a later date. The engineering notebooks or accountants' ledgers sold in office supply stores are ideal.

Cost: Around $10 to $20.

Requirements: This should contain evidence of your activity—everything that you do should be entered into the notebook, in sequence, and dated. This includes drawings, ideas that you consider, and discussions with vendors and customers, along with the date and time of each event and notes on whether the interaction was in person or on the telephone. It should have a dated signature of one and preferably two people on each page with the notation, "The above material is confidential, and I have read and understood this page." Note: Have witnesses sign the book at least every week.

Resources: Virtually all of the books listed under "Recommended Books" contain sections on filling out and using an inventor's notebook.

Advantages/Disadvantages: The main advantage is that it documents your invention's progress and can be useful with potential partners and investors. It can also be useful in case you need to demonstrate the date that you first conceived your invention and to show that the idea is indeed yours and that you didn't take it from someone else. The notebook can be easily kept up to date. You need only find one or two witnesses who can understand your invention. The disadvantages? The witnesses must not have a monetary interest in your invention, should not be close relatives, your patent agent or attorney, or people who have a working relationship with you on your invention. You must find people whom you can trust to keep your invention confidential.

Document Disclosure Program

Definition: The "disclosure document" is an explanation by you of what your invention is, what it is used for, and how to make it. A disclosure document is an official form of the USPTO, and it is kept on file at the USPTO for two years after you send it in.

Costs: $20.00.

Requirements: The document must explain in words and drawings everything about your invention. Photographs can be photocopied onto paper and included; however, a drawing of what is shown in the photograph should be provided. The document must be submitted on 8½-by-11-inch paper only. You must explain your invention so completely that someone can make your invention without asking you any questions (reduce it to practice).

Resources: See "Utility Patent" above for patent office information, or see any of the books listed at the end of the appendix.

Advantages/Disadvantages: The main advantage is that the document is proof of your invention just like your inventor's notebook. The document does not need witnesses, since the USPTO is the witness. The document provides an inexpensive solution when you are having trouble finding suitable witnesses for you inventor's notebook. The main disadvantage is that the document, just like the notebook, does not give you an intellectual property right. Unlike the provisional patent, you can't mark your product "patent pending," and it offers no foreign patent protection. The document does not stop the one-year publication and on-sale bars. The document will be thrown away in two years if you have not filed a utility patent application and requested in a separate letter that the document be made part of the application.

Patent Claims

The type of patent strategy you pursue is dependent on how much money you have, how you plan on selling your product, and on how well your patent will stop competition. Understanding the value of the different types of claims you can obtain is the important first step in determining your strategy.

A regular patent application must have at least one claim. A claim is your chance to say what you want others to be prohibited from making, using, or doing. A valuable patent has a broad claim, which means that it prohibits a wide variety of competitors. The patent office resists claims that are too broad, and your goal is to present the broadest claim possible that the patent office will accept. For example, if your invention is a device that prevents eyeglasses from sinking to the bottom of a pool, you could submit any of these three claims for the device:

Claim 1: A device for preventing eyeglasses from sinking to the bottom of a pool, said eyeglasses having a frame formed from a front and two temples, the device comprising a donutlike tube filled with air and said tube fitting around the temple.

Claim 2: In combination with a pair of eyeglasses having a frame formed by a front and two temples, a device for preventing the eyeglasses from sinking to the bottom of a pool, comprising a bladder filled with air and means associated with the bladder to attach said bladder to the eyeglass frame.

Claim 3: A method of preventing eyeglasses from sinking to the bottom of a pool, said eyeglasses having a frame, the method comprising trapping air in a substance and attaching the substance to said frame.

Your broadest claim is what protects you from competitors (your monopoly). Your competitors infringe on your claims if they make every element of the claim, do every step of the method of your claim, or enable others to infringe on your claim. In claim 1, your competitor could design around the claim by making the tube like a hot dog instead of a donut. Claim 1 can be easily circumvented by a competitor. However, claim 2 would be infringed on by the hot dog-shaped tube, since a bladder does not suggest any particular shape. Claim 2 is broader and better than claim 1. If your competitor thinks hard enough, they might come up with the idea of using a foam material that traps air in very small pockets, which they could argue is different than a bladder. Thus, the foam device would probably not infringe claims 1 or 2. Claim 3 is the broadest claim, as it covers any type of device that traps air. A foam material would read on (and infringe on) claim 3. Claims 2 and 3 are limited to the field of eyeglasses. However, under current U.S. patent law, claim 1 is too broad, as it could be considered as claiming any donut tube filled with air—which could apply to pool toys (with an inner tube shape) of much larger size. Of the three, claims 2 and 3 are the best. Of the two claims; claim 3 is very good, getting the best (or broadest) coverage, and the wording will get your application classified in the proper class and subclass and examined by the proper examiner.

Examiners will limit the scope of your claim based upon prior art. Prior art is technically any publication from anywhere in the world and in any language, but in reality the patent examiners work primarily from past patents. The examiner and you (or your agent or attorney) will be negotiating about how broad your claim will be. This negotiation is called the "prosecution of the application." You offer a claim, and the examiner rejects the claim if he or she does not think that the claim is different enough from the prior art. The fewer close references that the examiner finds, the better your chances to be granted a broad patent. When close prior art exists, the examiner will want you to spell out your claim with greater specificity as to your invention's design. Specificity is a sign of a weak patent claim because it is easier for a competitor to make a competing product by just avoiding one specific design criteria in your claim. Don't decide on your own how broad a claim your invention may be awarded. Take the results of a patent search to a patent agent or attorney and get his or her advice on how significant the claims you can file for will be.

Patent Strategies

Don't Bother

Explanation: If you don't need a patent to sell a product, you might want to avoid the expense if you are selling to a small market or if your invention can't support a broad patent claim.

Cost: Nothing.

Advantages/Disadvantages: Basically, it costs nothing to do nothing, but you can't prevent competitors. Products without patents are also much more difficult to license.

Patent Pending Strategy

Explanation: Once you have applied for a provisional, utility, or design patent, you can place "patent pending" on your product. The patent pending notice will scare away most companies from copying your invention. One way to use this strategy is to apply for a low-cost design patent or a provisional patent without any intention of filing a final patent. On short-term promotional items, or fad items with a short life span, the patent pending status might be all the protection an inventor needs.

Inventors will also use a patent pending strategy if it becomes evident that they cannot get a broad claim. They use a continuation-in-part (CIP) application, which is an application that changes the broadest claims of your original application and adds new developments in your invention, to keep patent pending on your product as long as possible. The patent office has to reexamine your patent every time you submit a CIP application, which can take six months to a year. This strategy can keep patent pending status for several years. You just need to be sure to file the CIP application before the USPTO declares your previous patent abandoned. Patents are typically considered abandoned if someone takes more than six months to respond to a letter sent by the examiner, or in the case of a final rejection, your response does not remove the rejection and you do not appeal the rejection to the Board of Appeals. To keep your patent pending status alive using a CIP, you only need to change your broadest claim by dropping one feature and adding a new feature.

Cost: Expenses range from $100 to $5,000, depending on if you file a provisional, design, or utility patent, if you file the patents yourself, or if you file through an attorney.

Advantages/Disadvantages: There are a number of advantages: Many competitors will not try to introduce a competitive product to one that is patent pending. Patent pending status is a better negotiating tool while getting a license, as the company won't initially know what your claims are. Patent pending status is almost as useful as an awarded patent when introducing a new product, and patent pending status can last for as long as 20 years if you keep changing your product's design. The main disadvantage: It doesn't provide any real protection for your product.

286 ← THINK BIG

Low-Quality Patents

Explanation: Design patents and utility patents with narrow claims don't offer significant barriers to competitors, but they still have a deterrent value for some competitors, still offer a marketing advantage, and still help inventors license their ideas. Since the patent will have limited real protection, inventors can save money by patenting the product themselves. *Patent It Yourself* by David Pressmen (Nolo Press) is an excellent resource for this (see "Recommended Books" on page 288). One thing that makes filing your own application easier is that the examiner almost always will help answer your questions about how to take care of the problems that he or she finds in your application. You can also proceed with a patent attorney.

Costs: From $500 to $5,000, depending on if you file a design or utility patent, if you file the patents yourself, or if you file through an attorney.

Advantages/Disadvantages: A low-quality patent allows you to have the marketing and psychological advantages of having a patent, but it doesn't offer significant intellectual property barriers to competition.

Broad Patent with Few Specifics or Limitations

Explanation: A utility patent with a broad claim is worthwhile, and you should use a patent agent or attorney to file the application for you. This claim will help prevent competition and leave you in the best position possible to license your idea.

Costs: As outlined in the "Utility Patents" section above, $5,000 to $15,000.

Advantages/Disadvantages: A broad patent offers strong protection from competitors and offers inventors a better chance of landing a licensing arrangement. The disadvantages are mainly monetary. As you proceed with the patent process, you may have numerous objections and rejections from the USPTO. It can easily cost $1,000 to $2,000 for each response to the patent office. You can end up spending well over $20,000—and in the end your final claim might be much more narrow than you expected, giving you nothing like the protection you had hoped for.

Many Weak Claims

Explanation: Sometimes inventions have close prior art that limits the scope of a patent. However, that prior art may not compete with the inventor's product, nor may it diminish the novelty of the product to the marketplace. One solution to this problem is to file as many specific claims as possible in an effort to tie up every possible design. When done correctly, this tactic, in effect, gives the product a broad patent. This will require the filing of many applications and the costly prosecution of each application to issue.

Costs: Expenses are hard to calculate, but from $25,000 and up.

Advantages/Disadvantages: This strategy can provide broad patent coverage for items unique to the market that have narrow patent claims due to prior art. A large number of patents discourages competitors and also provides a perceived edge in marketing the product. The disadvantage, again, is that it is an expensive process, as the attorney fees will climb rapidly when you add a large number of additional claims. There is also the possibility that someone will think of a unanticipated way to make the product that avoids infringing on all the listed claims.

Foreign Patents

Filing for a U.S. patent only protects you in the United States. To protect yourself elsewhere, you have to file foreign patent applications. The "patent cooperation treaty" (PCT) application can be used to file your invention in foreign countries that have signed the treaty.

The costs include $1,900 in PCT fees and $3,300 or more in patent agent or attorney fees to make and file the application. You may also need to pay $1,600 or more to rewrite a U.S. application into PCT form. In addition, you'll pay hundreds of dollars in yearly fees to each country that your application is filed in. The total cost will be at least $100,000 over the lives of your patents, assuming that you file in the richest countries.

The advantage of the PCT application is that you can file the same patent application in many countries. The disadvantage is that your patent rights can be 10 times more expensive than filing only in the United States. The total expense can be over $100,000 if you patent your product in the major countries of Europe and Japan. The violators of your patent rights will be more expensive to find. And the patent system and the courts that enforce the laws in foreign countries may favor their own citizens and companies over U.S. inventors.

Ultimately, I don't think inventors should ever bother with foreign patents unless they have a plan and the resources to market overseas. You would need to anticipate selling $5 million or more per year in a foreign country to make a foreign patent worthwhile.

Recommended Books

Elias, Stephen. *Patent, Copyright and Trademark*. Berkeley, CA: NOLO Press, 1999.

Fishman, Stephen. *The Copyright Handbook*. Berkeley, CA: NOLO Press, 1999.

Hitchcock, David. *Patent Searching Made Easy*. Berkeley, CA: NOLO Press, 2000.

McGrath, Kate, and Stephen Elias with Sarah Shena. *Trademark: Legal Care for Your Business & Product Name*. Berkeley, CA: NOLO Press, 1999.

Pressman, David. *Patent It Yourself*. 7th ed. Berkeley, CA: NOLO Press, 1999.

Stim, Richard. *License Your Invention*. Berkeley, CA: NOLO Press, 1999.

B

Prototyping for Inventors

Acknowledgments

This appendix has been prepared by Jack Lander, a prototyper for inventors and new product developers. He serves as an officer in three non-profit inventor organizations, writes a column on prototyping for *Inventors' Digest* magazine, and is a product development expert for Entrepreneur.com. You can reach Lander at 37 Seneca Road, Danbury, CT 06811; telephone 203-797-8955; fax 203-792-1377; or log on to www.inventorhelp.com.

Overview

Prototypes usually go through several stages of development, starting with a relatively crude "concept" model and hopefully finishing with a model that "looks like, works like" the eventual product. To aim for a prototype that approximates the final product, you need to select prototyping processes that imitate the volume-production materials and processes that will be used when the product is in full production. Much of this selection is common sense. Mass-produced products and product components today are made primarily in three ways: you can injection mold them out of plastic, stamp them from steel, or die cast them from a zinc alloy.

Prototypers are often specialists in certain processes, and you may need more than one source in order to complete your prototype. Also, there is usually more than one way to imitate any volume-production process, and you can often reduce your costs dramatically by knowing a bit about the options. For example, if the main component of your final product will be an injection-molded plastic part, you can imitate this in your prototype in several ways: by machining the component from solid plastic; by fabricating it by gluing together several pieces of plastic; by casting it from a two-part resin in a silicone rubber mold; or by using the "additive manufacturing" processes of SL (stereolithography) or SLS (selective laser sintering). Each has its place, its cost structure, and its characteristic time from start to completion. The process that is perfect for a corporation may be way too expensive for the average inventor, who is willing to wait a week or two for his or her parts in exchange for a low price.

This appendix covers the main options for imitating volume-produced parts. Some of these processes you can accomplish yourself. Others require enormously expensive machines and are only practical through job shops. In any event, it will pay to have a working knowledge of these processes to obtain the best prototype possible for the money. Page 301 lists "Resources" section listing the phone numbers and addresses of the suppliers and vendors that are mentioned.

Concept Models

A concept model typically shows only what a product will eventually look like. It helps investors, potential partners, and the people you contact for market research to get a better idea of your product's appearance. So-called "appearance models" are concept models that simulate the look of the final product, and they are used for initial brochures, publicity releases, and trade shows when the final product is not ready. It also helps the inventor get a sense of the proportion and style of the final product.

Using Balsa Wood

Description: This makes for an "odds-and-ends" prototype that is a do-it-yourself project. It uses tools and material found in the home workshop or readily available from hardware stores, craft supply shops, building supply "supermarkets," and auto supply stores. Balsa wood is perfect for products that have curves.

Products used for: Any.

Cost range: Free to $25 for most.

Resources: Local hobby shops and craft suppliers have useful publications that will guide you in a wide range of table-top processes for cutting and working with balsa wood.

Making your prototype: However crude, making a prototype out of balsa wood and other found materials is often useful as a concept model. Because such a prototype is fast to make and inexpensive, you can remake it several times until it looks and feels right.

Using Hobby Shop Products

Description: You can make concept models yourself using the foam, plastic, wood, glue, and metal parts found at most hobby shops.

Products used for: Any.

Cost range: Free to $25 for most.

Resources: Local hobby shops and craft suppliers have both materials and how-to books.

Making your prototype: One of the easiest materials to work with in making large items is foam board. This sign-making and self-supporting board consists of front and back surfaces of white cardboard laminated to a core of Styrofoam. It is approximately a quarter-inch thick and can be cut using a hobby knife or a jigsaw. Foam can also be easily curved. Start by making closely spaced parallel lines using a ballpoint pen or a dull butter knife on the inside of the part you want curved. Then curve the piece, and it will hold its new shape. You can join pieces of foam with a glue gun or one of the special glues (sold at craft supply stores) made for Styrofoam.

For thick sections, plain Styrofoam is sold at craft shops in a wide variety of shapes. If you intend to photograph the finished item, balsa wood, also available in thick pieces as well as thin, can be sanded and painted. Balsa wood's main advantage over pine or poplar is that it is very easy to carve. However, it is generally too soft for functional prototypes, which are best made from maple if strength is needed. Maple has a fine grain, and it can be sanded and painted for a near-perfect surface.

Bondo, which is a plastic filler used in automobile body repair work, can be added to wood, plastic, foam board, and so on to produce compound curves and fillets, as well as to fill joints. A compound curve is a secondary or more complicated curve than you can make with just a piece of foam or wood. For example, if you have a curved computer monitor with a small half moon on the top, that half moon is a compound curve that you could produce with Bondo. A fillet is a part that fits between two curved parts. For example, a fillet would be a one-inch flat molding in between two curved surfaces. Apply Bondo in layers no more that an eighth-inch thick to minimize cracking and shrinking. Bondo begins to harden in a matter of minutes, so be cautious about mixing too much or adding too much hardener, which affects its cure time. Bondo can be sawed, sanded, and painted for outstanding effects.

Sculpy is a ceramic imitation that can be "fired" in your kitchen oven. It can be molded into almost any shape, like modeling clay. It is available from craft stores.

"Looks Like, Works Like" Prototypes

Appearance and concept models are not functional. In fact, they will often fall apart if handled too hard. "Looks like, works like" prototype parts are not only functional but they look like the final product. The inventor uses them for market research with customers and for functional tests to see if the product will really work. They typically are not as strong as the final product, but they will last long enough for some product testing.

Using Stock Plastics

Description: This covers cutting and gluing together stock plastic shapes—such as sheets, tubes, and round and rectangular bars—using standard consumer hand and power tools.

Products used for: Many parts that will be plastic injection molded in production can be assembled from stock plastics shapes.

Cost range: $10 to $100.

Resources: National plastics suppliers such as AIN, Cadillac Plastics, and McMaster-Carr Supply Co. Smaller suppliers as well as plastic fabrication shops may be found locally.

Making your prototype: Stock plastics are readily available in a wide range of sizes: stock sheets of various thicknesses, bars and tubing of various diameters, and rectangular stock of various lengths and widths. These plastics can be divided into two main groups: commercial plastics and engineering plastics. The engineering plastics, such as nylon, Delrin, and polycarbonate, are so-called because they are not commonly used in high-volume consumer items due to their cost, and they have combined properties of strength, impact resistance, and resistance to chemicals that the less-expensive commercial plastics lack.

For prototyping, the main consideration, rather than cost, may be whether a plastic can be glued and successfully painted. Many common plastics are impossible to glue using off-the-shelf adhesives, and those that cannot be glued do not have acceptable paint adhesion either. The common plastics that are difficult to glue are nylon, Delrin (acetal), polyethylene, and polypropylene. Common plastics that are easily glued include acrylic, high-impact polystyrene, ABS, PVC (vinyl), and polycarbonate. Acrylic and polycarbonate are transparent; the others are opaque. Acrylic is brittle, but polycarbonate can be distorted or dropped without cracking. Acrylic is available in a scratch-resistant type. Polycarbonate, used for bulletproof windows, is more susceptible to scratching.

PVC and ABS are easy to machine using ordinary home workshop tools, including a table saw and router. If in doubt about which plastic to use for your prototype, start with PVC for opaque work and polycarbonate for transparent work. Glues for PVC and ABS are found at building suppliers and good hardware stores, or they may be ordered from plastics suppliers.

Using Stock Metals

Description: Applications include cutting a profile shape in sheet metal or bar stock, and optionally bending and/or joining to other parts by welding or screwing.

Products used for: Any part that imitates a punch press stamping or sheet metal fabrication.

Cost range: $100 to $500 for several pieces.

Resources: Job shops listed in the Yellow Pages under "Sheet Metal Fabricators," "EDM" (electrical discharge machining), "Laser Cutting," "Water Jet Cutting," and "Chemical Milling."

Making your prototype: Sheet metal fabricators are of two distinct types: those that make heating and air-conditioning ductwork and so on, and those that do precision work, which is nearly always what the inventor is seeking. Precision sheet metal fabricators cut shapes in sheet metal first by shearing from a large sheet, and then by stamping using a variety of steel in thicknesses from about .022 to about .1 inch. Less popular thicknesses are also available, and materials can be special ordered. Bending is done on a press brake. Drawing of metal, such as a bowl shape, is not a conventional process in most sheet metal shops, and must be prototyped by spinning. (Spinning vendors are found in the *Thomas Register of American Manufacturers*.)

Small parts that will be stamped when in volume production can be profiled using wire EDM, laser cutting, or water jet cutting. A wire EDM machine works something like a band saw, except the "blade" is a wire. The process is electrical, and it is essentially the opposite of welding. The metal being cut is deposited on the wire. The machine is computer driven, and, except for threading the wire through internal holes or other closed cutouts within the periphery of the part, it is automatic.

Laser cutting is accomplished by using a computer-driven intense laser beam that cuts the profile and any internal cutouts automatically. Parts may be cut in stock up to about a quarter of an inch. For thicker stock, abrasive water jet is typically more economical.

Abrasive water jet cutting is done by a computer-driven machine that jets a needle-thin stream of water containing a very hard grit at pressures up to 60,000 psi. This process can cut metal up to about eight inches thick. Precision is lost as the thickness increases. Plastics, including foam, can be cut by water jets without the abrasive grit. EDM, laser, and water jet cutting require a computer program that is developed from your mechanical drawing. CAD drawings can be inexpensively amended for this purpose.

Chemical milling (or chemical machining) is a photographic process that is generally used for relatively thin parts. A drawing is made of your part and then reproduced several times on a photographic negative by the "step and repeat process." A sheet of metal up to 24 inches long and up to about a 16th of an inch thick is coated with a photographic emulsion and exposed through the negative. It is then developed to expose the unwanted metal, which is etched away by a chemical spray. Blanks produced by any of the above processes can be bent to form parts that look convincingly as though they were produced by a punch press.

The cost of each of these processes varies according to the characteristics of your part, the kind of machinery a specific vendor uses, and how receptive the vendor is to working with a small job presented by an inventor. The only sure way to obtain the lowest cost is to submit a good mechanical drawing and request pricing from several vendors, perhaps two of each type of process for best results.

Many vendors of these processes also provide welding, usually TIG (tungsten inert gas) or MIG (metal inert gas) welding, either of which is much neater in appearance than "stick" welding. Parts that are around a 16th of an inch or thinner can be spot welded. Aluminum spot welding requires special machines that are not commonly found in sheet metal shops, but you can find them by calling shops listed under "Welding" in the Yellow Pages.

Machining Stock Plastics and Metals

Description: This involves removing material with cutting tools such as a drill press, lathe, and milling machine. Machining is purchased as a service from a prototyper or small machine shop.

Products used for: Any that are made from plastic or metal; usually for prototype parts that will be injection molded or die cast when in volume production.

Cost range: $50 to $1,000.

Resources: Prototypers and small machine shops found in the Yellow Pages, or in *Inventor's Digest* classified ads, and by referrals from fellow inventors met through networking.

Making your prototype: A lathe is something like a drill press turned on its side, except that the workpiece (the part being machined) is held in the chuck, rather than the cutting tool. Lathes create cylindrical shapes.

A milling machine—more precisely, a vertical milling machine—again resembles an upright drill press. The cutting tool, usually an end mill, resembles a drill, except it has a flat or round tip, and its edges are razor sharp. The workpiece is held in a vise, or clamped directly to the mill table, and is moved against the revolving cutting tool. Movement of the mill table is in any of three axes: X, Y, and Z, which are left to right, front to back, and up and down respectively. Manually operated milling machines produce rectangular shapes, although CNC (computer numerically controlled) milling machines can produce nearly any profile that can be drawn using a computer.

Lathes and milling machines are mainly used to machine metals, but they are also used for machining plastics. The best machining plastic is Delrin, though PVC, ABS, and nylon machine well. Polycarbonate, while easy to machine, does not produce a beautiful finish like the other plastics. And acrylic is touchy. When drilling any plastic, there is always the danger of the drill grabbing the plastic—which spoils the work and can injure the machinist—but acrylic takes first prize in this respect. Brass and copper are even more dangerous to drill. Never, never drill acrylic, brass, or copper without clamping it securely to the drill press table. Drilling any of these with a hand-held power drill is also dangerous, even when the workpiece (the part being machined) is held in a vise. The drill may be grabbed from your hand as the drill bit breaks through the far side. Experienced machinists can regrind drills to take the spiral edge off and thereby prevent the grabbing.

Prototypers usually have their own preferred suppliers, but small machine shops may work nearly entirely in metals and may not have convenient sources for plastics. You will usually be able to save money by hunting down the plastic stock yourself, in which case you are entitled to receive the unused portion back from the prototyper.

Casting Plastics at Room Temperature

Description: A two-component resin, similar to epoxy, is mixed and poured into a silicone rubber mold. The reusable mold is made from two liquid silicone components that are mixed and poured over a master pattern. The process can be learned for home shop production. A good source of information for this tactic is the *Model Makers Handbook* by Albert Jackson and David Day (Alfred Knopf). Another source is Castolite, Inc., a manufacturer of many prototype molding compounds; write to them at PO Box 391, Woodstock, IL 60098.

Products used for: This works for any parts that are made from plastic, but usually parts that will be injection molded when in volume production and are smaller than a grapefruit.

Cost range: $50 to $150 if you do it yourself.

Resources: Polytek Development Corporation's catalog. Vendors that cast parts are those that provide SL and SLS services.

Making your prototype: This process starts with a model of the part you intend to cast. This model can be made from metal, plastic, wood, or even Ivory soap if the part is not delicate. Molds are made in two steps. The model is suspended by a string half an inch above the bottom of a small container, such as a plastic refrigerator container, and a two-part mix of silicone rubber (which becomes the mold) is poured halfway up the model. This is allowed to cure overnight, and it becomes the first half of the mold. Then, a mold release (Vaseline is excellent) is applied to the exposed top rubber surface to prevent the next pour from adhering. (Silicone won't stick to anything except itself.) The model is then turned over and suspended over a container into a two-part mix of silicone rubber that just touches the first part of the mold. When the second pour is cured, the mold is removed from the container; the model is removed from the mold by splitting the mold where the two parts meet. Then channels are cut, or holes drilled, to provide an inlet for the plastic and an outlet for air.

A two-part plastic resin, usually polyurethane, is mixed and poured in the mold; this is cured for several hours. The cast part is removed, the inlet and outlet channel runners are trimmed off, and you have a part that closely resembles one that came from an expensive permanent injection mold. Polyurethane is available at hobby shops in a wide range of hardnesses, from soft as rubber to hard as acrylic.

Casting Metal Parts at Low Temperatures

Description: This covers the melting of alloys at less than 600°F and casting them in silicone rubber molds. This can be done at home.

Products used for: Parts that will be die cast when volume produced.

Cost range: $50 to $100.

Resources: Polytek Development Corporation, McMaster-Carr Supply Co., and building supply and plumbing supply stores.

Making your prototype: Cerro alloys are available in melting temperatures as low as 158°F. These alloys start at about $14 per pound. The lowest cost alloy is Cerroshield, which melts at just under the boiling point of water. McMaster-Carr's catalog number for Cerroshield is 8921K23. Plumbers solder, which does not contain (poisonous) lead, melts between 500 and 600°F and is less expensive than Cerroshield. Either of these alloys produces a part that is not as strong as the eventual die casting but is generally satisfactory for a prototype. Castings below 600°F can be made in the same silicone rubber molds as is used for casting plastics (see above). Dust the mold with talcum powder in order to produce the best surface finish.

Casting Metal Parts at High Temperature

Description: This is a foundry process of creating metal parts from various molds. It requires outsourcing to a vendor and cannot be done at home.

Products used for: Parts that will be die cast when produced in volume, or parts that will be cast using the same process in volume production.

Cost range: From one to several thousand dollars.

Resources: Thomas Register of American Manufacturers or the Yellow Pages.

Making your prototype: Investment casting (also known as the "lost wax" process) uses a wax pattern of the part you wish to cast. This pattern is invested (coated) with a plaster, the wax is melted out, and metal is poured in. This ancient process has changed little in four or five thousand years. Creating the wax pattern can be done by the SL, SLS or MJM methods (see "Computer-driven Additive Processes" below for descriptions of these methods).

Plaster casting is a service offered by some of the die-casting vendors for customers who must prototype their parts. The model used to make the plaster mold is made by any of the same processes that are used for investment casting. Plaster molds, like investment molds, are destroyed in removing the parts.

Sand casters represent the "smokestack" era of manufacturing, but they are still predominantly used in the casting of large parts, especially cast iron. The master pattern consists of a model of the part that is split in half and mounted on a board. A fence is placed around the board; a sand, clay, and binder mix is poured over the pattern; the half-mold is inverted; and the pattern is removed. The opposing half is made the same way. The two halves are put together, molten metal is poured, and when cooled, it is removed as the casting. The pattern is often made from wood, but for smaller parts it can be made from plastic by the SLS process.

Computer-driven Additive Processes

Description: A three-dimensional image is created using a computer that then drives a variety of equipment to produce prototype parts. The image is amended to create a machine program, which drive the X, Y, and Z axes of the machine.

Products used for: Any parts that will be made by injection molding when in volume production, or parts that become patterns for plastic or metal casting.

Cost range: $500 to several thousand dollars.

Resources: Thomas Register and Yellow Page listings under "Stereolithography," "Selective Laser Sintering," and "Rapid Prototyping."

Making your prototype: Rather than remove material, as in machining processes, these processes add material or solidify it to produce a net shape without waste. The SL (stereolithography) process uses a liquid plastic that is hardened by an ultraviolet laser beam. A platform is positioned about two human hairs below the top of the liquid. The machine program, which has "sliced" the 3-D computer image into hundreds of thin digital slices, scans and hardens the plastic, thereby creating the bottom "slice" of the prototype. The platform drops down one slice (about .005 inches), and scans again, bonding the new slice to the first. This process is repeated slice by slice until the entire height is reached. The plastic used in SL is relatively fragile, and it is often honeycombed to reduce the amount of material used and the process time. The parts are seldom used directly in prototypes except to check fits and to visually evaluate the concept. The selective laser sintering (SLS) process is much the same as SL, except that a powdered plastic is used. The plastics used are stronger than that of SL and can be used directly in prototypes.

Multi-jet modeling (MJM) is a wax jetting process that builds a wax prototype layer by layer, as in SL and SLS. The wax model can be used as a pattern for silicone rubber molds, or as a sacrificial pattern for investment casting or plastic casting.

Negotiating with Prototypers

The inventor should think carefully about exactly how many parts he or she will need, now and in the foreseeable future, before contacting any vendor. Much of the cost of making a prototype lies in the time spent planning the method, setting up machines, and communicating with the inventor. This time is the same whether the prototyper makes a single piece or ten, and of course, the cost of this time is spread across whatever quantity is bought. Thus, the cost of ten pieces may be only twice the cost of a single piece.

In any event, the inventor should always ask that the nonrecurring costs (programs, special tools, and so on) be spelled out as a separate item in the quote. And every RFQ (request for quotation) should ask for pricing in quantities of 1, 3, 10, and 25 (or whatever quantities you like) before the order is placed, while the vendor's "pencil is still sharp." Afterthought quotes solicited for repeat orders often come in high because the vendor holds the tooling and has the advantage.

Resources

▶ AIN Plastics. They have good service, a $50 minimum order, and are located mainly in the Midwest and the East, but they will ship across the country. Free catalog. Call 800-431-2451 for the nearest facility.

▶ Cadillac Plastic. They have retail stores in most large cities throughout the country. They have good service and require no minimum order if placed via the Internet or purchased for cash in a retail outlet. Free catalog. Cadillac fabricates as well as supplies stock plastics. Call 800-274-1000.

▶ *Inventor's Digest* magazine. They publish excellent articles on prototyping, patenting, and marketing for beginning as well as advanced inventors. Single issues are $5 postpaid; subscription are $27 per year for six issues. Call 800-838-8808.

▶ McMaster-Carr Supply Company. This is one of the largest national suppliers of a wide variety of industrial products. They have offices in most midsize and large cities. They have excellent service, no minimum dollar order requirement, and accept credit cards. But they won't send you their expensive catalog until you are a steady customer. Check their catalog on the Internet at www.mcmastercarr.com. Call 732-329-3200 to find the facility nearest you.

▶ Polytek Development Corporation. Their offices are located outside of Philadelphia, Pennsylvania. Excellent service and information, and there is a $40 minimum order. The catalog is well worth its $10 price because it includes a minicourse in plastic molding. Call 610-559-8620. Special price on first order.

▶ The Inventor's Bookstore. This is an excellent source of books and inexpensive reports that cover invention development, protection, and prototyping, and it is run by Jack Lander, who was instrumental in writing this appendix. Free paper catalog, or on Internet at www.inventorhelp.com. Call 800-214-2833.

▶ The *Thomas Register of American Manufacturers* is the most comprehensive directory of its kind. This multivolume set of large green books is found in the reference section of most libraries.

C

Funding Your Invention

Overview

Raising money has always been a problem for inventors, whether they are paying for a patent or prototype or trying to raise enough money to go into full production. Inventors today need more money than ever because of the high costs of today's production techniques and because of the need to get into the market with as much momentum as possible. But at the same time, inventors today have an easier time raising money, since manufacturers and marketers are willing to help fund new projects in innovative ways, and since new security rules (established by the Securities and Exchange Commission) make it easier for an inventors to raise money. Inventors can also benefit from community-based funding that rural areas offer to entice business. All this doesn't, of course, mean raising money is easy. You need a good plan, a good product, and lots of support from eventual customers. If you have this, combined with the proper strategy for introducing your product and for raising cash, you will find, however, that money is available.

This appendix is organized into two sections: The first takes you through the various steps of a product introduction, noting your cash needs and probable funding sources at each step, and the second looks more closely at the pros and cons of each investment source.

Funding Your Invention: From Concept to Final Product

Important Considerations

1. Don't rush to quit your day job. Many inventors use credit cards or personal loans to fund at least the first phase of their invention. These loans will be hard to arrange if you quit your job and are in effect self-employed with no income. Instead, apply for your loans or credit cards before you quit. You don't want to take out so much debt you'll go bankrupt, but it can help to have an extra $5,000 to $10,000 in credit if you need it. Finally, try to keep working for as long as possible, to maintain your income till you begin making sales.

2. Founders' equity. People always want to know how much you are investing in the next stage of the invention process. Many inventors don't have much funding in place and are hard-pressed to pay for more than the initial prototypes. One way around this problem when you are raising additional money is to have a group of founder investors that includes you. These could be family and friends, but it would preferably include an investor who is in the industry. Then when you take on additional investors, you can tell them how much the founders are investing.

   I personally like this approach because it gives the inventor more money to work with, and it provides a funding source if you need small amounts of additional money. Just ask people to put up $2,000 to $3,000 to start, a sum you match, and that is your founding investment. Typically, the inventor receives 500,000 shares or so of stock to start, since he or she created the idea, and the other founders get 10,000 to

25,000 in stock. The inventor can later get additional investments from the founders as more money is needed.

In general, it is very important to get outside investors as soon as possible, even if you have lots of money. It gives you several big advantages:

- It provides you with outside advice and expertise.
- Having several initial investors will help you add investors later, when you need more money. Investors feel more comfortable investing in a company that has always been able to attract investors.
- It reduces your financial risk if the project fails.
- Outside investors give you much-needed moral support (and sometimes a kick in the pants) when a project goes badly.

3. Business experience. You are not going to get money from any serious investors unless you have someone on your team who has experience either running a company or launching a new product. If you don't have that experience, work at getting a mentor, or even a business partner, to give your venture the business background it needs to succeed.

Early Investments

This is the money that helps you finalize your concept through the prototype stage, and it allows you to make your initial contacts with industry insiders.

1. Initial Seed Money
   Description: Money for a patent search, initial market analysis, and verification of the inventor's premise. The inventor might also attend a trade show to check out products and to conduct initial interviews with industry people.
   Amount needed: $100 to $1,000.
   Sources: Typically, self-funded with credit cards, savings, or through sale of personal property.
   Comments: This period gives the inventor a better understanding of the market potential of the idea. Inventors should be able to prepare a convincing presentation on why their invention might sell. They need

the presentation to get funds from family, friends, and hopefully industry investors.

2. Feeling Out the Market
Description: You'll need to start attending trade shows and association meetings to start networking and learning who your competitors are. You'll use the presentation you developed using your initial seed money to explain your product to industry contacts and potential investors. After this period, you should have a better presentation, and you should produce a sample brochure. You may need a concept model or prototype for the brochure.
Amount needed: $200 to $2,000.
Sources: Self-funding, family friends, and industry investors.
Comments: This is a good time to start adding investors, even if you don't need the money, because you only need to ask investors for small amounts. You could ask for $500 from three investors to prepare a concept model, prepare a sample brochure, and visit two trade shows. Your goal would be to line up industry insider contacts as early investors you can rely on during your invention process. You may want to apply for a provisional patent before attending the show so you can say that your product is patent pending.

3. Models, Prototypes, and Patents
Description: You want to make a high-quality prototype and possibly implement your patent strategy once you have solid information that your product has true market potential. Your goal in this period is to prepare a product, brochure, and ad package that you can use to conduct the research you need to land a private label, joint-venture, or license agreement. Be sure to consider your patent strategy carefully here, since you are about to research your idea in the market with end users.
Amount needed: $500 to $20,000 depending on your patent strategy and the complexity of the prototype.
Sources: Self-funded, industry investors, manufacturers through in-kind or outright investments, family and friends, and angel investors.
Comments: If you haven't done so yet, it is to your advantage to get industry investors and contract manufacturers involved in your

company around this stage. That's because they only have to invest a small amount now; later on, you'll want more money, and the easiest investments to get are ones from people who have already invested. If approached for the first time for large sums, investors will balk at the amounts involved. You can also self-fund this period and get money from family and friends, but those are not your best investor options.

4. Research Results

   Description: You have a product, a brochure, and an ad, and now you need to get out and interview people, both end users and people in the distribution channel, to see what they think. You may want to attend both trade shows and association meetings to meet as many industry people as you can to talk about your idea. In some cases, inventors will actually take out a booth at an industry trade show to gauge customer response.

   Amount needed: $300 to $6,000 depending on how close you are to the trade shows and key industry meetings.

   Sources: Self-funded, or money from family and friends.

   Comments: Your goal in this period is to prove your product can sell so you can get investors, companies, and industry insiders to help fund your preparations for production. That step is expensive, and you will need investors, and probably lots of them. With that in mind, try to get as many potential investors as possible to attend research events or trade shows. They are much more likely to invest if they see that end users get excited about your product.

Preparing for Production

1. Finalizing the Presentation

   Description: If you are hoping to get a private label contract or joint-venture agreement, you will need to have a "looks like, works like" prototype, an impressive demonstration, and research results that indicate your product can sell. This step would be to prepare a presentation illustrating these facts to show to interested parties.

   Amount needed: $1,500 to $4,000 depending on how many presentations you make and how far you have to travel.

Sources: Self-funded, family and friends, your contract manufacturer, and angel or industry investors.

Comments: Your best investor here is an industry insider—though it shouldn't be an employee of the company you are presenting to or one of their competitors. Having an industry insider on board implies that the product has strong sales potential. If you are proposing private label sales, your contract manufacturer may also be willing to help fund this step.

2. Finalizing Documentation

   Description: This is the stage where you do the engineering documentation, prepare preproduction models, and do preselling of your product to people in the distribution channel.

   Amount needed: $10,000 to $200,000 depending on the complexity of the product and on whether or not you hire salespeople to help presell the product.

   Sources: Angel investors, contract manufacturers, distributors, joint-venture partners, and industry investors.

   Comments: This step is necessary but somewhat difficult to get money for because you really don't do anything to further prove the product's sales potential. All you are doing is getting things prepared so they can be manufactured correctly. Your contract manufacturer may pick up these costs if you've done a good job researching the market and networking with key contacts. This step may be expensive, but the next step, producing the product, is even more so—so continue making contacts, getting positive feedback, and preselling your product.

3. Finalizing the Marketing Plan

   Description: In this step, you prepare a marketing plan for building sales momentum by preselling and to quickly penetrating the market once production starts. You write the plan to be sure you are doing all you can to presell and market the product, as well as to create the basis for a business plan, which you may need to get the necessary investments to start production.

   Amount needed: $1,000 to $5,000 depending on the extent of the plan and how much help you need to finish it.

Sources: Self-funded, industry investors, contract manufacturer, or angel investors.

Comments: As much as you can, utilize your industry contacts to help write the plan. A good tactic here is to get the help of a potential large industry investor. He or she will have great ideas, and it will help convince the writer to invest in your company.

Product Introduction

1. Manufacturing Start-up

   Description: Tooling, fixtures, inventory, packaging, and all other materials and equipment needed to manufacture the product.

   Amount needed: $5,000 to $1 million and up depending on the product.

   Sources: Private placements, venture capital, bank loans, community funding, angel investors, contract manufacturers, joint-venture partners, and distributors.

   Comments: You won't get the funding you need if you haven't carefully completed each step up to now. You definitely need lots of money, and you won't get it unless you have proven the product will sell.

2. Marketing Introduction

   Description: Your product introduction expenses including brochures, trade shows, advertising, promotions, distribution programs, hiring and training manufacturers, sales representatives, inside salespeople, and creating a Web site.

   Amount needed: $5,000 to $500,000 and up depending on the size of your market.

   Sources: Private placements, venture capital, bank loans, community funding, angel investors, contract manufacturers, joint-venture partners, and distributors.

   Comments: Don't skimp on your marketing plan, especially if you need a lot of money to produce your product. Your investors will want a big return on their money, and they'll want it fast. You want an ambitious marketing plan that will produce quick sales to get the product started.

3. Setting Up Company Operations
Description: This includes operating capital, fund-raising fees, buying computers, setting up phone systems, hiring an accountant, and paying legal fees.
Amount needed: $20,000 to $500,000.
Sources: Private placements, venture capital, bank loans, community funding, angel investors, contract manufacturers, joint-venture partners, and distributors.
Comments: I mention this section only because it is a big expense that most inventors tend to totally overlook. When inventors don't raise enough money, the culprit is often that they underestimated the administrative expenses in starting a company.

Funding Sources

Money from Individuals

1. Self-funding. This is money out of your pocket, either from savings, credit cards, or personal loans, or from the sale of personal property, homes, or stocks.

2. Family and friends. One of the tried-and-true forms of getting seed capital is to turn to those nearest and dearest to you. However, try not to take investments that represent any more than 10 percent of a friend or relative's total investment money. New products are a high-risk venture, and you don't want friends or family to lose too much. Be sure to have a written agreement. It avoids misunderstandings, plus you'll need those agreements for your corporate records once you start to operate as a real company.

3. Industry insiders. These are the best people to get investments from because they know the market, and they can even help you sell or make the product.

4. Angel investors. "Angels" can be anyone—your dentist, your neighbor, people at church, or local philanthropists and retirees. They are nonprofessional investors who invest in your company to help you get started, though they usually won't know much about your business

and rarely want any involvement. You probably know dozens of people who could become an angel investor for you. Don't be afraid to approach them once you get your first presentation ready. Angel investors usually want shares in your company in return. Be sure to have a lawyer draft a stock subscription agreement for each investor.

Money from Manufacturers

1. In-kind investments. This is when the manufacturer has his or her employees do work for you at no charge. It could be machining a part or doing engineering drawings. This usually pertains to jobs where the manufacturer would be paying the employee to do the same work anyway, so working on your project doesn't cost any extra money.

2. Options. If a manufacturer, joint-venture partner, private label customer, or potential licensee wants product changes, more research, or additional tests, you should comply, but do so only for a charge. In return, you can offer an option for anywhere from three to six months. The option means the party that paid you the money has exclusive rights to your proposed agreement (selling on commission, joint venture, private label, or license) for the designated time.

3. Extended terms. Normal payment terms are 30 days after the receipt of a service or finished product. The manufacturer could let you pay in 60 days or 90 days in order to stretch out your cash flow. If you are producing the product yourself, you can try to get extended terms from your suppliers.

4. Amortized tooling. Tooling are molds and other equipment accessories needed to make your product. Fixtures are items that manufacturers put into the manufacturing process to speed up the production process and to ensure high product quality. Typically, inventors have to pay for the tooling and fixtures up front, when the manufacturer obtains them. Amortized tooling means that instead of charging an up-front fee, the manufacturer charges an extra fee, say five cents, on every part manufactured.

5. Prototypes and product development. The manufacturer might offer to help you build prototypes and complete your product's development.

Manufacturers who have in-house prototype capability are often willing to bear much of the development costs if you can show your product has strong sales potential.

6. Outright investments. The manufacturer can also buy stock in your company, or loan you money to launch your product. Manufacturers will often loan you operating capital if you have strong orders when your product is introduced.
7. Joint-venture financing. You get this from companies that help you either manufacture or market your product. Your joint-venture or alliance partner can offer all of the investments that a contract manufacturer can. Joint-venture financing, or financing from a distribution partner or contract manufacturer, is the easiest form of funding for most inventors to obtain. You simply need to offer your main partners an opportunity to invest in your company. They do that if they believe in the inventor and his or her product.

Raising Big Money

1. Professional investors. These are investors who can put up $50,000 to $1 million into a project. They are much more like venture capitalists than angel investors. They check your product and market out carefully, and they negotiate a deal that is good for them. You typically learn of them from other start-up companies or by attending new venture and/or entrepreneurial conferences. Check with your local Small Business Development Center to see what conferences are in your area. Also check to see if there are any entrepreneur clubs or new venture clubs in your town.
2. Venture capitalists. These firms invest in companies with high growth potential, experienced management, and a sound business plan. They typically don't like to make investments that are less than a million dollars. They don't typically invest in companies without a sales history unless the company has a dramatic new technology. Most larger libraries have *Pratt's Guide to Venture Capital Sources* (published by Venture Economics), which contains a fairly comprehensive listing of venture capital companies.

3. Private placements. This is a method of raising money from investors where you hire a broker to sell stock. It is similar to a public offering, except that the stock from a private placement isn't listed on an exchange where it can be readily traded. Legal fees and broker fees for a $1 to $2 million private placement can run up to $250,000. Most investors in a private placement must be accredited, which means they either earn $200,000 per year or have a net worth in excess of $1 million. Stock sold through private placements can be difficult to sell. Investors hope you plan on growing your company and that you eventually have a public offering.

4. IPOs. An initial public offering, or IPO, refers to the time when you sell public stock that can be freely traded. The timing of your IPO is important to earlier investors, as it represents the first time that they can easily sell their stock. The advantage of an IPO is that it allows you to freely sell stock to anyone rather than mostly to accredited investors, and it allows you to sell stock to people you don't know. Technically, prior to a public offering, you are supposed to sell only to people you or someone in your company knows or to accredited investors. IPOs can raise huge amounts of money, but the legal fees are also very high, typically well over $250,000.

5. Community funding. Many rural communities have economic initiatives to bring businesses and jobs to their town. Inventors will also find investors in small towns who are more likely to invest in a local venture. Communities will offer low- or no-interest loans from the city or county, tax-increment financing, and outright grants. You can access some of this money if you start your own company in a rural area, but you can also access it if you work with a rural manufacturer. The manufacturer may be able to get funding from the community to expand his or her operation to include your new product. The manufacturer then passes those benefit on to you by building prototypes and absorbing tooling and fixture costs on your product.

6. Sales/lease back. Companies that own building or manufacturing assets can sell those assets and then lease them back. Real estate investors and equipment leasing companies are typically willing both to buy and then to lease back your assets provided you have a viable

business plan. This is a common strategy that even the largest companies use to preserve operating capital.

7. SCOR. The Small Corporation Offering Registration (SCOR) is a Securities and Exchange Commission (SEC) program that allows you to raise up to $1 million with much less paperwork and much lower legal fees. The program also frees you to take on investors you don't know or who aren't accredited. Contact your local Small Business Development Center or local entrepreneur club to find out more information and to locate attorneys who do SCOR registrations.

Other Types of Funding

1. Factoring. This is also called receivables financing. Factoring companies will buy your receivables from you for anywhere from 4 to 8 percent off their face value and then receive payment as customers pay their bills. This is a very expensive form of financing, as you may be paying 4 percent for, in effect, a two-month loan.

2. Cash deposits. Many inventor companies require customers to pay a down payment of anywhere from 25 to 50 percent on orders, especially for custom-made or industrial products. This funding can then help produce the products that you've sold.

3. Bank loans. Banks do give out loans, but they are not typically a good source of financing for new companies because they want collateral for their loans, and they want personal collateral if you don't have business collateral. Here are the most popular types of bank loans:
   - Installment loans, on which the business makes monthly payments for a certain number of years.
   - Term loans, which require the entire loan to be repaid after a predetermined term that can range from three months to five years.
   - Asset-based loans, which might be for inventory or equipment.
   - Revolving line of credit, which a business can draw upon when cash flow is low and then pay off when cash flow is high.

4. SBA loans. Small Business Administration (SBA) loans are similar to bank loans, except that they are guaranteed by the government, and therefore the banks are a little more flexible in their lending criteria.

5. Borrowing money off orders. If you have a big order from a reputable company, you may be able to get a term loan from a bank. Private investors will also issue short-term loans for a big order, but they will charge you a sky-high interest rate, and they will typically have a clause in their agreement that turns over substantial company assets to them in the event you fail to pay.

Glossary

accredited investor: Investors with an income of over $200,000 for at least two years or a net worth in excess of $1 million.

advertising specialty: A term that applies to products that businesses give away or sell at a big discount to promote their names. Could be pens, golf balls, or a magnetic message pad for the refrigerator.

affiliate agreement: Tactic that allows another Web site to sell your product or to get a commission or referral fee for sales that result from a customer linking to your site from their site.

alliances: A loose term that applies to any agreement in which two companies cooperate to help promote their products.

amortize: Turning a large payment into a series of smaller payments. For example, if a $10,000 tooling charge is amortized into the cost of a product, an inventor pays off part of the $10,000 cost on every production run.

angle: The focus of a press release or news story that is of interest to readers.

back order: Orders that are not shipped on time. For example, if normal delivery is two weeks and an order can't be shipped for eight weeks, the order would be identified as a back order.

banner exchange program: An Internet marketing tactic where you post banner ads on your site for no charge in return for other sites posting your banner ad.

blister pack: A piece of clear, hard, molded plastic that is glued to a paperboard backing. A popular package, especially for small toys.

brand name: Any well-known product or company name. Examples are Pillsbury, Betty Crocker, Mr. Coffee, Toro, and Sony.

branding: A strategy that helps customers and prospects remember your name, typically with a favorable trait. For example, Old Navy's branding message is that it sells affordable hip clothes.

cannibalizing: The practice of taking one product apart so that its parts can be used to make another product.

cavity: A part of a mold that can produce one unit. Injection-molded parts are usually produced from two-, four-, or six-cavity molds, which means that two, four, or six products are manufactured at once.

clip art: Black-and-white drawings of people, places, or events that can be cut out and used for ads, sales flyers, or promotional materials. Books of clip art are available at art and office supply stores as well as larger libraries.

confidential and nondisclosure statement: A form that specifies that the person you show an idea to can't disclose it to other people without your permission.

consignment: Giving a product, at no charge, to a store, sales representative, or dealer, with the understanding that the product will either be paid for when it is sold or else returned at a later date.

contract manufacturer: A manufacturer that agrees to make another manufacturer's or inventor's product for a fee.

co-op advertising: A promotional program in which manufacturers and retailers split the cost of ads promoting the manufacturer's products. A co-op advertising program rebates retailers a percentage of their purchases back when they advertise the manufacturer's products. When a manufacturer offers a 10 percent co-op advertising allowance, it will pay for half of the retailer's ads for its products with an upward limit equal to 10 percent of a retailer's purchases.

copy: All the words used on an ad, package, or promotional display.

creative expenses: Costs relating to the preparation of literature for printing, including art work, graphic design, and copywriting.

dealer: A type of distributor that often offers full service to industrial or professional customers.

design patent: A low-cost patent that only covers the product's visual appearance.

direct mail: Any type of promotion in which materials are mailed or delivered to homes, apartments, or businesses.

direct-response ad: Any ad—whether in print, on radio, or on TV—that requests an immediate order from customers. Direct-response TV ads can be either short form, which are less than two minutes, or infomercials, which are typically 30 minutes long.

distributor: A company that buys products from a supplier and later resells them to retailers, other companies, or consumers. A distributor owns the products it sells, in contrast to a manufacturers' representative, who never buys the product.

engineering documentation: Refers to the part drawings, assembly drawings, and part and final product specifications that need to be prepared before a product can be produced by most manufacturers.

exclusive agreement: An agreement by which one party agrees to sell only to one customer, distributor, or retailer.

extended dating: Offering payment terms to customers that are in excess of 30 days.

factoring: The practice of selling receivables for immediate cash. For example, if a manufacturer ships a $20,000 order to a customer, the invoice statement is a receivable. If the manufacturer needs immediate cash, it will sell the receivable or "factor" it to a commercial finance company. The charge for factoring ranges from 4 to 10 percent of the receivable's value.

fixture: Something a manufacturer uses to ease manufacturing. For example, a fixture could be added to a bending machine so the machine would bend a bar four times to make the perfect shape. A fixture could also be a device to hold a part while it is polished or shrink-wrapped.

flash: A trade show term that refers to moving in and around the booth to attract booth visitors.

focus group: A market research term for a group of 5 to 15 people brought together for the sole purpose of evaluating a product.

four-color artwork: Also called *full color.* Four-color printing uses black, yellow, red, and blue ink to produce all the possible colors. One-color artwork means only one color of ink is used. Two-color artwork uses two colors. Four-color artwork is expensive because it requires both a color separation (the process that turns a photograph into four printing plates, one for each color ink) and a larger printing press.

grinding: A trade show term for trying to sell everyone who walks by your booth. Needed when show traffic is low.

guaranteed sales: A manufacturer's or distributor's promise to issue a refund for any unsold merchandise.

infringement: When a product "reads on," or has all the elements of, another invention's patent claim(s). Patent holders can sue parties infringing on their patent to get them to cease and desist their infringement, and sometimes they can collect damages.

injection molding: A common way of making small plastic parts. An injection mold shoots plastic into a mold, cures it (heats and then cools the plastic so that it becomes solid), and then pops the part out of the mold. Ideal for high-volume, automated production. The process has high start-up costs because of expensive tooling charges.

in-kind investments: Investments of free services or materials rather than money. Examples are free rent, working without pay, or use of a proto-type laboratory.

IPOs: Stands for "initial public offering," the first offering of stock that can be freely traded. Typically sold through a broker, IPOs can range from several million to hundreds of millions of dollars.

job shop: A manufacturer that doesn't sell any of its own products but rather just manufacturers jobs for other companies.

joint venture: Two or more companies that invest in a product, project, or venture. Their investment doesn't have to be equal, nor does their share in the venture.

license: A contractual arrangement in which an inventor agrees to allow a manufacturer to produce his or her idea in return for a royalty (a pre-determined share of either the manufacturer's sales dollars or its profits). A 5 percent royalty based on sales will give an inventor an amount equal to 5 percent of a company's net sales of the inventor's product.

manufacturers' representative: A person who acts as a sales representative for several manufacturers, never taking possession of a product, but fun-neling orders to the manufacturers in return for a commission (usually 10 to 15 percent). Manufacturers' representatives are used by companies whose sales are too low to justify having their own sales forces.

margins: The percentage of profit that a company makes. Gross profit mar-gin is equal to the selling price minus the manufacturing cost, divided by the selling price. Net margin is the selling price minus all costs—manu-facturing, marketing, administration, and so on—divided by the selling price.

markings: The proper way to indicate on your product or brochure that you have a trademark, service mark, copyright, or patent, or that your patent is pending.

markup: The percentage a retailer or distributor increases the price of a product. If a retailer buys a product for $1 and sells the product for $2, the retailer has a 100 percent markup. The formula for determining markup is:

$$\frac{\text{Dollar amount increase in the product's price x 100\%}}{\text{Purchase price of the product}}$$

mock-up: A crude model of a product that helps an inventor to visualize what the final product will look like. Often made out of cardboard, papier-mâché, or other easily shaped materials.

model: A representation of what the product will be like, usually structurally sound and functionally similar to a production unit. A model is different from a prototype in that a model will not be quite like the final product; it may have different materials, a different size, or some other different feature. A prototype is very close to, if not exactly like, the final product.

OEM: Original equipment manufacturers (OEMs) supply parts that are used in finished parts. A bearing manufacturer selling to auto manufacturers would be considered an OEM supplier.

on-sale bar: A patent regulation that says that a product can't be sold for more than one year before a patent application is filed or else the right to a product patent is forfeited.

option: Offering another party exclusive rights to negotiate or buy something in the future in return for a payment. Options are for a specific time period, often as short as three to six months.

outsourcing: Turning certain parts of a company's operations to an outside vendor.

overhead: Any expense that occurs regularly, such as rent, salaries, utilities, telephone, and so on. Sometimes referred to as *fixed expenses*.

override: A commission override pays a percentage of sales for every product sold. Called an *override* because this commission is over and above any other commission paid on the sale.

patent claims: The section of a patent that awards inventors the right to exclude others from manufacturing an infringing idea.

patent pending: This indicates that your patent application has been received by the U.S. Patent and Trademark Office. It doesn't mean you'll be awarded a patent, only that you have applied.

PCT patent application: An application that registers a patent in all the countries that have signed the Patent Cooperation Treaty (PCT), which includes most major industrial countries.

per-unit surcharge: A charge by which a contract manufacturer recovers tooling or other costs. If a manufacturer has absorbed $10,000 in up-front setup costs, those costs might be recovered by charging 25¢ per unit over and above the product's manufacturing cost.

pilot production run: A short production run, sometimes with temporary tooling, that manufacturers frequently make to be sure they uncover any potential difficulties in manufacturing a product. Output of a pilot run is frequently used to test market a product.

portal site: A comprehensive informational site targeted at a Web community, such as a site for singles, a site for young investors, or a site for model railroaders. Also sometimes called a *magnet site*.

positioning: A marketing term that relates to the practice of adding features and benefits to a product so that target customers will perceive it in a certain way, such as by considering it "technologically advanced" or as a "value leader."

premise: The reason why end users are expected to buy a product.

preproduction model: A model that is exactly like an actual production unit. It may be made with more handwork and machining than will be done during actual production.

press release: An information kit regarding a product or inventor that is sent to media outlets in the hopes of getting a story published or a media interview.

price/value relationship: A comparison between the actual selling price and what the product is worth to customers. Products with a good

324 ▼ THINK BIG

price/value relationship have a price that's lower than the customer's perceived value.

private-label manufacturing: A manufacturer's production of an item that is then sold under another company's name. For example, manufacturers that make products that are then sold under the Sears brand name are producing private-label products.

private placement: A private sale of stock, primarily to accredited investors. Stock sold in a private placement is not freely traded.

product liability insurance: Insurance that covers potential lawsuits from any injury that your product might cause an end user.

pro forma: A projected income and cash-flow statement. Most loan documents require an income and cash-flow statement for at least 12 months in the future.

promotional allowance: A type of price discount that pays for a customer's promotional programs. A 10 percent promotional allowance, for instance, gives a retailer reimbursement for its promotional costs in an amount equal to 10 percent of its purchases.

promotional products: Also called *advertising specialty products.* Giveaway items used to promote a company's name or brand.

prototype: A sample of what a product will look like once it's produced. Prototypes are usually manufactured with a different technique than will be used for the final production unit.

provisional order: An order that is contingent on the buyer inspecting and approving the product prior to taking delivery.

provisional patent: A patent that is sent to the patent office and then held for one year or until a regular patent application is filed. A regular patent must be filed within a year of the provisional patent or the inventor loses his or her patent rights.

public domain: When an idea becomes known to the public, it is said to be in the public domain, and it loses its confidential status. Selling the product, publishing press releases, and attending trade shows are means of placing a product in the public domain.

publicity: Any mention that your product or company receives in the media.

read-on: A patent office term that indicates a product has every element of a claim of an existing patent.

receivables: The money that is owed by customers to a manufacturer or distributor.

royalty: A payment made by a licensee to an inventor based either on a percentage of sales or on the unit volume of products sold.

sampling: A marketing term for passing out samples at supermarkets, major events, or any other venue.

service mark: The official term for registering the name of a service. It has the same rights as a trademark. Markings are SM before the mark is officially registered, and ® after it's registered.

slotting allowance: A payment to a store that is required before a manufacturer can obtain shelf space. Grocery stores are among the stores that require this payment.

targeting: A process in which a manufacturer or inventor identifies a small segment of the market as having potential customers, and then directs all of its promotion at that segment. *Targeting* and *niche marketing* are often used interchangeably.

temporary tooling: Tooling that is expected to last for only a short production run.

terms: A period of days after which payment is due. For example, "30-day terms" means payment is due for a product or service 30 days after the product is shipped or the service performed.

tip: A trade show term for the first person who comes over to see a demonstration.

tooling: Molds, stampings, embossers, and other devices that are inserted into production equipment to make a specific part.

trade magazines: Magazines geared toward businesses rather than consumers. Can be targeted at manufacturers, distributors, or retailers in a certain market.

trade shows: Conventions that are geared toward one market, such as tire wholesalers, gift galleries, novelty distributors, or semiconductor manufacturers.

trademark: Intellectual property right that prevents others from using the same symbol, design, or words.

turnover: How long it takes for a store to sell its inventory. If a store sells out of a product in two months, then the product has a two-month turnover.

utility patent: Protects a mechanical design or a method of use for a product. The strongest patent protection available for most products.

vacuum-forming: A manufacturing process in which a sheet of plastic is placed over a mold. Then the plastic is heated and a vacuum is applied to draw the plastic tight over the mold. Used for fairly large products where high strength is not required.

value added: Typically used when referring to dealers or distributors and indicating that they perform a certain task that adds value to customers. A dealer that offers installation would be considered a value-added dealer.

vendor: Another term for a supplier.

virtual company: A company that outsources most or all of its functions, including manufacturing, R&D, customer service, and sometimes sales and marketing. A virtual company might have three or four employees with annual sales of over $1 million.

wholesale price: The price at which a product is sold to distributors.

working capital: Money that is needed to buy inventory, pay workers, and pay other bills until invoices are paid by customers. Most companies like to have a six-month working capital reserve.

Index